Social Consequences of Religious Belief

SOCIAL CONSEQUENCES OF RELIGIOUS BELIEF

EDITED BY
WILLIAM R. GARRETT

A NEW ERA BOOK

PARAGON HOUSE
NEW YORK

First edition, 1989

Published in the United States by

Paragon House
90 Fifth Avenue
New York, NY 10011

A New Ecumenical Research Association Book

Library of Congress Cataloging-in-Publication Data

Social consequences of Religious Belief / edited by William R. Garrett. —
—1st ed.
    p.   cm.—(God, the contemporary discussion series)
"A New ERA book."
  ISBN 1-913757-99-3   0-89226-065-3 (pbk.)
  1. Religion and sociology. I. Garrett, William R. II. Series.
Includes index.
  BL60.S614 1989
  306'.6—dc19   88-30121
                                         CIP

Manufactured in the United States of America

Contents

Preface

The essays collected in this volume—with three exceptions—were originally prepared for a conference entitled, "God: The Contemporary Discussion," held in Coronado, California, from December 29, 1986 to January 3, 1987, sponsored by the New Ecumenical Research Association. More specifically, the contributions printed herein were initially presented in Theme Group VI of a larger conference under the heading of "Social Consequences of the Belief in God." Theme Group VI was designed with both a disciplinary and substantive orientation, that is to say, it was expected that most of the contributed papers would be grounded in the several branches of the social sciences—as opposed to comparative religion, philosophical theology, biblical studies, and the like—and that religious consequences would be investigated on both the individual and organizational/societal levels. Beyond these broad guidelines, scholars were free to pursue whatever topical issue they chose and by whatever means of analysis they deemed appropriate to their research endeavors.

Latitude of this proportion represents a rather risky procedure, even under the best of circumstances. And when many of us read the submitted papers which were circulated prior to the opening of the conference, I think it is fair to say that we were somewhat apprehensive over whether the session would ever congeal around a thematic center. The papers, quite literally, covered the waterfront. They included analyses of religious patterns in Japan, South Africa, Germany and India. We explored Mormanism and the new Evangelicals, missionology and the thought of Josiah Royce, liberation theology, and classical Hindu thought. Some were psychologically oriented, while others were of a distinctive sociological bent.

Pre-conference misgivings about the disparate nature of the papers swiftly dissipated once the discussions actually got underway. Indeed, in a rather remarkable fashion, a collegial spirit quickly emerged as those who presented papers and those who offered critiques entered into dialogue. Perhaps this collegial spirit was due to the fact that we were situated in a non-academic setting where disciplinary turf did not have to be protected or, perhaps, it was due to the magnanimous character of the participants. (This participant leans heavily toward the latter explanation, but his view is not altogether objective.) At any rate, each contribution was treated critically and, yet, each criticism was couched in a general framework of civility wherein the overall objective remained a search for genuine insight. And perhaps most important, humor pervaded our discussions—both inside and outside our formal deliberations.

One of our more startling discoveries, however, was that a common theme was emerging from our collective enterprise. We came to realize that our initially quite diverse topics were actually grounded in a common polarity between the societal and individual consequences of religious belief, or what we have chosen to describe in the more sociological categories of this volume as the macro- and micro-levels of social reality. The nature of this polarity was more profound, however, than simply the split between psychological and social consequences. What our discussion increasingly brought to the foreground was the intrinsic connection between these two levels. That is to say, the more we pursued personal consequences of religious belief, the more this quest drove us ineluctably toward the wider social grounding of those individually held claims, and vice versa.

The recovery of a sense of the linkages between these two segments of social reality was, I believe, the newsworthy feature of our deliberations. Thus, in editing these discrete essays, a concerted effort has been made to highlight the lines of inter-penetration between self and societal, personal and social, and individual and organizational developments in the forging of a vibrant religious faith. Moreover, our discovery of these linkages corresponded with a larger discussion going on within the social sciences generally relative to the integration of the micro- and macro-levels of social reality and the increasingly prominent dichotomy between particularism and universalism.

Perhaps it should also be noted that the publication of this particular sets of papers from the "God Conference" represents something quite distinctive for this series of volumes. Heretofore, the volumes have largely been devoted to comparative, historical, philosophical, or historical theology. We trust that the inclusion of these essays concerned with social scientific and social ethical issues will add another dimension to this already distinguished series of volumes.

A number of people have made enormous contributions to this project. I would like to mention, first, the two co-chairs who set the collegial tone for our discussion, Richard Quebedeaux and James Wood. Both formally and informally, M. Darrol Bryant has provided sound advice as to how we ought to proceed in bringing this volume to completion. Franz Feige, both as contributor and then as Executive Director of New ERA, has given encouragement and guidance to the project from its inception. The lion's share of the labor that brought these manuscripts to their final form, however, was contributed by John Gehring. John's patience and good humor have been unflagging over what has become a more drawn out process than all of us had initially hoped. That the book has finally come to see the light of day is as much John's doing as anyone else. And finally, I would like to thank the contributors for their lively, cooperative, and scholarly achievements which made this volume possible.

—William R. Garrett

Part I
INTRODUCTION

The essays which comprise this volume were originally drafted, with a few exceptions to be noted later, quite independently from one another and without reference to the organizational theme of the micro and macro consequences of religious belief. The original topic was to be the "Social Consequences of Belief in God," a theme designed to elicit contributions from a broad spectrum of disciplinary and substantive areas. Thus it was only after the fact that those two general substantive areas were selected as an appropriate conceptual scheme for ordering these papers in published form.

The overriding purpose of Chapter I is to provide a basic background to the larger issue of the nature and linkage of micro and macro social processes in the contemporary scientific study of religion. This effort has been designed to demonstrate that the focus on the micro/macro dimensions of religiosity and its manifestations does not really constitute a new research interest. Although the precise parameters of the issue may have been stated somewhat differently in earlier eras, both theologians and social scientists alike have long wrestled with the personal and collective integuments of religiosity. More recently, however, the relationship between these two levels of socioreligious reality has been thrust into sharp relief by the controversy surrounding the issue of secularization, its dynamics, character, and probable consequences. By a somewhat circuitous route, in fact, secularization theories have ineluctably fostered a renewed focus on what may perhaps best be defined as the emerging patterns of sacralization at both the micro and macro levels.

1

The Micro/Macro Linkage in the Scientific Study of Religion: The Problem of Assessing the Influence of Religion on Individuals and Society

WILLIAM R. GARRETT

The assertion that religion represents a vital social force capable of generating profound consequences over the diverse spheres of individual conduct and collective affairs will meet with little resistance nowadays, except perhaps from a few diehard secularists or an occasional rationalist with atheistic or agnostic leanings. Even social scientists from the Soviet bloc who follow the official line of opposing religion as a pernicious institution now recognize, implicitly if not explicitly, that religious faith does affect both individual behavior and the course of institutional dynamics, however unfortunate from their point of view this state of affairs may be.[1] And conversely, proreligionists are now beginning to recognize—in light of the fratricidal holy wars springing up around the world—that the power attributed to religion cannot always be naively heralded as benign. Closer to home, the multiplying scandals among TV evangelists of the religious right wing have simply served to underscore that somber conclusion.

Whether the influence accorded to religious forces is ultimately construed as edifying or malevolent, however, is not the major concern of this introductory chapter—even though this issue does warrant serious reflection and several of the contributions to this volume do provide information pertinent to its adjudication. Simply put, the overriding aim of this introduction is to set the various essays collected in this volume into a general analytic framework which will provide a means for apprehending their inherent linkage with a formidable debate in the contemporary scientific study of religion. This debate has to do with whether the function of religion in the present age is to provide meaning and comfort to individual participants or, by contrast, whether religion has its most substantial influence on the collective level of culture and social institutions by legitimating values, by encoding symbolic universes or world views, and by framing organizational patterns of behavior. Or, indeed, whether religion will be able to retain an enduring significance at either level with the coming of postindustrial society. Thus, the problem of the micro/macro influence of religious forces represents today one of the central interpretive issues sinuated throughout the whole length and breadth of the scientific study of religion.

Background to the Problem of Micro/Macro Linkage

Theologians and social scientists alike have long grappled with the ramifications devolving from the collective and individual aspects of organized religion. During the early days of neo-orthodoxy's ascendency, for example, Reinhold Niebuhr penned a powerful critique in "Moral Man and Immoral Society," of liberalism's naive campaign to usher in the kingdom of God on earth through social reform. The central polemical interest of this essay was to establish a thesis which, in essence, drove an analytical wedge between self and society by asserting that, while individuals were capable of love and altruistic action, social groups could not transcend their vested interests or exhibit the sort of moral behavior of which selves are capable.[2] The conclusion toward which Niebuhr pressed was that we should not expect that type of religio-moral consequence to manifest itself at the collective level. To be sure, Niebuhr was not proposing that religion was irrelevant to either national or international political affairs; he was, in fact, quite certain that religious perspectives could promote justice and equity on the macro level of collectivities, even though they could not ultimately generate love. The realistic perspective Reinhold promulgated was designed, above all else, to scale down the expectations of religionists to attainable goals. He was not so much disparaging the role of religion as trying to delineate the boundaries within which it could effectively operate.

Reinhold's brother, H. Richard Niebuhr, predicated his ethical reflection on an altogether different set of assumptions. Adhering to a Calvinist rather than a Lutheran theological perspective, H. Richard linked together the micro and macro levels in a framework that facilitated a more dynamic interrelation between these two analytical integuments. Although faith was transmitted, in H. Richard's view, by a process of socialization which entailed face-to-face interaction among believers, nonetheless, persons could—and regularly did—transform the institutions and communities in which they were situated so as to achieve a more responsible relationship to the continuing activity of God in history and the social order. The image of believers "transforming culture" in response to their own *metanoia,* or inward transformation, undergirds H. Richard's model of the responsible self in which God, self, and community exist in dynamic interrelation. Accordingly, selves manifest their responsibility to God by participating in a reflexive manner in "what God is doing" within the realm of time and history and the structures of societal existence.[3] The upshot of H. Richard Niebuhr's pioneering effort, therefore, was to forge together inseparably the micro and macro dimensions of human existence.

In this manner, H. Richard transcended the analytical perspective bequeathed to him by Ernst Troeltsch, the theologian sociologist from whom Niebuhr derived his early insights relative to the self-community problem. Troeltsch, in his classic tome on *The Social Teaching of the Christian Churches,* had in effect treated the micro/macro problem in terms of historical periodization.[4] This is to say that, during the Middle Ages and into the early modern period, Christendom had embraced a "church type" solution to the question of its role in the larger social order. The Church—both Roman Catholic and early Protestant branches—sought to Christianize cultural forms and direct the conduct of ordinary citizens by concentrating its influence at the macro level of the social order. Entering into an alliance with the ruling classes, church leaders at once secured a monopoly over the religious dimension of society, fostered a state-supported church on the masses, and ultimately relied on a "trickling down" process whereby religiosity established at the macro level gradually permeated the whole of the lower orders of society. The liability attending this solution to the "social question" of Christianity was, of course, that micro-level participants stood at such a social distance from the framers of religious thought and behavior that little influence actually filtered down to mold the lives of the rank-and-file. Low levels of religious knowledge and ethical practice typically characterized those nations where Christianity was legally established.

The quest for greater depth and integrity for the faith resulted in the emergence of the sect-type response. Although the monastic movement was regarded by Troeltsch as a forerunner to mature sectarianism, it was only out of the Protestant Reformation that separatist enclaves emerged. These religious communities sought to

live apart from the corrupting influence of the world and to nurture
piety within the sheltered context of their primary group relations.
Here the emphasis was squarely fixed on maintaining proper belief
and leading morally upright lives. Yet, the cost of this micro-level
focus was to render almost null and void the influence of sectarians
on the larger structures of social and cultural life.

The sect-type response was not the most radical, micro-level
orientation to arise within the historical parameters of Christian
social thought. This distinction was reserved for what Troeltsch
labeled the third type, or mysticism. Especially in the modern age,
Troeltsch insisted, and especially among the educated, middle
classes, a relatively new form of religiosity has emerged. Unlike
classical mysticism with its quest for the vision of God and a union
of the human/divine spirit, modern mysticism exhibits a radical
individualism, free inquiry, an eclectic combination of theological
symbols drawn from a variety of religious traditions, and an idio-
syncratic behavioral style fashioned on a set of moral precepts selected by the self. Modern mysticism embodies, in short, Jefferson's
famous concept of a "church of one."

With the two Niebuhrs and Troeltsch, essentially four quite distinct approaches are introduced relative to the issue of the linkage
between micro and macro levels of religious life. Reinhold's stance is
to insist that each level operates according to its own inherent laws,
and hence it is only on the micro level of individual piety that the
fuller expression of religiosity is rendered possible, for it is only on
this level that altruism, love, and transcendence of vested interests
can be realized. H. Richard contends, by contrast, that such a sharp
cleavage between the self and community is an empirical distortion
of the situation in which persons come to faith and subsequently
manifest that faith in responsible social action. There is, in other
words, an essential sociality to the appropriation of religious belief
and the expression of moral responsibility. Authentic faith manifests
itself in the transformation of social collectivities, just as communities provide the occasion for the nurturing of individual piety.
Hence, religious life entails a reciprocity between the poles of self
and society.

While these two stances might be described as the dualistic and
transformational, respectively, Troeltsch proffered yet two other
possibilities. The church type represented the option of concentrating the forces of religious influence on the macro level through
aligning the church with the ruling classes, the state, and the instru-

ments of cultural formation. The alternative of modern mysticism constitutes a privatization of religion wherein selves devise their own belief and moral systems, often not connected with organized religion at all. These two stances can be described as the elitist and radically individualist alternatives. The former represents a macro response to the problem of religious institutionalization, while the latter clearly presses toward a micro-level solution.

Although there are, no doubt, additional alternatives to the dualist, transformational, elitist, and radical individualist options surveyed above, these types do serve to underscore the fact that no general consensus abounds on how best to relate the micro and macro levels of the religious institution, nor, indeed, on the extent to which it is even desirable to press for such an integration. Some religionists—and even nonreligionists, for that matter—are content to regard religion as essentially a social institution which performs certain societally useful functions (such as social control, value legitimation, moral solidarity, collective ritual celebrations, and the like) but whose relevance beyond that range of functions is quite appropriately limited. (In contemporary Sweden, for example, religion is largely relegated to the role of marking rites of passage for crucial life events, such as baptism, marriage, and funerals. Apart from these occasions, many Swedes never darken their church doors and apparently feel little compulsion to pursue religious matters further.) Still others regard religious sentiments as purely personal preferences, matters of the heart, which require no institutional expression; and, indeed, they shun formal participation in religious organizations as a means of protecting the privatized integrity of their spiritual orientation. Both extremes tend to view the integration of the micro/macro levels of religious faith and practice as wholly unnecessary.

Recent trends in theory development and empirical research in the scientific study of religion, meanwhile, suggest that religious culture cannot be fully understood with sufficient clarity and precision so long as the micro and macro social processes of religiosity remain starkly segregated from one another. How these two integuments are to be articulated has, as yet, not been quite so apparent, however, as the need for such an articulation. An exploration of some of the problems emerging from the part/whole, micro/macro dichotomy, as well as avenues for securing a resolution to some of these problems, most specifically those relating to the scientific study of religion, is the prime concern of the following section in this essay.

Classical Formulations of the Micro/Macro Linkage Problem: Self and Society

Because the disciplines which comprise the scientific study of religion utilize the theoretical paradigms, language, and constructs of the social sciences, the sociology, anthropology, and psychology of religion inherit willy-nilly, although often in somewhat more particularistic forms, the controversies swirling around the explanatory efforts of economists, political scientists, anthropologists, psychologists, and sociologists. Accordingly, while the problem of macro/micro linkage is certainly not unique to the scientific study of religion, neither can this issue be summarily avoided in those subdisciplines focused on an analysis of religion and its social dynamics. By the same token, the lack of insulation from these larger controversies also means that religious analyses can benefit from the insights and breakthroughs registered in other sectors of social scientific research, just as the investigation of religious organizations can also provide insights for ongoing debates in the secular domain of theory formulation and the interpretation of empirical phenomena.[5]

From the early days of theorizing about the social order, differences have emerged among the leading figures relative to the proper alignment between micro and macro influences. John Locke, it may be recalled, contributed a crucial foundational statement for this debate at the onset of the modern era by contending that the basic building block of society is the individual.[6] Hence, society emerges when selves enter into a social contract and agree, through legislative processes, on the terms, laws, and organizational structure their particular society will embrace. Lockean social theory clearly presupposed that the macro structures of society are contingent on actions undertaken at the micro level, that is, on the actions initiated by individual actors.

One of the founding fathers of sociology, Emile Durkheim, explicitly took exception to Locke's claim.[7] Motivated by a powerful concern to separate sociology from individualistic or even social/psychological explanations of collective phenomena, Durkheim proposed that society was a reality *sui generis,* that is, that macro forces were ultimately responsible not only for the creation of social order itself, but also for the creation of individual selves who populated a given social order. In Durkheim's view, then, society was not a product of individual action in the Lockean sense. Rather, civilized individuals (as opposed to human animals) constituted a product of society. Durkheim's point, which is still worth taking with a great deal of seriousness, is that individual actions are constrained on all sides by the forces of collective life. Selves receive from society such essential elements for their existence as culture, language, values, norms, role patterns, and institutional structures which give purpose, guidance, and direction to the course of their everyday lives. Therefore, it is not society which derives from individuals, but rather individuals which are the foremost product of societal forces.

An attempt to chart a mediating course between the alternatives of Locke and Durkheim was forged by the American pragmatist, social psychologist, and philosopher, George Herbert Mead. One of the most seminal minds in American social science, Mead sought to devise a theoretical perspective which gave appropriate salience to the influence of socially established systems of meaning and role acquisition, while still holding out for the autonomy of the self to exercise genuine freedom and voluntarism with respect to those collectivities within which the self was enmeshed.[8] Unfortunately, the Meadian perspective has, in retrospect, lacked the requisite resources for resolving the micro/macro problem, largely because Mead labored so diligently to provide an account of micro dynamics with respect to role acquisition, socialization, and the participation in meaningful systems of self-to-self interaction that he never managed to describe in cogent terms how society is possible or how massive and complex organizations contribute significantly to the development of individuality. Indeed, the very concept of society emerges in Mead's reflection as a relatively ambiguous construct.[9] And although Mead asserted that self and society were "twin born" phenomena, thereby seeking to eschew the alternatives proposed by Locke and Durkheim, the fact of the matter is that ultimately Mead was more at home describing micro processes than the processes of macro social relations.

Meanwhile, in Germany, by all accounts the hotbed of theoretical advancement in the early decades of the twentieth century, Max Weber was framing his classic essay on the Protestant ethic and the spirit of capitalism.[10] One of the more productive themes to arise out of the lively debates which greeted this perspicacious account of how modern, rational capitalism appeared on the social scene centered on the role of individual believers who were armed with a new conception of the world and to their response to those cultural forces which defined their sphere of secular action. Weber's account was not simply a fixation on the social/psychological mind-set which Calvinists introduced into the world as a means for validating systematic, diligent labor so crucial for the take-off of modern, rational capitalism. Rather, as he delineated more fully in his brief but seminal essay. "The Social Psychology of the World Religions," Calvinists represented a "status carrier" (*standische traeger*), that is, a class group whose ideal religious interests synchronized with their material interests as emergent bourgeoisie to legitimate a new order of capitalist enterprise.[11] Once the new order had been institutionalized as a coherent world view (*Weltanschauung*), however, and once the appropriateness of rational labor had been established as a necessary social psychological correlate to the effective functioning of the capitalist system, then the religious motivation provided by Calvinism was no longer essential for the performance of this type of business activity. The "ethic" could be secularized in due course (and, indeed, historically was over the next two hundred years after Calvin), so that persons from all religious traditions could now readily participate in the mentality as well as the economic structure of modern, rational capitalism.

Given our present concern with the micro/macro linkage in understanding religious forces, Weber has provided a substantial advance over other conceptions. The essential thrust of Weber's contention was that the individual mentality inspired by Calvinism was insufficient by itself to foster the sort of massive transformation occasioned by the emergence of capitalism. What was required in addition was a set of social modifications at the macro level, including a renovated concept of the world which encompassed a value complex legitimating economic acquisition on the part of selves, a new set of legal codes (allowing for contracts, the creation of corporations, the collection of interest on money lent for speculative purposes, and the like), rational capitalistic organization of free labor, the development of economic enterprises responding to market forces, a class structure permitting social mobility based on individual achievement, and eventually political freedoms to allow for the pursuit of group interests through the formation of power blocs.[12] Thus the rise of modern capitalism as the dominant economic system in the West necessitated a simultaneous transformation of individual consciousness at the micro level *and* cultural and social changes at the macro level. Modifications on only one level would almost certainly not have allowed for the breakthrough necessary to supplant the traditional economic and political order of medieval society.

While Weber's accentuation of the role of religious beliefs and practices in providing psychological sanctions for practical ethical conduct and a systemization of everyday life has generally received the most attention from supporters and critics alike, the more penetrating insight developed in his Protestant ethic essay centered on the role of the status carrier in bridging the gap between individual and societal levels of social reality.[13] The status-carrier concept denotes a class-specific group which has managed to oversee the installation of its originally limited religious perspective into the position of a dominant cultural orientation within a given society. Weber attributed extraordinary importance to status carriers because they promoted a set of ideas which at once reflected both their material and ideational interests. Included among successful status carriers are not only the Calvinist groups that promoted capitalism, but also the literati who oversaw the triumph of Confucianism in China, the Brahmans who successfully institutionalized the caste system in India, the Arabic warrior class responsible for the spread of Islam, the urban middle classes who disseminated early Christianity, and so on. In each instance, the influence of religious ideas is redoubled because they answer the material interests of status carrier members, even as they legitimate social structural patterns for society as a whole, wherein the status group emerges as the prime beneficiary. Thus classical Chinese social structure promoted by the literati accorded a special, governing role to certified scholars. Indian society constituted on Hindu principles allocated the highest social status to Brahmans. And capitalist society supported by an emerging Calvinist bourgeoisie provided a secure position for entrepreneurs.

The status carrier construct not only supplied an analytical bridge between micro/macro–level social processes, but it also afforded Weber a means for accommodating the Marxian emphasis on material interests. That is to say, ideas acquire inordinate motivative power when they foster the class or economic interests of constituents and, then, lead to the structuration of a societal order wherein those twin interests can be realized.

Even Weber was convinced, however, that the historical evolution of the capitalist system would ultimately produce a bureaucratized social system wherein the sheer dynamics of this organizational structure—with its rationalism, specialization, and efficiency—

would effectively overwhelm any ideological commitment to individual freedom, creativity, and self-expression. What originally developed out of an efficacious linkage between micro and macro forces in capitalist society had, in the course of its maturation, inevitably created a mass society dominated by bureaucratic structures. As a result selves now increasingly find themselves encompassed on all sides by the "iron cage" of bureaucratic controls.[14]

To Weber's mind, quite clearly, the relationship between micro and macro social structures, the relative strength of each, remained a precarious issue in any social system and ever open to renegotiation. And the Weberian contention that macro forces were coming to prevail in an inexorable fashion over the micro systems of individuals and local communities in the late modern era is a theme still widely accepted by commentators writing today.[15]

Contemporary Formulations of the Micro/Macro Problem: Secularization Theory

Secularization theory is frequently used to justify the contention that there has been a triumph of secular, macro social forces over the cultural hegemony of religious ideas, practices, and social organizations. The larger domain of the "world" is defined more explicitly today by the rubrics of science, politics, and economic ideology, so this thesis runs, than it is by the ethereal constructs of religion. Forced into a position of increasing irrelevancy, organized religion should expect wholesale defections of practitioners from its ranks as a prelude to the eventual demise of the puissance of religious forces altogether. The possible exceptions, perhaps, are a few timid souls who cannot confront the terrors of the human condition without some "superstition" about a supernatural being or force to relieve their anxieties.

It follows from this line of argument, therefore, that one of the more critical upshots of the rise of modernity has been the systematic relegation of religion to a marginal role wherein its function is largely reduced to providing meaning, direction, and purpose for individuals and primary-group enclaves, while the major issues relating to the polity at large are resolved on other grounds, with a distinctly this-worldly cast. Although the Judeo-Christian tradition certainly played a formative role in laying the cultural foundations for Western civilization, that influence has now largely—and latently—been eclipsed by the secular, cultural, scientific, political, and economic forces which it originally inspired.

During the early decades of the twentieth century the advocates for this "decline of religion" conception of the processes of secularization were mainly confined to European scholars and social analysts, who were drawn almost exclusively from outside the ranks of professional theologians. By midcentury, however, this had all begun to change; and in the decade of the 1960s, secularization theory emerged as a dominant theme in both the social sciences and theological studies.[16] Although no unanimity emerged among theological interpreters relative to the precise meaning to be accorded to the rubric of secularization, agreement did arise with respect to the waning influence of religion in public life, especially, and to a lesser degree in private affairs as well.

A differentiated response typically marked the reaction to this state of affairs. One contingent of theologians—including Robinson, Macquarrie, and the death of God theologians in particular—viewed secularization as an opportunity for religious folk to break out of traditional formulas for the faith and experiment with new forms of theological conceptualization. Others—led by Cox and the more activist wing of theological liberalism/radicalism—boldly asserted that religious adherents must move out of the stained glass, gothic fortresses of their churches into the streets, marketplace, and political arena where the "real action" was already underway, and participate in those processes as a means of being responsible to the demands of the Gospel.

The first, or what we might tentatively label the intellectualist, response by and large accepted the fact that religion no longer prevailed at the macro level as a potent cultural force giving definition to the course of ongoing societal action and development. Relieved of this responsibility, religion was now freed to be religion, that is to say, to devise coherent systems of belief for nurturing piety among those still eager to experience the ministrations of religious organizations.

The activist cortege, meanwhile, was fundamentally attuned to issues of macro significance. The cultivation of personal piety paled in comparison to addressing such overriding concerns as injustice, economic exploitation, poverty, war, discrimination, political powerlessness, and the like. Moreover, this whole range of issues could only be adequately ameliorated by collective action and massive restructuring of the basic institutions of American society. And if the church proved unwilling or incapable of initiating movements directed toward the realization of these moral ends, then activists had no real alternative but to defect from the church in favor of organizations for whom these issues were matters of utmost concern.

Theologians and church leaders who wrestled seriously with the implications of secularization, then, tended to come to two mutually exclusive conclusions. Either religion would retreat from the public marketplace of ideas in the hope of devising systems of meaning for giving comfort and direction to privatized selves, or religion must forsake individual concerns for the larger issues of moral consequence troubling the body politic.

The 1960s also witnessed a revival of interest in secularization theory on the part of social scientists, and especially sociologists of religion. Like their theological counterparts, sociologists ascribed a wide range of meanings to the construct of secularization. Bryan Wilson, for example, defined the term from within the decline-of-religion tradition as "the process whereby religious thinking, practice and institutions lose social significance."[17] And writing on the basis of somewhat different religious presuppositions, Peter Berger sounded a similar theme when he defined the term as "the process by which sectors of society and culture are removed from the domination of religious institutions and symbols."[18] For others, secularization pointed toward a pattern of compartmentalization whereby religion retained a degree of social significance, but only with respect to discrete areas of collective life. The most radicalized version of this stance is, perhaps, best represented by Thomas Luckmann, who contended—much as had the earlier classical theorists Spencer, Durkheim, and Troeltsch—that religion had become a privatized phenomenon in the contemporary age whose primary function was to help facilitate the development of an individual identity, particularly in juxtaposition to the impersonal, mass institutions of modern, industrial, and bureaucratized societies.[19] According to Luckmann, religion was not in danger of being eradicated altogether from human experience because all selves have a need for meaning which transcends their basic, biological nature. But the institutional expression of religion was in the process of being radically marginalized by the strategic forces of science, economics, politics, and culture, which had now assumed the primary responsibility for defining the perimeters of the world in an empirically cogent fashion.

An alternate approach to the secularization conundrum that pressed in very nearly the opposite direction of Luckmann materialized in the position expounded by Robert Bellah. Out of his concern for the fragmented nature of contemporary culture, a fragmentation which has subsequently made it almost impossible to communicate an integrated set of meanings to the youth generation, Bellah has at once both identified and sought to enhance a generalized religious interpretation of American society and its moral destiny through the construction of a rubric now familiarly known as civil religion.[20] This genre of religiosity prevails at the macro level. More precisely, civil religion transcends the particularity of churches and their formalized belief systems to provide an institutionalized religious dimension to societal culture. It bequeaths to the American republic a collection of sacred beliefs, symbols, and rituals which appertain to the collectivity as a whole and which express in religious form the special purposes, nature, and destiny of American society. And although Bellah expects that individuals will find guidance and a revivified devotion to ultimate societal goals through their participation in and acquiesence to the tenets of civil religion, the real center of gravity for this national religious self-understanding exists at the highest level of the cultural system rather than at the micro level of individual citizens.

Very much like their theological colleagues, then, sociologists can be separated into two groups, one intent on defining the post-secularist role for religion as one mainly confined to providing meaning to individual identities at the micro level, and the other regarding religion's most important contribution as providing symbolic forms of meaning at the macro level for societal collectivities as a whole. The very divergence of these two strands of interpretation, each proposed almost simultaneously, contributed to a growing sense among members of the discipline that a viable theory of secularization had not yet been articulated. And as the decade of the 1970s ushered in an era of renewed religious activity—first signaled by the Jesus freaks, then by the rise of new religious movements and the coming of the Moral Majority, and finally by the TV evangelists—it became increasingly clear that simplistic theories of secularization simply would not suffice to account for the sort of activism reverberating through the religious institution—and not only in the United States but in other nations as well.

The challenge to sociological imagination aroused by the problems associated with secularization theory swiftly generated a succession of efforts aimed at devising a more elegant and complex theory to answer the sundry difficulties associated with earlier endeavors. One such enterprise was that undertaken by Richard Fenn in *Toward a Theory of Secularization,* wherein he proposed a five-step model for delineating the long-term trajectory of the secularization process.[21] Fenn's account postulates a process of differentiation first internal to the religious organization itself, then between the sacred and secular society, and finally culminating in a generalized set of religious symbols for society as a whole (civil religion), the secularization of political authority, and the dispersion of the sacred as individuals become separated from the dominant institutions of corporate life. Although this process is not strictly described as unilateral in its direction or irreversible with respect to its developmental stages, nonetheless, the general thrust of the model tends toward the view that secularization occurs on *both* the micro and macro levels. Privatization of individual meaning systems and the emergence of civil religion as a societal phenomenon represent differing consequences of what should be properly understood as one overall social process.

Operating on an alternative set of presuppositions and preoccupied with a rather different data base, David Martin also concentrated his analytical focus on the grand process of social differentiation to elucidate his general theory of secularization.[22] In sharp juxtaposition to Fenn, however, Martin predicated his empirical theory on a vast range of cross-national data, especially as these data pertained to the interrelation between religious organizations and political structures. The resulting typology gave definition to the modes by which ecclesiastical bodies entered into monopoly relations with the political order and the extent to which the religious environment was characterized by pluralism set within a disestablished political framework. And although the dominant focus of Martin's analysis was firmly fixed on the macro level, the model did allow for varying observations concerning the range of individual voluntarism accorded within each typological frame. Thus the sort of bifurcation between the macro and micro levels characteristic of Fenn's interpretation of the secularization process, Martin relegated to the status of a subtype within his more generalized analytical construct.

A final contribution to this unfolding debate was provided by Bryan Wilson, who reentered the lists in order to provide fresh support for his older conception of secularization.[23] In keeping with his earlier assessment, Wilson reiterated his claim that the phenomenon of religion was an attribute of what has come to be known since Toennies as community (*Gemeinschaft*). Yet, the salient trend in the modern era has been toward a diminution of community and a corresponding expansion of society (*Gesellschaft*), a social form characterized by a marked increase in rationality, efficiency, impersonality, and sheer growth in size of its organizational units. In the process of societalization—that is, the ongoing, large-scale, internally coordinated, and complex social system process of state formation—religion simply has no role to play except at the margins, the interstices, the domain of private lives, and this only for a steadily decreasing number of modern selves who still find it possible to respond affirmatively to the message of salvation proclaimed by religious functionaries. Industrial society with its bureaucratically organized technological, economic, and political systems no longer requires the sort of religious legitimation once commonly bestowed on local community patterns of value, meaning, group interaction, and custom. Indeed, Wilson even discredits civil religion as nothing more than a "feeble remnant of what remains of the latent functions of religion in providing social cohesion."[24]

Among these three recent approaches to the problem of micro/macro linkage insofar as the processes of secularization are concerned, Wilson's certainly remains the most starkly critical with respect to the future of religion, since in his view religion has no macro-level function to perform and only a marginal—and no doubt shrinking—micro-level contribution. Fenn discerns an ongoing marginalization process at both the macro and micro levels and finds the whole issue of linkage distinctly problematic. And for his part, Martin develops a whole succession of scenarios that allow for a wide variety of linkages depending on the theological tradition (especially Catholic versus Protestant), the degree of traditional and modern elements embedded in the cultural/societal structure, the alignment of religion with ethnic or class formations, the historical frame bequeathed by a revolutionary tradition, and so forth. Thus the message implicit in Martin's writing is caution against too swiftly assuming that there is but one grand trend in the secularization process which resolves in a definitive fashion the question of linkage between micro and macro religious forces.

Toward Micro/Macro Linkage in the Scientific Study of Religion

In a recent survey of the current status of the secularization model, Phillip Hammond observed that "(t)he sacred obviously is persisting, but the secularization thesis—as traditionally understood—is not sufficient to allow us to understand why."[25] Part of the reason, Hammond continued, may be that religion and the sacred have too frequently (and mistakenly) been employed as synonymous terms, while in the empirical domain of historical experience it now appears that religion can undergo a period of decline without necessarily being accompanied by a corresponding disappearance of the sacred. That, indeed, Hammand concludes, would seem to describe the current situation in the religious life of modernized, industrial nations.

The substantive chapters designed to cover the more significant research areas in the scientific study of religion provided little in the way of further definition to a recrudescent theory of secularization, however, and several contributors expressed satisfaction with much of the inherited wisdom relative to the dynamics of secularization processes. What did emerge from these sundry reflections on the current status of our knowledge of religious behavior was a recurrent theme that postulated the regenerative capacities of the sacred, especially at the micro and macro levels. Moreover, the evaluation assessments of these tendencies stood at sharp variance with previous conclusions predicated on the earlier versions of secularization theory. Most pronounced was the absence of any suggestion that the micro (self-transformational) and macro (global) developments were intrinsically marginal to ongoing societal dynamics.

And not only were the patterns of resacralization construed as critical developments in postindustrial societies, but they were also typically depicted as correlative developments. That is to say, the resurgence of interest in the sacred at the micro level necessarily found its intrinsic theoretical counterpart in the global community at the macro level. This inherent linkage derived in no small part from the fact that, increasingly, both self and society were coming to be understood by social theorists as anchored in that general orientation toward the world which Parsons described under the rubric of the "human condition paradigm."[26] The analytical advantage proffered by this framework centered preeminently in its emphasis on the telic, meaningful concerns shared by humanity at large, albeit crystallized in individual as well as in transsocietal forms of consciousness.[27] Or, to recast the issue in slightly different terms, the conceptualization of self and society may now be understood to be taking place primarily within a single categorical context, so that self-consciousness comes to fruition under the circumstances of modernity only in conjunction with the more encompassing generation of societal consciousness. Ineluctably, therefore, the micro and macro integuments through which manifestations of sacredness are conjoined in advanced societies constitute a kind of reenchantment project, whose relevance in the emergence of a global polity we are just beginning to comprehend.

If the trends toward a new phase of sacralization have been rightly apprehended, then the conclusion would appear intractable that some mechanism for delineating the particularistic features of the rapproachement between the micro/macro poles of social reality and the role of religion within that sociocultural matrix represents a task of some urgency. Before such an undertaking is launched along these or similar lines, however, there is considerable merit in carefully weighing the appropriate methods for arriving at what might be heralded as a series of reasonably cogent interpretive conclusions. Two divergent approaches readily spring to mind as potentially fruitful research strategies. Should one proceed by closely scrutinizing the secular processes of privatization and globalization in tandem and then strive to discern the place of religiosity within those patterns? Or, should one concentrate primarily on religious processes and draw in materials from secular life as these become appropriate for fleshing out the contextual background to the discussion?

It would be difficult to deny that most research in the contemporary scientific study of religion proceeds on the basis of the latter alternative. That is to say, analysts start from the familiar territory of the religious institution and then endeavor to trace the lines of its influence outward into the larger secular domain. The salient difficulty with this procedure is that it tends to encourage a more insular conception of religion than may actually be the case. There results, in fact, an almost methodological begging of the question, because investigators are implicitly constrained toward the view that religion persists as an influential and strategic institution in societal life. The more fundamental question, however, is really whether and how that supposition is a correct reading of the empirical situation?

A more neutral tack would entail an empirical account of dominant social trends in advanced social orders and the role, if any, which religious ideas, actors, or institutions have to play in those unfolding social processes. Perhaps the most serious defect in conventional secularization theory—and the cause of its myopic misreading of contemporary societies so that the resurgence of

fundamentalism, interfaith conflicts, and new religions took experts
by such surprise—was its focus on what was happening *to* religion
itself instead of to society as a whole.

Of course, no methodological strategy is any better than the
quality of those questions which its practitioners pose. Even if the
point of departure for one's research venture is the fundamental
issue of "what is going on" in the secular social arena, the contribution of the religious institution to those dynamics may well not be
highlighted until that issue is explicitly raised. The thrust of the
analysis developed throughout the larger body of this introductory
chapter tends to suggest, however, that the emerging focus of religious influence may well be situated at both the micro level of
individual self-consciousness wherein there persists a vital search
for identity, meaning, and purpose, and at the macro level of societal
consciousness wherein there persists a quest for collective legitimation of the polity, a concern with the normative structure of intergroup relations, and a redefining of the ultimate *telos* toward which
we should be striving in our collective endeavors. We have also
claimed that, in a programmatic sense, neither of these central
concerns can be adequately addressed *in vacuo,* since they exist
empirically as merely separate facets of the same general problem.

A final observation needs to be registered as these comments draw
to a close. A comprehensive theoretical model for interpreting the
role of religion, which adequately integrates the micro and macro
dimensions in a coherent fashion, will almost certainly prove to be a
collective enterprise based on numerous, but discrete, contributions
from empirical and theoretical researchers alike. The chapters collected together in this volume constitute one—and we hope a significant—contribution to that larger enterprise. Indeed, while each of
these separate studies has its own story to tell, its own disclosures to
reveal relative to a specific aspect of religious life, there is in addition
a larger significance to these research endeavors which ranges beyond the sum of their parts. For each substantive chapter illuminates
another dimension to the problem we have labeled herein as the
micro/macro linkage in the scientific study of religion.

NOTES

1. See, for example, A. Barmenkov, *Freedom Of Conscience in the USSR* (Moscow:
    Progress Pubs., 1983).

2. Reinhold Niebuhr, *Moral Man and Immoral Society* (New York: Scribners, 1960).

3. See in this connection, H. Richard Niebuhr, *The Meaning of Revelation* (New York: Macmillan, 1960); H. Richard Niebuhr, *Christ and Culture*. (New York: Harper, 1951); and H. Richard Niebuhr, *The Responsible Self* (New York: Harper, 1963). For a secondary interpretation which highlights the theoretical foundations to Niebuhr's theological reflection, see William R. Garrett, "The Sociological Theology of H. Richard Niebuhr," in *Religious Sociology: Interfaces and Boundaries,* ed. William H. Swatos, Jr. (Westport, CT.: Greenwood Pub. Co., 1987), pp. 41–55.

4. Ernst Troeltsch, *The Social Teaching of the Christian Churches* (London: George Allen & Unwin, Ltd., 1931).

5. Two recent attempts to address the sundry problems of micro/macro linkage can be found in: Michael Hechter, ed., *The Microfoundations of Macrosociology* (Philadelphia: Temple University Press, 1983); and Jeffrey C. Alexander et al., eds., *The Micro-Macro Link* (Berkeley, CA: University of California Press, 1987).

6. Cf. John Locke, *The Works of John Locke,* vol. 5 (London and Germany: Scientia Verlag Aalen, 1963). For a recent and insightful interpretation of Locke's social theory, see Ian Shapiro, *The Evolution of Rights in Liberal Theory* (New York: Cambridge University Press, 1986), pp. 80–148.

7. The most direct critique of Locke can be found in Emile Durkheim, *The Division of Labor in Society* (New York: Free Press, 1964). Also relevant is Emile Durkheim, *The Elementary Forms of the Religious Life* (New York: Free Press, 1965).

8. For the classical statement of Mead's position, see George H. Mead, *Mind, Self, and Society* (Chicago: University of Chicago Press, 1934).

9. See, in this connection, Jonathan H. Turner and Leonard Beeghley, *The Emergence of Sociological Theory* (Homewood, IL: Dorsey Press, 1981), pp. 480–6.

10. Max Weber, *The Protestant Ethic and the Spirit of Capitalism* (New York: Scribners, 1958)

11. In Max Weber, *From Max Weber,* Trans. and ed. H. H. Gerth and C. Wright Mills (New York: Oxford University Press, 1958), pp. 267–301.

12. Weber set forth these conditions in their most explicit form in his brief introduction to *The Protestant Ethic and the Spirit of Capitalism,* op. cit., pp. 13–31. Although Talcott Parsons placed this "Introduction" at the beginning of the Protestant ethic volume, Weber originally penned these remarks as an introduction to his three volume, *Gesammelte Aufsaetze zur Religionssoziologie* (Tubingen, 1922–1923).

13. This concept reappears consistently in Weber's extensive literature. See, Weber, *From Max Weber,* op. cit., p. 287; Weber, *Wirtschaft Und Gesellschaft,* 5th ed. (Tubingen: J.C.B. Mohr [Paul Siebeck], 1972), p. 311; and in English translation, *Economy and Society,* 2 vols. (Berkeley, CA: University of California Press, 1978), I:502–3.

14. Weber not only articulates this theme at the end of the Protestant ethic essay, but also in two addresses presented in Munich very near the end of his life. See

"Science as a Vocation" and "Politics as a Vocation," in *From Max Weber,* op. cit., pp. 77–156.

15. Several of the more important thinkers who predicted the demise of religion or at least its radical secularization are: Auguste Comte, *Auguste Comte and Positivism,* ed., G. Lenzer (New York: Harper, 1975), pp. 393–476; Karl Marx and Frederick Engels, "Manifesto of the Communist Party," in Karl Marx, *Political Writings, Vol. I,* ed., David Fernback (New York: Random House, 1974); Ferdinand Toennies, *Community and Society* (New York: Harper 1963); and Emile Durkheim, *The Division of Labor in Society,* op. cit., Emile Durkheim, *The Elementary Forms of the Religious Life,* op. cit.

16. The opening wedge to this spate of literature was John A. T. Robinson, *Honest to God* (Philadelphia: Westminster Press, 1963), a volume inspired in part by Dietrich Bonhoeffer's cryptic observations in *Letters and Papers from Prison* (New York: Macmillan, 1962), especially pp. 161–9. Meanwhile, just as the Death of God movement was being launched, Harvey Cox published, *The Secular City* (New York: Macmillan, 1965). This was followed in short order by a succession of studies including, John Macquarrie, *God and Secularity* (Philadelphia: Westminster Press, 1967); Martin E. Marty and Dean G. Peerman, eds., *New Theology No. 2* (New York: Macmillan, 1965); Marty and Peerman, eds., *New Theology No. 4* (New York: Macmillan, 1967); Paul M. Van Buren, *The Secular Meaning of the Gospel* (New York: Macmillan, 1963); and James F. Childress and David B. Harned, eds., *Secularization and the Protestant Prospect* (Philadelphia: Westminster Press, 1970); to cite but a few of the more important or representative contributions.

17. Bryan Wilson, *Religion in Secular Society* (Baltimore: Penguin Books, 1966), p. 14.

18. Peter L. Berger, *The Sacred Canopy* (Garden City, N. Y.: Doubleday, 1967), p. 107.

19. See Thomas Luckmann, *The Invisible Religion* (New York: Macmillan, 1967).

20. Robert Bellah, *Beyond Belief* (New York: Harper, 1970).

21. Richard K. Fenn, *Toward a Theory of Secularization,* Monograph Series, no. 1 (Storrs, CT: Society for the Scientific Study of Religion, 1978).

22. David Martin, *A General Theory of Secularization* (New York: Harper, 1978).

23. Bryan Wilson, *Religion in Sociological Perspective* (New York: Oxford University Press, 1982), especially pp. 148–179.

24. Wilson, op. cit., 1982, p. 169.

25. Phillip E. Hammond, "Introduction" to *The Sacred in a Secular Age,* ed. Phillip E. Hammond (Berkeley, CA: University of California Press, 1985), p. 3.

26. See Talcott Parsons, *Action Theory and the Human Condition* (New York: Free Press, 1978).

27. See in this connection, Roland Robertson, "The Sacred in the World System," in *The Sacred in a Secular Age,* op. cit., pp. 347–8.

Part II

SOCIAL CONSEQUENCES OF BELIEF ON THE MICRO LEVEL

The distinguishing feature of micro-level analysis turns on the fact that individual selves constitute the starting point of research enquiries. Thus patterns of interpersonal relationship, meaning acquisition, and role definition figure prominently in the sorts of concerns addressed at the micro level. To be sure, the differentiation between micro and macro levels defies precise delineation since the two levels, rightly understood, represent end points along a continuum. Individual belief structures invariably build into larger symbol systems carried by denominational bodies or sociocultural conceptions of reality. While conversely, macro patterns of meaning can be traced downward toward those individual participants whose personal outlooks they inform. Nonetheless, the relative sphere of influence for these two segments of reality possesses sufficient analytical specificity to warrant their usage in this volume.

In this section, the essays presented primarily treat micro issues. The first two contributions examine, largely from within a sociological perspective, the influence of belief in God for channeling the course of individual behavior. James R. Wood, for example, raises the issue of whether and to what degree a belief in God eventuates in humanistic behavioral styles for religious adherents. Armand L. Mauss concentrates his attention on a specific religious tradition, namely, the Mormons, and delineates how specific religious doctrines translate into specific patterns of behavior for members of the Mormon faith.

The next essay is focused on the philosophical, religious thought of Josiah Royce. The provincialism of Royce, derived in part from his early upbringing in California, is the subject of John K. Roth's essay. Roth's thesis is that Royce's concept of loyalty and its implications for contemporary religiosity can best be understood against the backdrop of his early life.

The final two chapters in this section on micro-level interpretations examine how religious beliefs motivate actors with respect to what we commonly call "social action." Rita M. Pulliun tackles the difficult issue, at least for committed religionists, of why some devout believers embrace positions of intolerance, discrimination, and hostility toward other selves. She develops a thesis which contends that certain types of religiosity can be expected to take negative attitudes toward others, while other forms of religiosity can result in humanitarianism. Using the metaphor of "the family," Irene K. K. Jensen examines how religious themes informed by this concept can result in concern for the material and spiritual needs of others. Jensen's point of departure is the missionary experience, but she also applies this family metaphor to the issues which trouble modernized societies.

Taken together, there is a common theme which unifies these essays. This has to do with how conceptions of God exert influence on individuals' definitions of their religious responsibility to enter into service to humankind, even as these prescriptions also define the religious reality within which particular participants are to understand their own religious situation and destiny. Yet, each of these essays has its own avenue toward the larger issues of macro-level religiosity, which invariably impinges willy-nilly on micro-level dynamics.

2

Sociological Conditions for Humanitarian Consequences of Belief in God

JAMES R. WOOD

In the United States belief in God is part of the general culture that is often learned almost automatically. Whether belief in God has social consequences is problematic. I will argue that certain beliefs about God, when salient to the individual, draw him or her into religious activities that have humanitarian consequences.

More than twenty years ago, Glock and Stark noted "agreement among religions that consequences follow, or should follow, from religious commitment." These consequences include both "what the individual can expect to receive as a result of being religious"—such as peace of mind or promises of eternal life—and what he or she is expected to give—such as "avoiding certain kinds of conduct and actively engaging in others."[1] Though what a person expects to receive from religion may also have social consequences, I will focus on the other aspect of Glock and Stark's "consequential dimension" of religion: what a religious person is expected to do. Glock and Stark find little research that treats the effect of religion on *behavior* as distinguished from attitudes. The only major such work they cite is Gerhard Lenski's *The Religious Factor.* Lenski presents evidence that religion

> is constantly influencing the daily lives of the masses of men and women in the modern American metropolis. More than that: through its impact on individuals, religion makes an impact on all the other institutional systems of the community these individuals staff. Hence the influence of religion operates at the social level as well as the personal level. . . . Depending on the socio-religious group to which a person belongs, the probabilities are increased or decreased that he will . . . vote Republican, favor the welfare state, take a liberal view on the issue of freedom of speech, oppose racial integration in the schools, migrate to another community, maintain close ties with his family, develop a commitment to the principle of intellectual auton-

omy, have a large family, complete a given unit of education, or rise in the class system.[2]

Later I will discuss Lenski's work as well as more recent work relating religion to behavior. I will also consider studies relating religious beliefs to attitudes and values that may be presumed to have consequences for social behavior.

Humanitarian Consequences

A recent study by Hoge and De Zulueta reviews the literature and brings new data to bear on the issue of the social consequences of religious beliefs:

> The main theoretical conclusion is that the consequences of religion vary greatly from value area to value area. In many value areas there are no consequences of religion; in some there are direct consequences; in a few there are consequences only among educated, high-salience persons. General statements about "religion and values" or "religion and politics" are worth very little. Future research must be precise about the specific value areas it is studying.[3]

I will argue that religion has important social consequences in two areas: (1) recruiting individuals into helping people outside their families; and (2) enlisting individuals in the support of social changes that more directly help others. First, I will ask whether certain beliefs are directly related to humanitarian consequences; then I will discuss the relation of these beliefs to religious activities that have these consequences.

Variation in Belief about God

In a survey by the Princeton Research Center in 1985 it was found that 92 to 99 percent of the people in the United States believe in God. This contrasted to 88 percent in Northern Ireland, 70 percent in Great Britain, 64 percent in West Germany, and 58 percent in Sweden.[4]

Content of belief

A major variable in belief itself is content. The survey just cited found that substituting "personal God" for "God" reduced the number of Americans believing to 66 percent (compared to 70 percent in Northern Ireland, 31 percent in Great Britain, 24 percent in West Germany, and 19 percent in Sweden).

Roof and Roof have shown not only that there is a great deal of variation in images of God among American believers, but also that this variation is associated with education, class, and denomination.[5] For example, 71 percent of those with less than a high school education were extremely likely to imagine God as Father, compared to 48 percent of those with a college education; similarly, 77 percent of Baptists studied, compared with 46 percent of Episcopalians, were extremely likely to imagine God as Father.

I found no studies relating content of belief in God to humanitarianism. However, Broughton found that "traditional" imagery (forgiving, helpful, trustworthy) was positively associated with the importance attributed to church membership and to the frequency of devotional and ritual activities.[6] Later in this paper, I will show that these variables are related to humanitarianism.

Salience of belief in God

Another way to increase variation in belief in God is to take into account the salience of belief. For example, among Americans sampled, 61 percent considered "following God's will" very important, compared with 92 percent who favored "good family life," and 81 percent who favored "good physical health."

In 1973, David Gibbs, Samuel Mueller, and I offered a theoretical explanation for why there is relation between religious belief and social consequences only when the religious belief is salient to the individual.[7] Our theory is based on the symbolic interactionist concepts of identity—"an analytically discrete aspect of the Meadian self [and] identity salience"—"the probability, for a given person, of a given identity being invoked in a variety of situations." Within an individual, "the discrete identities that comprise the self are arranged in a hierarchy of salience." However, certain social situations may call forth more than one of an individual's identities at the same time.[8]

Symbolic interactionist theory predicts that "the higher an identity lies in the salience hierarchy, the higher will be the probability of role performance consistent with the role expectations attached to that identity."[9] Focusing on the degree of overlap between an individual's religious and political identities, we proposed that "the greater the degree to which an individual regards himself as a religious person, the greater will be his tendency to conform to the secular attitudes and behavior—perhaps implicitly—in the content of his [or her] religious beliefs." In other words, the relationship between one's belief in God and the consequences of that belief should be a function of salience.

The theory predicted well for clergy, and for laity when the dependent variable was church related, but not for laity's attitudes about secular actions. We interpreted the results to mean that an even higher level of salience would be needed for belief to predict consequences. Indeed, Hoge and De Zulueta, using a better measure of salience, concluded that our theory was supported in the case of political values.[10] Where religious salience was high, there was a positive relationship between conservative belief and conservative political values.

Devotionalism

I am not aware of studies that relate belief in a personal God or the salience of belief in God to helping behavior or social action. However, both the Lenski study of Detroit and the Nelson and Dynes study of a Southwestern city link to humanitarianism a measure of devotionalism that implies both a personal belief in God and the salience of that belief.

Lenski found that devotionalism, unlike doctrinal orthodoxy, was linked with humanitarianism. Doctrinal orthodoxy is

> linked with (and we suspect fosters) a *compartmentalized view of life*. It seems to foster the view that one's religious commitments are irrelevant to one's political and economic actions and other aspects of secular life—except, of course, that in interpersonal relations one should be honest and fair. Devotionalism by contrast, seems linked with problems of social injustice.[11]

For example, among both Protestants and Catholics, those high on devotionalism but not on orthodoxy were the strongest supporters of foreign aid. "Evidently the cultivation of a personal relationship with God through prayer and meditation is a phenomenon with significant social consequences, while intellectual assent to doctrines seems socially irrelevant."[12]

Using frequency and importance of prayer as a measure of devotionalism, Nelson and Dynes found that devotionalism was related to helping behavior, though more strongly related to "ordinary" helping behavior than "emergency" helping. Ordinary helping included regular contributions to social service agencies, donations of goods through such agencies, taking food to bereaved families, and regular participation in formal voluntary social service work.

Church participation and humanitarianism

More refined measures of belief may help to establish meaningful relationships between beliefs and social consequences. However, a more fruitful approach to the issue of social consequences of belief in God may be to ask whether beliefs provide a means of leverage by which leaders of religious organizations can involve their members in humanitarian actions?

Lenski's major concern was with socioreligious groups—the networks of social interaction through which particular religions are manifested. Of particular interest here is that Lenski found different social consequences for the communal (friendship-network) and the associational (church-participation) aspects of socioreligious group membership.

> There is only a very limited relationship between the degree to which individuals are involved in a formal religious association and the degree to which they are involved in the corresponding subcommunity. Hence, the subcommunity is a vehicle by means of which large numbers of persons are effectively indoctrinated with the norms of the group. . . . Thus the subcommunity becomes an important instrument for extending the influence of religious groups in the life of the community.[13]

Nevertheless, the norms of the group, especially the humanitarian ones, are apparently translated into action primarily by those who are involved in church activities. The subcommunity is only imperfectly coordinated with the religious association. "At times, in fact, it exercises an influence which brings it into conflict with the formal association."[14] For example, unfavorable images of other groups are linked with having a high proportion of ones primary relationships in the socioreligious group, but not with a high degree of church attendance. At least among Protestants, there was evidence that church attendance had the opposite effect. And among both Protestants and Catholics, support for racial integration was highest among those who were regular church attenders but had a low proportion of their primary relationships in the religious subcommunity. It appears that it is the subcommunities rather than the churches that foster intolerance, narrow-mindedness, and other negative attitudes so often cited by critics of the churches.

The relationship between church attendance and humanitarianism gains further support from other surveys. Nelson and Dynes, for example, found that frequency of church attendance is related to helping behavior, especially emergency helping behavior (e.g., donation of funds to relief organizations, provision of relief goods for victims of disasters, and the performance of disaster relief services for victims). They concluded that "a primary way churches mobilize members to participate in emergency helping behavior is through the provision of organizational means for such activity."[15]

A national survey found that those persons high on religious commitment—which included participation in a church—were most likely to do volunteer work for a local organization. Thirty-eight percent of those with high religious commitment volunteered frequently, compared with only 6 percent of those with low religious commitment. Those with high religious commitment were also more likely to attend community meetings, discuss local issues with friends and neighbors, and hold office in local associations.[16]

In a current project, I am examining in much greater detail the relationship between participation in the church and humanitarianism. Preliminary analysis shows that 85 percent of those who belong to or attend a church perceive that their church encourages them to participate in activities that help other people. We determined how many hours persons in our sample spent in volunteer activities assisting people who needed help trying to change their community's policies for helping people. Almost two times as many frequent church attenders spent at least one hour per week in such activities. This included taking meals to shut-ins, taking the sick for doctor's appointments, and serving on the community school board.

Impact of the Church on Society

As important as humanitarián activities are, they vastly underestimate the impact of the church on the community. Firstly, the church as a corporate body gets involved in the community. When I examined 58 churches representing denominations in Indianapolis, I found, for example, that 57 of them supported the church federation which sponsored a number of community action projects; 46 contributed to the principal group sponsoring racial justice programs; 35 contributed to social service centers; 16 provided tutors for innercity schools; 14 took liberal stands on such controversial issues as busing, integrated housing, integrated schools, abortion, and

Table 2–1   Churches' Participation in Social Action

Form of action	Number of active churches (out of 58)
Local church programs and policies	
Black members (or active recruitment)	22
Innercity tutoring (or similar innercity work)	16
Liberal stands on such controversial issues as busing, integrated housing, integrated schools, abortion, redlining	14
Recreation programs for the surrounding neighborhood	9
Headstart and similar programs	7
Community forums on controversial issues	5
"Adoption" of underprivileged children	5
Thrift shop	5
Black staff member(s) (other than janitor)	4
Direct support of community organizations	
Church Federation	57
Social service centers	35
Interracial understanding	11
Community action programs	11
Health care centers	10
Housing opportunity programs	9
Minority opportunity programs	7
League of Women Voters	6
Civil rights organizations	4
Community improvement associations	3
Support for activist organizations through denomination	
Indiana Interreligious Commission on Human Equality (a group sponsoring racial justice programs)	46
Minority opportunity programs	9
United Presbyterian Metropolitan Center	7
Welfare rights organizations	6
Community action programs	4

redlining; and 11 cooperated in some way with community action projects. Table 2-1 gives a more complete picture of their involvement. Bear in mind that the activities noted in the figure are controversial ones; hence the example actually understates the humanitarian impact of the churches. My study found the following:

Many of the churches' noncontroversial activities are valuable services to segments of the population most affected by social change.
For example, consider the actions of the 10 churches that were *least*
involved in the controversial issues treated in this study. Five of the
churches spent sizable amounts of money on food and clothing for
needy families; 3 allowed innercity 4-H clubs to use church facilities;
and 2 were centers for Meals on Wheels, a plan for distributing hot
meals to elderly people in the community. In addition, service projects of Sunday school classes and various other groups within the
churches involved important one-on-one acts of charity and human
kindness.[17]

Beyond these local community involvements, local churches support financially, and often cooperate actively with, denominational
leaders and agencies that play an important role in bringing about
social change at a national level. Here is how Robert Spike described
the role of the churches in the passage of the 1964 Civil Rights Bill:

> Congress became aware that the religious community was aroused in
> a startling way. The participation of the religious groups in the March
> on Washington was another bit of evidence. Over 40,000 white
> church people participated in that March. . . . White church people
> followed through during the long months of 1963 and 1964 with
> unparalleled persistent attention to the legislative process. Thousands
> of calls were made on Congressmen and Senators. . . . At one point,
> Administration leaders felt their only chance of passage lay in a
> watered-down bill. Church pressure insisted on the stronger version
> which was finally passed. . . . When it was finally passed, friend and
> foe alike credited the passage of the bill to the persistent power of the
> church. Senator Humphrey, the leader of the struggle in the Senate,
> and other veteran fighters for civil rights legislation, insisted that the
> churches' efforts had made the difference which had been lacking in
> other struggles for such bills. Senator Russell declared that it had
> passed because "those damn preachers had got the idea it was a moral
> issue."[18]

Though not quite so dramatic, the recent political battles over aid to
the Contras have evidenced the similar lobbying strength of
churches.

Belief in God as a Basis of Leverage for Religious Leaders

How can we explain the influence of church participation on humanitarianism? And how is that influence related to belief in God?

Elsewhere, I have developed a theory of leader's legitimacy that is based on raising members' consciousness of certain beliefs and then connecting those beliefs with the actions their leader believes necessary to carry out the mission of the organization.

> In the case of religious organizations, leaders frame policies on social action to reflect the fundamental values of the church, such as the servant of a just and compassionate God. They then use those values as a basis for claiming legitimacy for controversial policies by bringing to consciousness the members' belief in those general values—thus raising the rank of those values within members' value hierarchies (Rokeach, 1973)—and by encouraging members to apply the general values to the specific policies. . . . As Peter Berger and Thomas Luckmann have suggested (1966:95), the fundamental legitimating explanations are built into the vocabulary of faith (for example, the fatherhood of God and the brotherhood of man). But to establish a link between general values and a specific policy, such as busing or contributing to a welfare rights organization, involves a new construction of reality. Murray Edelman saw this clearly: "If legislative, administrative, and judicial procedures significantly influence how people see leaders, issues, and themselves, then those procedures are less likely to reflect the people's will than to shape it." More precisely, they reflect it only after they shape it (1971:175). In contrast to broader political processes, however . . . the church [has] a more central set of values to which members have been socialized and of which they are continually reminded, for example, through the use of the Bible and of Biblically based rituals in weekly services. Thus, at least in a general sense (often embedded in Jesus' parables or in descriptions of events in his life), these values are well known among church members. Hence leaders have these Biblical values as reasonably clear guides to the way in which they shape the will of the people and as a basis for shaping that will.[19]

This logic can be extended to less controversial involvements. Church appeals for visitors to nursing homes, people to take groceries to the poor, and volunteers to serve in a soup kitchen are made in the context of serving God. Figure 2-1 presents an actual bulletin insert from a local church. Here is an appeal based on belief. Most of the items on the list involve work in and for the congregation, but "Soup Kitchen" and "Scouting" are specific community activities and the "Church and Society" and "Missions" committees involve other activities in the community.

Of those individuals who believe that God commands us to love our neighbor as ourselves, the ones who are reminded of this in weekly church services and in that context are provided specific avenues for expressing concrete love for neighbor, are more likely to perform humanitarian deeds.

Figure 2–1   Your Gift

"There are different kinds of spiritual gifts, but the same Spirit gives them. There are different ways of serving, but the same Lord is served. There are different abilities to perform service, but the same God gives ability to everyone for their particular service. The Spirit's presence is shown in some way in each person for the good of all." Cor. 12:4-7

What is your gift? Each of us has some gift from the Spirit to share, some ability which we can contribute to help the whole church. What is your ability? If you know, St. Mark's needs you. If you are uncertain, St. Mark's would like to help you discover them. Below are several opportunities for you to share your spiritual gift or to discover your gift. If you need more information about any of the following, please place a question mark in the blank. If you would like to participate in any of them, just place a check mark in the appropriate blank. Then place your name, address, and telephone number and drop it in the offering plate on Sunday as a tithe of your gift and time.

_____ Missions   _____ Scripture Reader
_____ Communications   _____ Handiwork (carpentry,
_____ Evangelism   electrical, grounds,
_____ Finance   painting, etc.)
_____ Administrative Board   _____ Money Counter
_____ Finance Campaign   _____ Money Courier
_____ Church and Society   _____ Educ. Ministries
_____ Family Ministries   _____ Library Worker
_____ Acolyte Ministries   _____ Campus Ministries
_____ Usher   _____ Children's Ministries
_____ Visitation (homebound,   _____ Crib-room worker
         newborns, etc.)   _____ Child-care worker
_____ Choir (adult or youth)   _____ Teacher (specify age level)
_____ Soup Kitchen   _____ Bell Choir (adult or youth)
_____ Other   _____ Scouting
_____ Youth Ministries   _____ Worship
_____ Greeter   _____ Transportation
_____ Hosts   _____ Shepherding

NAME _____ PHONE _____

ADDRESS _____

Conclusion

Whether or not belief in God has social consequences depends upon the content of that belief and its salience to the individual. I have explored possible ways of measuring the content and salience of such belief. Though empirical work has not as yet established the relation between particular beliefs about God and humanitarian behavior, there is some evidence that devotionalism, which implies salience of belief in a personal, caring God, is related to such behavior.

Far more important, however, is belief's role in drawing people into collective religious activities that expose them both to persuasion that their belief should have humanitarian consequences and to structures of opportunity for acting out the humanitarian implications of their faith.

Stark and Bainbridge, in glorifying future religions in which people will be drawn into a career of successive religious involvements seem unaware of the potential for loss in humanitarianism if traditional religious organization is weakened in the United States.[20] The Unification church might be an example of a new religious organization that will have an important humanitarian influence, but whether Unificationism will be a permanent feature in America likely depends on the extent to which it has adopted much of the organizational apparatus of traditional religion.

Implications for Theoretical Development and Research

Deliberation in this paper suggests numerous theoretical and research issues. I will briefly discuss two of them.

(1) Is belief in God any more likely to lead to humanitarian consequences than to the opposite? In two previous studies, I have demonstrated that the same value-based leadership processes that lead members into liberal social action can lead members into conservative social action. For example, 36 percent of Moral Majority members in Indiana reported shifts toward more conservative values because of Moral Majority involvement.[21] More specific to the question of antihumanitarian actions, the Good News movement within the United Methodist church effectively defeated that church's proposal to urge Congress

> to ban discrimination against homosexuals, [to seek] an executive order banning discrimination based on sexual orientation in all agen-

cies of the federal government, [to seek] the end of discrimination against homosexual parents in child custody cases, and [to urge] all church agencies not to discriminate in employment regardless of sexual orientation.[22]

Certainly some conceptions of God would be congruent with inhumane, vindictive, and even violent behavior. We need studies that take seriously the possibility that the same sociological mechanisms of value-based leadership that have led to so much humanitarianism are also implicated in violence, conflict, and persecution throughout the world.

(2) We need cross-national, cross-cultural, and historical studies of the social consequences of belief in God. I have shown above that there is great variation in belief in God across nations. Undoubtedly, there is even more variation in the content and salience of that belief. A Gallup International Research Institute survey asked respondents in fifteen nations "to rate, on a scale of 1 to 10, how important God is in their lives." The results are shown in Table 2–2.

Table 2–2

United States		8.21
South Africa	Whites	8.55
	Blacks	8.45
Republic of Ireland		8.02
Northern Ireland		7.49
Italy		6.96
Spain		6.39
Belgium		5.94
Great Britain		5.72
West Germany		5.67
Finland		5.35
Netherlands		5.33
France		4.72
Japan		4.49
Denmark		4.47
Sweden		3.99

Despite this variation, I found few comparative studies. Chalfant and Heller's finding in a British sample that frequency of church attendance "does have a liberalizing influence on the tendency to positively evaluate government welfare spending" suggests the generalizability of one aspect of the present study.[23]

Regarding religious belief as leverage for leading religious people into social action in the community, Shupe's findings on the relation between religion and political participation are suggestive. Among Shinto and Buddhists in Japan, he found

> religious preference-holders who find their church or temple located *within* their local community are more likely to be drawn into political involvement through the community's social structure than are religious preference-holders whose church or temple is situated outside the local community.[24]

Shupe's interpretation is that religious identification and participation are measures of integration into the community social structure and that

> it is within this social structure that villages are mobilized for political participation. The differences between the two types of Buddhists can then be explained in terms of this social structural engagement: they are differentially involved in their local community, a key area for the stimulation and encouragement of political activity.[25]

Though Shupe offers no basis for determining whether community integration leads to shrine, church, or temple participation, or whether that participation leads to further involvement in the community, his findings suggest that the general approach of the present paper is testable in a cross-cultural context.

The kind of comparative research most needed would ask such questions as: Is there anything in common between the value-based leadership that supported the civil rights movement in the United States and the leadership that supported the Islamic revolution in Iran? Hamid Dabashi argues that semisecular Islamic intellectuals have used Islam for their political objectives "This metamorphosis of faith-turned-ideology is best concealed in terms like 'progressive Islam.' "[26]

> "Progressive Islam" betrays those utilitarian uses of faith for radical revolutionary purposes that became inevitable once secular, necessarily Western, ideologies failed to provide the political ideologues with a banner under which to mobilize a resistant traditional society. Having failed to supplant the traditional common symbolic otherwise known as Islamic culture, with a progressive rationalism, and disenchanted by its stubborn perseverance, the Muslim intellectuals of modernity sought to utilize whatever revolutionary trait in Islamic history they could salvage and resuscitate for the same revolutionary ends."[27]

Are there really any social consequences of belief in God that do not reflect "faith-turned-ideology"? Certainly much of the history of Christian doctrinal disputes from Cyprian to Luther to King to Falwell can be interpreted that way. Given the values of our culture, we find more congenial those social consequences that are both humanitarian and nonviolent, but the same sociological mechanisms that leveraged people into the struggle for civil rights in the United States may be operating to foster violent struggles like those in Iran and Northern Ireland.

Most belief systems contain rudiments both of humanitarianism and of its opposite. By providing an understanding of how religious leaders' goals and strategies shape the social consequences of belief, sociologists of religion can fuel the flickering flame of hope for peace on earth and good will to humankind.

NOTES

1. Charles Y. Glock and Rodney Stark, *Religion and Society in Tension* (Chicago: Rand McNally, 1965), pp. 34–5.

2. Gerhard Lenski, 1963 *The Religious Factor* (Garden City, N.Y.: Doubleday, 1963) p. 320.

3. Dean R. Hoge and Ernesto De Zulueta, "Salience as a Condition for Various Social Consequences of Religious Commitment," *Journal for the Scientific Study of Religion* 24 (March 1985): 21–38.

4. Princeton Religious Research Center, "God and the American People: 95% Today Are 'Believers,' " in *Emerging Trends* 7 (June 1985): 1–4.

5. Wade Clark Roof and Jennifer L. Roof, 1984 "Review of the Polls: Images of God among Americans" *Journal for the Scientific Study of Religion* 23 (June 1984): 201–5.

6. Walter Broughton, "Theistic Conceptions in American Protestantism," *Journal for the Scientific Study of Religion* 14 (December 1975): 331–44.

7. David R. Gibbs, Samuel A. Mueller, and James R. Wood, "Doctrinal Orthodoxy, Salience, and the Consequential Dimension," *Journal for the Scientific Study of Religion* 12 (1973) :33–52.

8. Sheldon Stryker "Identity Salience and Role Performance: The Relevance of Symbolic Interaction Theory for Family Research," *Journal of Marriage and the Family* 30 (1968) :560.

9. Ibid., 563.

10. Hoge and De Zulueta, op. cit.

11. Lenski, op. cit., p. 329.

12. Ibid., p. 207

13. Ibid., p. 327

14. Ibid., p. 328

15. Russell R. Dynes and L.D. Nelson, "The Impact of Devotionalism and Attendance on Ordinary and Emergency Helping Behavior," *Journal for the Scientific Study of Religion* 15 (March 1976) 55.

16. Research and Forecasts, *The Connecticut Mutual Life Report on American Values in the '80s: The Impact of Belief* (Hartford: Connecticut Mutual Life Insurance Company, 1981), pp. 71–81.

17. James R. Wood, *Leadership in Voluntary Organizations: The Controversy over Social Action in Protestant Churches* (New Brunswick, N.J.: Rutgers University Press, 1981), p. 59.

18. Robert W. Spike, 1965 *The Freedom Revolution and the Churches* (New York: Association Press, 1965), pp. 106–8.

19. Wood, op. cit., pp. 85–6.

20. Rodney Stark and William Sims Bainbridge, 1985 *The Future of Religion: Secularization, Revival and Cult Formation* (Berkeley: University of California Press, 1985).

21. Wood, op. cit.,

22. Ibid., p.

23. H. Paul Chalfant and Peter L. Heller, "A Cross-National Perspective on Religiosity and Social Justice: A Research Note," *Review of Religious Research* 26 (March 1985): 261–8.

24. Anson D. Shupe "Conventional Religion and Political Participation in Postwar Rural Japan," *Social Forces* 55 (March 1977): 613–629.

25. Ibid., p.

26. Hamid Dabashi "The Revolutions of Our Time: Religious Politics in Modernity," *Contemporary Sociology* 13 (November 1984): 673–676.

27. Ibid., p. 675–6.

3

God of Gods: Some Social Consequences of Belief in God Among the Mormons

ARMAND L. MAUSS

Social scientists do not claim much competence in matters pertaining to God. We do, however, assume that whatever may be the Ultimate Source of divine revelation, such revelation will be received by human vessels. It will always be human cultures, then, and their constituent human beings, that provide the a priori premises and cognitive categories through which revelation and its implications will be understood. In every culture, the accumulated genius of revelation has interacted across time with historical experience to produce "images" of God and man—that is, understanding of what God is like, what humankind is like, and how the two are related. Derivative of these "images" are certain "explanatory modes" which deal with the universal questions of existence and meaning in the face of the incomprehensibly complex or tragic in human experience. Whether, how, and to what extent the explanatory mode of a people makes use of divine intent or divine intervention is, of course, culturally variable to a very large degree.[1]

The revelations received by Joseph Smith, the youthful founding prophet of Mormonism, were, on the one hand, startling and heretical enough to attract the attention and interest of thousands of spiritually discontented seekers. On the other hand, however, those revelations were understood and expressed by the prophet and his followers largely in terms of the religious, social, and scientific wisdom and issues familiar to their time and place: namely, the early nineteenth-century western frontier. This environment has been thoroughly described elsewhere and need not concern us here to any great extent.[2] Suffice it to say that there was much flux and ferment surrounding such religious issues as the nature of God, of man, of grace, of salvation, and of the millenium; such social issues as freedom versus equality, slavery, alcohol abuse, family obligations, and women's roles; and such scientific issues as the nature of the universe, the place of magic and the supernatural in that universe, the origin of life, and the preservation of human life. The Mormon prophet's revelations addressed many of these issues in one way or another, and Mormon teachings from that time to the present have evolved in a kind of dialectical relationship with the changing American social and intellectual milieu.

Space will permit only the most cursory and concise discussion of the social implications and consequences of Mormon beliefs and images concerning God. As a result, I shall perhaps be open to a certain amount of criticism for a *post hoc ergo propter hoc* line of reasoning. Yet, I am hopeful that my culpability in this respect will be mitigated somewhat by two considerations. One is the empirical evidence presented in much of the scholarly work that I shall cite. The other is the sheer implausibility, given such high levels of belief in (their own) God among the Mormons, that alternative causal explanations (other than religion) would be as compelling for those social traits that are uniquely Mormon.[3] In any case, I shall proceed now to outline the Mormon teachings about God, man, and their relationship, and then later I shall discuss some of the social consequences and implications thereof.

God and Man in the Mormon Cosmology

Beginning with the prophet Joseph Smith, Mormons have shown a great deal of ambivalence toward the work of professional theologians, in the belief that the latter have made theology largely inaccessible to the common man. Accordingly, scholarly and systematic theological literature relating to the Mormons is quite rare. There is a small official literature produced by an earlier generation of scholars among the Mormon leadership. These were not theologians, however, and while their work is articulate and persuasive, it is ultimately still of an amateur nature.[4] More recently, secular scholars with more appropriate qualifications have provided brief but informative treatises on Mormon theology.[5] All have made extensive use of the unique, revealed scriptures of Mormonism (e.g., the *Doctrine and Covenants*) and of the lectures of Joseph Smith in particular. From these sources, it is possible to sketch out a fairly consistent statement on the basic Mormon beliefs about God, many of which, as we shall see, are quite heterodox in terms of traditional Christianity.

To begin with, Mormonism rejects entirely not only the notion of *ex nihilo* creation, but also the belief in a Great First Cause. In the

Mormon cosmogony, matter, life, and intelligence have *always* existed in varied and changing forms; they are eternal, infinite in time and space, and uncreated—a conception fully in line, of course, with the emerging science of Joseph Smith's time. God is not the First Cause, therefore, but simply "co-eternal" with all that is in the cosmos. He is the creator in the sense of *organizer* of our world and of our known universe. All of His creations, furthermore, and all of the so-called miracles attributed to Him, have been accomplished by the application of natural laws, many of which remain unknown to us (and thus His works seem miraculous). However, all is potentially knowable, through either scientific discovery or revelation, or both. In one sense, then, God might be thought of as "super scientist," an idea not far from the naturalistic God of the Deists of Joseph Smith's time.

This is not the end of the Mormon "heresies." God is not only not the First Cause; He is *not even the first God*. The cosmos has been generating Gods eternally. Indeed, the acquisition of Godhood is the potential destiny of every human being. Though there is a definite Mormon soteriology, in which Jesus Christ plays an indispensable role, it is subsumed by the Mormon *plan of salvation,* which refers to a natural cosmic process by which Gods are produced. The process begins (insofar as one can speak of a beginning in infinity!) with an uncreated and vaguely described entity called an "intelligence," which is somehow the ultimate essence of the person. The beginning of the process *for each person* is the acquisition by the "intelligence" of a "spirit body," or in other words, the intelligence becomes a spirit. The spirit (corresponding probably to "soul" in conventional Christian theology) is a person with a body comprised of matter that is "refined" (or less dense) than that of mortal bodies. (Joseph Smith taught that "there is no such thing as immaterial matter"; whatsoever is not made of *some* kind of matter simply does not exist.)

The spirit has a meaningful existence of indefinite duration in the immediate presence of God, a phase called "the pre-existence." In due time, however, through the event we know as "birth," the spirit acquires a mortal body and enters the next stage in the cosmic process. Following the stage of mortality comes "death," and a disembodied stage called "the spirit world," where the spirit is again temporarily without mortal characteristics but still enjoys a conscious existence and continues in intellectual and spiritual growth until the resurrection. All, including evildoers, are ultimately resurrected, with bodies and spirits inseparably reunited forever. At that point, however, the cosmic process yields three divergent paths: a celestial glory, a terrestrial glory, and a telestial glory.

The first of these glories (or eternal paths) is reserved for those who, through obedience to God's eternal laws, have achieved a sufficient spiritual and intellectual level to continue toward God-hood. However, not all who qualify for celestial glory will achieve it. The resurrected beings in the other two glories (presumably the overwhelming majority of humankind) will also enjoy a pleasant, eternal existence, but not eligibility for Godhood. And all resurrected beings, like God himself, will live in or on particular worlds or planets somewhere in the greater universe. Indeed, those who ultimately achieve Godhood will be creating (organizing) new universes (or sections of the universe) of their own, having completed the destined cycle like their great parent God before them. Since the universe is infinite in time, space, and matter, there is room in it for an infinite number of realms and Gods, all of whom are progressing eternally. The process has been going on eternally and will continue to do so, just as the earth continues to produce monarch butterflies from cocoon-bound worms (to use a finite analogy).

Notice in all of this that the naturalism, materialism, and anthropomorphism which are so antithetical to mainstream Christianity, serve to eliminate the troublesome duality or dichotomy between spirit and matter, between the spiritual and material modes of existence. In Mormonism, God and man belong to the same great cosmic "species," and members of that species (in accordance with their respective stages of progression) move easily from one kind of existence to another (and back again, if they need to communicate with people at the earlier stages). The traumas that we call birth and death are just gateways to the next level, never to oblivion. This more "naturalistic" image of the relation between God and man, again, is more easily reconciled than traditional theologies with modern physics and astronomy, not to mention today's science fiction!

While all of this obviously adds up to polytheism in a *theoretical* sense, Mormonism is nevertheless a monotheistic religion in *operational* or practical terms. The infinite multiplicity of Gods produced by our species throughout eternity, while fully and freely acknowledged as part of the Mormon cosmology, in no way constitutes a *pantheon;* for Mormon *worship* is directed singularly and exclusively

to *our* God, our Eternal Heavenly Father, through the mediation of
Jesus Christ. The Holy Ghost is a deity with certain auxiliary
functions. These three, in Mormonism, constitute a "Godhead" of
three separate (but coordinating) Beings, **not** a trinity in the traditional sense.

At most, then, Mormonism might be considered "tritheistic"
rather than monotheistic, but even its tritheism is hierarchical, for
God the Father is always considered preeminent and is always the
sole object of worship. No other deities (aside from those three here
mentioned) have names or symbols of special identity. Thus closely
related to the concept of God the "super scientist" is the image of
God as "cosmic role model"—He who has become all that we aspire
to become. Or, in the words of one of Joseph Smith's prophets, "As
man is, God once was, and as God is, man may become." This was a
powerful idea in the radically egalitarian environment of Jacksonian
America: If Jackson was often taken to personify the ideal that any
man could become president, Joseph Smith surely demonstrated
that any man could become a prophet. And he went still a step
further in teaching that any man could become a God!

Another recurring theme in Mormon theistic imagery is that of
God as Eternal Family Head or Patriarch. At first glance, this may
seem merely an expression in Mormonism of a fairly classical Puritan and Old Testament image; but it has a literalism for Mormons
that it apparently lacks in those earlier traditions. In the plan of
salvation outlined above, the birth of spirits into mortal bodies here
on earth has its precedent and its type in the preexistent birth of
intelligences into spirit bodies. Our spirits are thus in some way
born to our Heavenly Father, so that He is our Father in rather a
literal (if spiritual) genealogical or even genetic sense.

This idea has many implications. Perhaps the most obvious and
humanitarian one is that the brotherhood and sisterhood of humankind for Mormons is theoretically both literal and eternal. A more
unconventional implication, however, is that such a Father must
have a spouse—a Heavenly Mother—in order for a *literal* father-
hood to have any meaning. This logical implication has indeed
become explicit in Mormon theology, though it is only rarely mentioned in official Mormon literature. Interestingly enough, it was a
female poet and associate of Joseph Smith (Eliza R. Snow) who
spelled out the idea of a Heavenly Mother, in one of her stanzas of a
still often sung Mormon hymn. He, however, definitely validated
her idea, providing Mormon women also with a potentially powerful "cosmic role model."[6]

Whatever the ultimate source of this idea in Mormonism, its prominence has waxed and waned with the general status of women in the Mormon subculture. Incongruous though it may seem the status of women in the polygynous Mormon subculture of the nineteenth century was relatively high compared to their contemporaries outside that subculture, and the Mormon church was one of the leading advocates for woman's suffrage in those early days. Then, after World War I, the status of Mormon women and women generally, declined with the reassertion of a more "traditional," patriarchal definition of ideal family life. For the past two decades, however, the strong patriarchal ideal in Mormonism has collided with the resurgence of feminism in American society, and even within the church to some degree. Accordingly, Mormons are starting to hear more about their Heavenly Mother, though the theology about her is terribly underdeveloped, and her role seems still to be interpreted largely in traditional patriarchal terms when she is mentioned at all.[7]

At a very minimum, however, Mormons understand themselves to be the literal, spiritual offspring of two Heavenly Parents in the preexistence, loving parents who want only to see all of their children succeed in the great cosmic quest for eventual Godhood of their own. One of the logical requirements for this accomplishment would seem to be a marriage covenant that would outlast the relatively brief period of mortal life. Thus it is that while Mormons recognize as legitimate (and even perform) conventional marriages for mortal time only, these are not considered "celestial" marriages. The latter (also called "temple marriages") are performed only in Mormon temples, and only for Mormon couples in good ecclesiastical standing.

In the temple marriage, the phrase "til death do us part" is replaced by "for time and all eternity," so that only temple-married Mormon couples are eligible for Godhood. Only such couples may eventually create worlds and people them with spirit offspring of their own. Furthermore, since "Father" and "Mother" inevitably imply the existence of each other, neither man nor woman can achieve Godhood without an eternal bond to the other. Once again, the essential egalitarianism of Mormon cosmology can be seen here, despite the shortage of both revelatory and systematic theology about a maternal deity, which we would expect to be the case in a patriarchal social and ecclesiastical structure.

So that we all have to learn to walk by faith in this mortal life, God has erased from each of us the memory of our preexistent life with our Heavenly Parents and all of our brothers and sisters. By revelation, however, we have learned a certain amount about what transpired in that important phase of our eternal existence. Mormonism teaches, for example, that there occurred an occasional "Council of Heaven," in which the entire celestial family of our Heavenly Parents met under God's leadership, to plan the creation and future of our mortal experience. God would need prophets and other leaders, and some of his children were selected by mutual consent to fill those roles.

This constituted *not* predestination but "foreordination," since the future realization of the mission would be problematic, given free will and the many hazards of the mortal setting. Nor were all equally well equipped for the same mortal missions. God did not, after all, create the "intelligences" that were born to Him and our Heavenly Mother; they took their children as they came, just as mortal parents do. Nor is it in God's nature to compel obedience at any point in our eternal progression; so in the preexistence, as in mortality, some of us, in the exercise of our free will, were more obedient than others, progressed more rapidly, and thus qualified for more favorable circumstances in mortality.

Some entire categories of our brothers and sisters in the preexistence were given special missions or roles for mortality, and were to be identified by distinct mortal lineages. Thus some were designated as "God's chosen people" and received mortal birth only through Israelite lineage. Potentially, any group or individual might have been given a special mortal mission, but revelation has identified only a few of these special assignments. Notice how all of these concepts about the preexistence and God's part in it set the stage for a Mormon theodicy and for a certain "explanatory mode" with important social implications in this world: God is not responsible either for evil or for human failure, individual or collective.

To begin with, He did not create the intelligences that He found, in infinitely varied quality, in the natural economy of the cosmos. He and our Heavenly Mother simply gave those intelligences spiritual birth and launched them (us) on the plan of salvation. Since launching, all humankind has been morally responsible for what has happened, whether in the mortal or the premortal existence, since all of us have had our free agency to obey or disobey divine commands, to accept or reject divine missions and assignments, and to make the best of whatever the mortal circumstances in which we find ourselves.

In sum, Mormons understand mortals to be of the same cosmic species as God and created (born) with divine potential, whether male or female, and with the freedom and the responsibility for their own eternal progression. They see God as having the *initiative* in history, but not necessarily a determining control, since, by his nature, He is constrained by the consequences of human free agency. He can teach, persuade, and direct, but He cannot compel. Many have been given special mortal missions, but they may fail to fulfill them adequately, so God is perforce a contingency planner. In identifying with God as a role model (theoretically both male and female), Mormons also see Him as the ultimate scientist and engineer, manipulating nature wisely and rationally, not arbitrarily; as loving Eternal Parent, forever and always offering direction and succor to his eternal children, finding ultimate joy and fulfillment in the cosmic accomplishments of those children.

Mormon Familism

Let us now turn to some of the apparent social consequences of the Mormon theology and cosmology. Of course, the Mormons are not unique in valuing a stable and wholesome family life, but the family institution receives in Mormonism a theological and ecclesiastical centrality that constitutes almost a religion in its own right. The image of the Father God and Mother God, surrounded by multitudes of righteous, striving children preparing for the next stage in their eternal progression, is not only the model for Mormon family life in the here and now, it is also the aspiration for the eternal future of the successful Mormon family. As characterized in church literature, this model is both patriarchal and matricentric: The ultimate authority in the home (as in the heavens) is the father, but the mother is the foundation.

In part, this model fits well with traditional ideas about family governance in many cultures of the earth. In part, also, it is derivative of the earlier, polygynous period in Mormon history, when the presence and authority of the father had to be distributed among two or more households. In those days, it was the mother who by necessity provided the main source of stability and continuity in the home. (In those days, too, God the Father was often characterized in church literature as a polygynist!). Nevertheless, the righteous Mormon father, like the Mormon Heavenly Father, exerts his authority not in Victorian or Ibsenian fashion but benignly, in close consultation with his wife, and with "gentleness, meekness, and love unfeigned" in all relationships with either wife or children.[8]

As would be expected, real Mormon family life approaches this model only imperfectly. Mormons have by no means been spared the tragedies of marital discord, divorce, juvenile delinquency, youthful suicide, teenage pregnancy, and other such banes of modern family life.[9] Nevertheless, the influence of church teachings is apparent, both in the institutional supports given to the family and in the actual social behavior of Mormons. Institutionally, the church sponsors many family-based social and recreational activities. It designates Monday evening throughout the world as Mormon family-home evening, on which families are to meet together in council, after the model of the Council in Heaven (in the preexistence); and no church activities are permitted on that night. The church also promotes and subsidizes a great deal of genealogical research and the compiling of family histories, all intended to emphasize the enduring nature of family life. A common motto in the church is "Families are forever," an aphorism that no doubt evokes different feelings in harried Mormon parents on different days!

Where individual and family social behavior are concerned, the professional literature makes abundantly clear that, compared with people of other major religions in America, Mormons marry and establish families earlier and more often, and have more children. These generalizations obtain despite differences in, for example, education. Where divorce is concerned, the Mormon case is complicated by the two levels of marriage : For ordinary civil or church marriages, the Mormon divorce rate is at least as high as the national average, but for the temple marriages (available, remember, only to Mormons in good ecclesiastical standing), the divorce rate is much lower, probably bespeaking a more thorough internalizing of the ideal model.[10]

Although Mormons accept and use modern birth control, they still produce twice the number of children found in American families generally. This suggests that the large families among Mormons are not the result of either ignorance or religious scruples, but rather of a consciously pronatal philosophy derived from Mormon religion. For Mormons are taught to see births and parenting as collaboration with the Eternal Father in bringing spirits from the preexistence into the next (mortal) stage of their eternal progression.[11]

At the same time, however, Mormon family values and norms

have been mediated in practice by secular economic and social forces. For example, while family size has always remained about double the national average, it still seems to have yielded to the same influences as has family size more generally. In other words, the graphic curve showing the rise and fall in Mormon family size across time closely resembles the corresponding curve for the nation as a whole, but at a *higher absolute level*.[12] Furthermore, changing definitions of women's roles, and other byproducts of modern feminism, have mediated considerably the classical patriarchal expectations of Mormon couples. Official church literature is starting to present models of womanhood other than the traditional "mother in Zion" model, and the meaning of "the patriarchal order" is undergoing some modifications.

These rather painful changes in church traditions are reflected in recent findings which indicate that Mormon women are relatively well educated compared to their American sisters outside the community. In actual practice, Mormon couples tend to rely on the kinds of egalitarian decision-making practices common in most American families, no matter how much patriarchal rhetoric may still be heard. On balance, however, despite some mediating influences from the outside, Mormon familism, derived as it is from the Mormon conception of God, continues to have concrete and definable social consequences for Mormons, and, derivatively, for their neighbors as well.[13]

Mormon Social Conservatism

During recent decades, the Mormons church has acquired such an image of conservatism that some scholars have considered the prospect of a political alliance between Mormons and the New Christian Right. While there are many historical and theological reasons for dismissing such a notion, its origins are understandable.[14] Ezra Taft Benson, one of Mormonism's most powerful apostles and currently its church president, has often given public support to right-wing causes during the past thirty years. More recently, of course, the church entered the national political arena in full force to oppose the Equal Rights Amendment.[15] Yet, it would be an oversimplification to conclude from such examples that either Mormons, Mormonism, or the Mormon church are part of the political Right here or anywhere else. Non-Mormons, especially in the media, generally fail to understand how little support there is among Mormons for the extreme political views of President Benson. This is particularly so among his colleagues in the ruling hierarchy of the church.

Mormon political opinions are influenced by all the same factors that influence others: education, occupation, region, family, and so forth. Any generalizations about Mormon political tendencies, therefore, that fail to take into account such variables, are questionable. Even Utah, the center of Mormonism, has generally voted with the majority of the nation in presidential elections. Mormon voters are almost equally divided between the two majority parties, and the most nearly accurate political generalization that could be made about Mormons would probably be that they are centrist and moderate in their preferences, all things considered. The ERA issue excepted, the intervention of church leaders in national politics, has been rather rare and not very obtrusive.[16]

Much of what gives Mormons a public image of political conservatism is not political at all, in the strictest sense, but is rather a deep-seated *social* conservatism that is fully understandable in terms of Mormon theology. The generally conservative Mormon attitudes on abortion, homosexuality, pornography, and women's rights, for example, are all tied to the familism.[17] That is to say, those practices are all perceived in the Mormon subculture as subversive to God's plan of salvation and eternal progression: abortion and homosexuality because they frustrate the natural, God-ordained process for bringing the spirit-children of our Heavenly Parents into this next and necessary stage in their eternal progression; pornography because it encourages attitudes and practices that subvert or downgrade the sacred marital bond and trivialize the procreative act; and equal rights for women because of the expectation that it would undermine the matricentric nature of family life.

Even in these matters, however, Mormons do not assume an extremist posture: neither Mormons nor their church, for example, advocate prohibition of abortion under any circumstances. Furthermore, the church has never advocated restrictions on civil liberties for homosexuals, or denial of equal rights for women. On the latter point, it was only the *constitutional amendment* that was officially opposed. National survey data show that Mormons feel like others about the role of women in politics or in the workplace (e.g. 75 percent of Mormons surveyed would be willing to vote for a female candidate for president).[18] In other words, Mormon social conservatism is not only an expression of preference for certain norms relating to sex, sex roles, and family life; it also expresses a fear that national policy (especially at the constitutional level) might come to interdict *church* norms for its own members, and thus interfere with the efforts of believing Mormons to act out their own model of family life in the image of their Heavenly Parents.

The Mystique of Mortal Mission

The mandate which believing Mormons endorse for their model of ideal family life is supported by another theological notion mentioned earlier: what might be called "the mystique of mortal mission." As God's children move from the preexistence to the mortal stage of their eternal progression, they may bring with them certain special missions, roles, or responsibilities (it is important to emphasize here again that free will remains paramount in this conception; so that we are talking about a kind of "fore-ordination," and *not* predestination). We do not always know if we have any special mortal missions, individually or collectively, but we can infer that most of us have missions at least as parents. Also, Mormons have learned through revelation that certain entire *categories* of God's children have been set aside for mortal missions or roles of one kind or another, and these categories are distinguished from the rest of us by separate *lineages* during their mortal lives.

One of these is the lineage of *Israel* or Jacob. To a large extent, Mormon theology about Israel converges with that of other Christian religions, especially the more evangelical ones, in emphasizing the role of Israel as "God's chosen people," the historic carriers of the covenant of Abraham and of the messianic expectation. In some important respects, though, the Mormon conception is unique: There were, after all, *twelve* tribes of Israel, of which the tribe of Judah, or the Jews, constitutes only one. In preparation for the messianic return, prophecy tells us, God will gather *all* of scattered Israel, and not just the Jews.

Through a mystical, spiritual process, the descendants of the tribe Ephraim, wherever they are in the world, have been called out of the world as Mormon converts. They have been especially susceptible to God's voice, through the Mormon church, in these last days, and have constituted the overwhelming majority of Mormon converts for at least the first hundred years or so. In the gathering process, according to Mormonism, God has assigned a special *vanguard* mission to the descendants of both Judah and Ephraim. Thus, by foreordination and through lineages especially set aside, today's

Jews are preparing for their gathering, the gathering of the historic
kingdom of Judah, in and around Jerusalem; while today's
Ephraimites (Mormons) are preparing for the gathering of the historic northern kingdom, the kingdom of Israel, in North America.
The Messiah will eventually come to both places.

Are their any social consequences to this rather unusual conception of the *mortal mission* of Jews and Mormons? I have made a special
study of this question and reached the following conclusions.[19] One
social consequence is also quite an important political one: Mormons are obviously inclined toward Zionism in today's world, like
many evangelicals, as a concomitant of theology. For Mormons,
though, it is not only a matter of Old Testament prophecy, but also
of mortal mission deriving from long-laid plans in the premortal
life. Furthermore (and, no doubt, much to the chagrin of Jews!),
Mormons are *doubly Zionist,* seeing an important role for North
America as another Zion sharing in the Israelite premillenial mission. There is another social consequence as well: Survey data show
that among believing Mormons there are relatively low rates of anti-
Semitism.[20] Mormons who accept the church teachings about mortal missions, and about the joint Israelite lineage of most Jews and
Mormons, seem to see themselves as "blood brothers" to the Jews,
and not merely their spiritual brothers.

This mystique of mortal mission expresses itself also in Mormon
attitudes toward the American Indians. The *Book of Mormon* is for
believers a scripture equal in authority to the Bible. This book is
understood by Mormons as a history of the ancestors of the native
American, that is, the Indian. Indians are identified as Israelite in
origin, and therefore also "blood brothers" to both Jews and Mormons. The ancient Indians brought a Hebrew religion with them
when they left Palestine, shortly before the Babylonian captivity,
and eventually the resurrected Christ appeared among them and
established his religion, too. Book of Mormon prophecy predicts
both the miserable fate of the Indians at the hands of white gentiles,
and the eventual redemption, recovery, and flowering of Indian
civilization with the help of the Mormons.

In pursuit of that mission, Mormons have tried a variety of
programs involving Indian tribes. Chief among these has been, of
course, an extensive proselyting program, especially during the
past few decades. Placement programs, whereby Indian children
have been taken into white Mormon homes for the school year in an
attempt to upgrade their educational experiences, have also been

undertaken. Brigham Young University, too, has provided hundreds of scholarships to Indian students, and for twenty years has carried on a kind of technological and agricultural extension program on some of the reservations.

The consequences of this theologically inspired Mormon mission among the Indians have been quite mixed and are rather difficult to evaluate. Among the Indians themselves, there has been a variety of opinion, depending on whether the Indians were Mormon or non-Mormon, and whether they were tribal leaders, movement activists, and so forth. The evaluations from the Mormon side have also been ambiguous, but, on balance, are not too encouraging, which probably explains the severe reduction in such church programs during the past decade. Reductions in North America, however, have been accompanied by increased efforts in South America, where the Indian populations have apparently been more responsive to the Mormon efforts at both proselyting and community development.

There is but little data available on the attitudes of Mormons as individuals toward Indians, but such as there is indicates considerable ambivalence. The Mormon theology about Indians, after all, has been mediated by the typical white American hostility toward Indians throughout the nineteenth century, especially in the western mountains and prairies of the Mormon homeland. The overwhelming majority of contemporary Mormons have no personal contact with Indians whatever, so perhaps we should not expect Mormon attitudes to differ much from those of other Americans, despite the unique Mormon theology.[21]

Another aspect of race relations where Mormon theological conceptions have played some role is the case of black Africans and Afro-Americans. There is by now a rather extensive and definitive literature about the changing history and policies involved in relationships between white Mormons and blacks.[22] Until 1978, Mormon church policy denied to members of black African ancestry the lay priesthood available to nearly all other Mormon males. There was not, however, a clear theological or canonical basis for this restrictive policy, and the exact historical basis for it has remained partly obscured. In any case, the clash of this racially restrictive policy with the American civil rights movement caused an extensive and painful reassessment of the policy within the church, and particularly on the parts of Mormon historians and social scientists. One of the results was the realization that the Mormon concept of *mortal mission,* which had given Jews and Indians a favorable and fraternal identity for Mormons, had instead been used to give a negative definition to blacks.

Since it is antithetical to Mormon theology to think of God as arbitrary (to say nothing of irrational or unjust), the only possible rationalization for denying the priesthood to black Mormons was that in the premortal world, while they were still spirits, they must have somehow failed to measure up in God's eyes, so that they were sent to earth in an unfavored lineage. In designating Cain as the founder of that lineage, and Canaan (son of Ham) as its perpetuator after the flood, Mormons were able to link up their theory with the one so common among other Christians until recent times— namely, that blacks were descendants of Cain and bore his curse and mark.[23]

This kind of "countermission" assigned to blacks in mortality was not to be found in Mormon scriptural canons but was instead a part of Mormon folk religion, which was encouraged by certain key leaders. The main point here is that it represented a potentially damaging social application of the mystique of mortal mission. When in 1978 an explicit revelation to the Mormon prophet removed prescriptions against black priests, most Mormons breathed a great sigh of relief; the few Mormon blacks were all given the priesthood and some meaningful leadership responsibilities in the church; and a vigorous proselyting effort was launched both in North America and in the predominantly black countries of Africa and the Western hemisphere.

Mormon relationships with the three ethnic groups discussed here, blacks, Jews, and American Indians, illustrate both the social consequences of certain notions about God *and* the mediating power that surrounding secular society has upon those notions. Where blacks were concerned, Mormon folk theology ran headlong into a social climate hostile to such its notions. Accordingly, as survey data have shown, the potential in Mormonism for engendering antiblack social attitudes was largely offset and neutralized by secular influences. That is, when controls were imposed on the data for differences in social class, education, region, and the like, Mormon attitudes toward blacks closely resembled those of other Americans—suggesting that without the unique Mormon folk theology, Mormons might have been less racist than other Americans. Indeed, since the 1978 change in church policy, Mormon attitudes toward blacks have converged toward national norms to the extent that polling data now show Mormons among religious groups *least* negative toward blacks.[24]

In the case of the Jews, Mormon theology has been *reinforced* by a surrounding social milieu that has been both pro-Israel and inhospitable to anti-Semitism. Accordingly, Mormons have appeared in surveys to be less anti-Semitic than other Americans. Finally, where the American Indians are concerned, a generally favorable Mormon theology has been partly neutralized by the traditional animosity of the white man, and by decades of hostile and condescending media portrayals of Indians. Accordingly, Mormon attitudes toward Indians seem rather ambivalent.[25]

In sum, we have seen that Mormon social conservatism expresses itself in generally unfavorable attitudes toward abortion, homosexuality, pornography, and constitutionally mandated equality for the sexes, as well as in certain traditional attitudes toward blacks, Indians, and Jews. These attitudes can be understood in large part by reference to the Mormon theology of familism and the mystique of mortal mission. Such concepts portray God (or, more accurately, our Heavenly Parents) as the founders and proponents of a great cosmic family, which is in turn made up of constituent families bound in eternal marital and filial relationships and charged with the responsibility for helping God bring his spirit children into the mortal stage of their existence and successfully through to the next stage in their eternal progression.

Besides this mission, which all Mormon parents have been given, certain other missions have also been given to categories of God's children identified by certain mortal lineages. These other missions have been based not only upon God's own needs in human history, but also upon the greater or lesser premortal merit earned by the individuals involved. While the social and secular outcome of all this theologizing might be often to make Mormons look pretty much like other social conservatives, it is important to recognize that Mormons get to their social conservatism by a different route.

Conclusion

The social consequences of Mormon beliefs about God is a subject about which much more could be written. However, we have considered probably the most important, or at least the most conspicuous, examples of the connection between Mormon theology and social behavior in our discussions of *familism* and *social conservativ-*

ism, and there is room here to consider but little more. In closing, however, I would like to introduce another interesting possibility for future investigation, and that is Mormon *scientism*. We observed early in this essay that much in Mormon theology and cosmology accords reasonably well with modern science; that, indeed, it is only slightly facetious to understand the Mormon God as a kind of super-scientist who operates according to principles that are at least potentially accessible to mortal scientists. In seeing this as one of God's attributes, Mormons in effect provide for themselves a kind of divine model for emulation that might even carry a potential for influencing the occupational preferences and other cultural attributes of Mormons. Is there any evidence that such is the case?

At present, the evidence is largely impressionistic, but it ought to be possible, for example, to do a survey of occupations among Mormons and thereby determine whether Mormons disproportionately choose careers in the hard sciences. If the Protestant ethic could influence career choices in nineteenth-century Europe, then presumably Mormon scientism could have a similar cultural impact. A certain amount of systematic evidence does, in fact, already exist. More than forty years ago, the psychologist Thorndike published a study of the origins of American scientists and scholars. This study was replicated and expanded just a decade ago. Both studies determined that people of Utah origin were unusually numerous among the most accomplished scientists of the nation.[26]

This Mormon tradition is perhaps personified in the recent appointment, for a second time, of devout Mormon James Fletcher to head the nation's space agency (NASA). A culturally related observation would point also to Glen Larson and science fiction writers of Mormon origin who have become prominent in the media. Larsen, for example, wrote material for the TV series "Battlestar Galactica" and for the *Star Wars* films, both of which seem to draw on Mormon cosmology.[27] On this somewhat whimsical note, I shall issue the usual call for additional research and end this paper.

NOTES

1. Charles Y. Glock, "Images of 'God', Images of Man, and the Organization of Social Life," *Journal for the Scientific Study of Religion* 11 (1972): 1–16; R.A.

Apostle, C.Y. Glock, T. Piazza, and M. Suelzle, *The Anatomy of Racial Attitudes* (Berkeley,: University of California Press, 1983).

2. Representative works on this topic include Fawn M. Brodie, *No Man Knows My History: The Life of Joseph Smith, the Mormon Prophet,* 4th ed. (New York: Knopf, 1972); Richard L. Bushman, *Joseph Smith and the Beginnings of Mormonism* (Urbana and Chicago: University of Chicago Press, 1984); Whitney R. Cross, *The Burned Over District: The Social and Intellectual History of Enthusiastic Religion in Western New York, 1800–1850* (Ithaca, N. Y.: Cornell University Press, 1950); Klaus J. Hansen, *Mormonism and the American Experience* (Chicago: University of Chicago Press, 1981), Thomas F. O'Dea, *The Mormons* (Chicago: University of Chicago Press, 1957); D. Michael Quinn, *Early Mormonism and the Magic World View* (Salt Lake City, UT: Signature Books, 1987); and Jan Shipps, *Mormonism: The Story of a New Religious Tradition* (Urbana, IL: University of Illinois Press, 1985).

3. Marie Cornwall, S.L. Albrecht, P.H. Cunningham, and B.L. Pitcher, "The Dimensions of Religiosity: A Conceptual Model with an Empirical Test," *Review of Religious Research* 27 (March 1986):226–244; Armand L. Mauss, "Saints, Cities, and Secularism: Religious Attitudes and Behavior of Modern Urban Mormons," *Dialogue: A Journal of Mormon Thought* 7 (Summer 1972):8–27.

4. Representative works include Parley P. Pratt, *Key to the Science of Theology* (Liverpool, Eng.: F.D. Richards, 1855); B.H. Roberts, *The Mormon Doctrine of Deity* (Salt Lake City: Deseret News Press, 1903); James E. Talmage, *The Articles of Faith,* 12th ed. (Salt Lake City: Deseret News Press, 1924); and John A. Widtsoe, *A Rational Theology* (Salt Lake City: Deseret News Press, 1915).

5. Thomas G. Alexander, "The Reconstruction of Mormon Doctrine," *Sunstone* 5 (1980):24–33; Sterling M. McMurrin, *The Theological Foundations of the Mormon Religion* (Salt Lake City: University of Utah Press, 1965); O'Dea, op. cit.; and Shipps, op. cit.

6. The Mormon concept of the Mother in Heaven is discussed in Hansen, op. cit, 81, 170; J. Heeren, D.B. Lindsey, and M. Mason, "The Mormon Concept of Mother in Heaven: A Sociological Account of Its Origin and Development," *Journal for the Scientific Study of Religion* 23 (1984):396–411; and Linda Wilcox, "The Mormon Concept of a Mother in Heaven," *Sunstone* 5 (1980):9–15.

7. On the changing status and definition of Mormon women, see, e.g., Lavina F. Anderson, "Mormon Women and the Struggle for Definition: Contemporary Women," *Sunstone* 6 (1981):12–16; Lawrence Foster, "From Frontier Activism to Neo-Victorian Domesticity: Mormon Women in the 19th and 20th Centuries," *Journal of Mormon History* 6 (1979):3–21; Tim B. Heaton, "Role Remodeling in the Mormon Family," *Sunstone* 11 (1987):6; Heeren et al., op. cit.; Linda K. Newell, "A Gift Given, A Gift Taken: Washing, Anointing, and Blessing the Sick among Mormon Women," *Sunstone* 6 (1981):16–25; Margaret M. Toscano, "Beyond Matriarchy, Beyond Patriarchy," *Dialogue: A Journal of Mormon Thought* 21 (Spring 1988):33–57; and Linda Wilcox, op. cit.

8. H.M. Bahr, "Religious Contrasts in Family Role Definitions: Utah Mormons, Catholics, Protestants, and Others," *Journal for the Scientific Study of Religion* 21

(1982):200–17; Lawrence Foster, *Religion and Sexuality: Three American Communal Experiments of the Nineteenth Century* (New York: Oxford University Press, 1981); T.B. Heaton, op. cit.; and Toscano, op. cit.

9. H.P. Bluhm, D.C. Spendlove, and D.W. West, "Depression in Mormon Women," *Dialogue: A Journal of Mormon Thought* 19 (Summer 1986):150–5; T.K. Martin, T.B. Heaton, and S.J. Bahr, eds., *Utah in Demographic Perspective: Regional and National Contrasts* (Salt Lake City: Signature Books, 1986).

10. Tim B. Heaton, "Four Characteristics of the Mormon Family: Contemporary Research on Chastity, Conjugality, Children, and Chauvinism," *Dialogue: A Journal of Mormon Thought* 20 (Summer 1987):101–14; T.B. Heaton and K.L. Goodman, "Religion and Family Formation," *Review of Religious Research* 16 (1985):343–59.

11. The generalizations here about Mormon family life and norms are based upon H.M. Bahr, S.J. Condie, and K.L. Goodman, *Life in Large Families: Views of Mormon Women* (Washington, D.C.: University Press of America, 1982); L.L. Bean, G. Mineau, and D. Anderton, "Residence and Religious Effects on Declining Family Size: A Historical Analysis of the Utah Population," *Review of Religious Research* 25 (1983):91–101; L.E. Bush, Jr., "Birth Control among the Mormons: Introduction to an Insistent Question," *Dialogue: A Journal of Mormon Thought* 10 (1976):12–44; B.L. Campbell and E.E. Campbell, "The Mormon Family," in *Ethnic Families in America* ed. C.H. Mindel and R.W. Habenstein (New York: Elsevier, 1981), 379–416; H.T. Christensen, "Stress Points in Mormon Family Culture," *Dialogue: A Journal of Mormon Thought* 7 (1972):20–34, and "The Persistence of Chastity: A Built-in Resistance within Mormon Culture to Secular Trends," *Sunstone* 7 (1982):7–14; T.B. Heaton, "How Does Religion Influence Fertility?: The Case of the Mormons," *Journal for the Scientific Study of Religion* 25 (1986):248–258, and "Four Characteristics." (1987); T.B. Heaton and S. Calkins, "Family Size and Contraceptive Use among Mormons, 1965–1975," *Review of Religious Research* 25 (1983):102–13; Heaton and Goodman, op. cit.; Phillip R. Kunz, ed., *The Mormon Family: Proceedings of the Annual Family Research Conference at Brigham Young University, 1975* (Provo, UT: BYU Family Research Center, 1977); G.P. Mineau, L.L. Bean, and M. Skolnick, "Mormon Demographic History 2: The Family Life Cycle and Natural Fertility," *Population Studies* 33 (1979):429–46; M. Skolnick, L.L. Bean, D. May, V. Argon, and P. Cartwright, "Mormon Demographic History 1: Nuptiality and Fertility of Once-Married Couples," *Population Studies* 32 (1978):5–19; J.C. Spicer and S.D. Gustavus, "Mormon Fertility through Half a Century: Another Test of the Americanization Hypothesis," *Social Biology* 21 (1974):70–6; A. Thornton, "Religion and Fertility: The Case of the Mormons," *Journal of Marriage and the Family* 41 (1979):131–42; D.L. Thomas, "Family in the Mormon Experience," in *Families and Religions* ed. W.V. D'Antonio and J. Aldous (Beverly Hills, CA: Sage Publishing Co., 1983), 267–88; and J.M. Wise and S.J. Condie, "Intergenerational Fertility Throughout Four Generations," *Social Biology* 22 (1975):144–50.

12. Spicer and Gustavus, op. cit.; Wise and Condie, op. cit.; and Heaton, "How Does Religion Influence Fertility" (1986).

13. On changes in spousal relationships and in attitudes toward women among the Mormons, see Note 7 above; see also S.L. Albrecht and T.B. Heaton, "Secularization, Higher Education, and Religiosity," *Review of Religious Research* 26:43–58; S.J. Bahr and B.C. Rollins, "Crisis and Conjugal Power," *Journal of Marriage and the Family* 33 (1971):360–7; S.L. Albrecht, H.M. Bahr, and B.A. Chadwick, "Changing Family and Sex Roles: An Assessment of Age Differences," *Journal of Marriage and the Family* 41 (1979):41–50; Bahr, "Religious Contrasts . . . ," (1982); Kunz, ed., op. cit; and the national survey about Mormons and others reported in Wade Clark Roof and William McKinney, *American Mainline Religion: Its Changing Shape and Future* (New Brunswick, N.J.: Rutgers University Press, 1987).

14. On the problematic prospects for coalition or even cooperation between the Mormons and the New Christian Right, see M.B. Brinkerhoff, J.C. Jacob, and M.M. Mackie, "Mormonism and the Moral Majority Make Strange Bedfellows? An Exploratory Critique," *Review of Religious Research* 28: (March 1987) 236–51; A.D. Shupe, Jr. and J. Heinerman, "Mormonism and the New Christian Right: An Emerging Coalition," *Review of Religious Research* 27 (December 1985):146–57; and O. Kendall White, Jr., "A Review and Commentary on the Prospects of a Mormon/New Christian Right Coalition," *Review of Religious Research* 28 (December 1986):180–8.

15. Robert Gottlieb and Peter Wiley, *America's Saints: The Rise of Mormon Power* (New York: G.P. Putnam, 1984).

16. D.E. Mann, "Mormon Attitudes toward Political Roles of Church Leaders," *Dialogue: A Journal of Mormon Thought* 2 (1967):32–48; A.L. Mauss, "Moderation in All Things: Political and Social Outlooks of Modern Urban Mormons," *Dialogue: A Journal of Mormon Thought* 7 (1972):57–69; A.L. Mauss and M.G. Bradford, "Mormon Politics and Assimilation: Toward a Theory of Mormon Church Involvement in National U.S. Politics," in *The Politics of Religion and Social Change* ed. A.D. Shupe, Jr. and J.K. Hadden (New York: Paragon House, 1988); Roof and McKinney, op. cit.; and J.D. Williams, "The Separation of Church and State in Theory and Mormon Practice," *Dialogue: A Journal of Mormon Thought* 1 (1966):30–54.

17. Empirical data and other information on Mormon views toward abortion, homosexuality, and pornography will be found in, e.g., K.R. Hardy, "Controlling Pornography: The Scientific and Moral Issues," *Dialogue: A Journal of Mormon Thought* 2 (1967):89–103; A.L. Mauss, "Mormons as Ethnics: Variable Historical and International Implications of an Appealing Concept," in *The Mormon Presence in Canada* ed. B.Y. Card and H.C. Northcott (Edmonton: University of Alberta Press, 1988); J.T. Richardson and S.W. Fox, "Religious Affiliation as a Prediction of Voting Behavior in Abortion Reform Legislation," *Journal for the Scientific Study of Religion* 11 (1972):347–359, and "Religion and Voting on Abortion Reform: A Follow-up Study," *Journal for the Scientific Study of Religion* 14 (1975):159–64; Roof and McKinney, op. cit.; M. Rytting, "The Need for Moral Tension," *Sunstone* 6 (1981):20–4; M.C. Segers, "Abortion Politics and Policy: Is There a Middle Ground?" *Sunstone* 6 (1981):10–16; and A. Van Alstyne, "Obscenity and the Inspired Constitution: A Dilemma for Mormons," *Dialogue: A Journal of Mormon Thought* 2 (1967):75–89.

18. See Mauss, "Mormons as Ethnics . . ." (1988); and Roof and McKinney, op. cit. for current survey data on Mormon attitudes toward civil liberties.

19. A.L. Mauss, "Mormon Semitism and Anti-Semitism," *Sociological Analysis* 29 (1968):11–27, and "Mormons and Minorities: A Study in the Social Consequences of Religious Ideas," book manuscript forthcoming.

20. Compare data in Mauss, "Mormon Semitism . . ." (1968) with comparable data in C. Y. Glock and Rodney Stark, *Christian Beliefs and Anti-Semitism* (New York: Harper and Row, 1966).

21. The above discussion of Mormons and native American Indians is based upon E.D.L. Douglas and A.L. Mauss, "Religious and Secular Factors in the Race Attitudes of Logan, Utah, Residents," *Proceedings of the Utah Academy of Sciences, Arts, and Letters* 45 (Fall 1968); Mauss, forthcoming; and the following articles, all of which appear in a special issue of *Dialogue: A Journal of Mormon Thought* 18 (Winter 1985): J.N. Birch, "Helen John: The Beginnings of Indian Placement," 119–29; E. England, " 'Lamanites' and the Spirit of the Lord," 25–32; P.J. Hafen, " 'Great Spirit Listen': The American Indian in Mormon Music," 133–42; L.A. Harris, "To be Native American—and Mormon," 143–52; K. Parry, "Joseph Smith and the Clash of Sacred Cultures," 65–80; and D.J. Whittaker, "Mormons and Native Americans: A Historical and Bibliographical Introduction," 33–64.

22. The major works on historical and contemporary attitudes of Mormons toward blacks are: N.G. Bringhurst, *Saints, Slaves, and Blacks: The Changing Place of Black People within Mormonism* (Westport, CT,: Greenwood Press, 1981); G.L. Bunker and M.A. Johnson, "Ethnicity and Resistance to Compensatory Education: A Comparison of Mormon and Non-Mormon Attitudes," *Review of Religious Research* 16 (1975):74–82; G.L. Bunker, H. Coffey, and M.A. Johnson, "Mormons and Social Distance Multi-Dimensional Analysis," *Ethnicity* 4 (1977):352–69; L.E. Bush, Jr. and A. L. Mauss, *Neither White nor Black: Mormon Scholars Confront the Race Issue in a Universal Church* (Salt Lake City: Signature Books, 1984); P.R. Kunz, "Blacks and Mormonism: Social Distance Change," *Psychological Reports* 45 (1979):81–2; and A. L. Mauss, "Mormonism and Secular Attitudes toward Negroes," *Pacific Sociological Review* 9 (1966):91–9, Roof and McKinney, op. cit., also contains data comparing Mormons with others on this topic.

23. For non-Mormon Christian folk doctrines on blacks, see T.F. Gossett, *Race: The History of an Idea in America* (New York: Schocken Books, 1965), and H.S. Smith, *In His Image, But . . . Racism in Southern Religion, 1780–1910* (Durham, N.C.: Duke University Press, 1972).

24. Mauss, "Mormonism and Secular Attitudes . . ." (1966) and forthcoming; A.L. Mauss, "The Fading of the Pharoahs' Curse: The Decline and Fall of the Priesthood Ban against Blacks in the Mormon Church," *Dialogue: A Journal of Mormon Thought* 14 (Fall 1981):10–45; and Roof and McKinney, op. cit.

25. Historic Mormon ambivalence in attitudes toward Jews and native American Indians will be apparent from the works cited in Notes 19, 20, and 21 above.

26. K.R. Hardy, "Social Origins of American Scientists and Scholars," *Science* 185

(1974):497–506; E.L. Thorndike, "The Origins of Superior Men," *Scientific Monthly* 56 (1943):424–32.

27. See J.E. Ford, "Battlestar Gallactica and Mormon Theology," *Journal of Popular Culture* 17 (Fall 1983):83–87, for more on this point.

4

Josiah Royce's Provincialism
JOHN K. ROTH

I speak of course as a native Californian, but I do not venture to limit even for a moment my characterization by reference to my own private experience.

Josiah Royce (1855–1916)

The statement by Royce that opens this chapter first appeared in an address that the American philosopher gave to the National Geographic Society in 1898. It serves well not only as a departure point for this essay, but also as a motto for Royce's intellectual career. Royce valued his California upbringing. Those formative experiences in the American West remained fundamental as he developed the far-reaching theories that brought him fame in the cosmopolitan academic centers of the American East and in their trans-Atlantic counterparts as well.

Ever the keen observer of life in the West, this California youth transmuted into Harvard philosopher never knew a "golden state" replete with urban sprawl, freeways, smog, Hollywood, and Disneyland. He would find much to deplore in contemporary California, just as he did during his lifetime. But Royce always appreciated that California was different. He believed, for example, that its climate and geography encouraged distinctive types of individuality. They enriched the One and the Many that Royce took reality to be.

Shortly before his death, Royce located the origin of his philosophical interests in a sense of wonder at once provincial and universal. Royce's early home was the California mining town of Grass Valley, a place only five or six years older than himself. He heard his elders describe it as a new community. The boy, however, noticed abandoned mines, rotting structures, and graves. They all looked old. The land's majesty, moreover, was anything but recent. Ages were in it. What, the young Royce wondered, was really new in this particular California dwelling-together where his life began? Such puzzlement led him to many destinations, few of them reached by routes that a gold-country lad could guess in advance.

As a philosopher, Royce was intensely interested in what religions have in common. That broad concern, however, never led him to lose sight of religion's particularity. On the contrary, when Royce wrote about the social consequences of belief in God, his philosophy included a place for *provincialism*. This chapter concentrates on that latter aspect of his thought. Its inferences are Roycean, which is to say that they are not new insights. But like many of the points that Royce drove home, they may be overlooked because they are so basic as to be obscured. Specifically, then, this chapter explores the following propositions: (1) Contrary to conventional wisdom, provincialism has much in its favor; (2) Lacking "a wise provincialism," as Royce called it, religion in particular is impoverished; and (3) A critical human need—the upbuilding of loyalty to loyalty—depends largely on religion's ability to nurture the right provincial touch. However, we use the verb "explore" advisedly. This essay's style is not to argue directly for the truth of those ideas, but instead to let Royce's thought encourage wonder about their validity.

California: A Symbol of Provincialism

Royce published his National Geographic address—"The Pacific Coast: A Psychological Study of the Relations of Climate and Civilization"—in his 1908 book *Race Questions, Provincialism and Other American Problems*. He regarded this collection of essays as "an effort to apply, to some of our American problems, that general doctrine about life which I have recently summed up in my book entitled *The Philosophy of Loyalty.*"[1] Royce's paper on the Pacific Coast noted how California's regional identity developed. The changes, Royce believed, were important for understanding loyalty and provincialism's place within it.

Beginning with the "forty-niners," Royce discerned three stages in the more than half-century of California life he knew. Early on, he recalled, "nearly everything was imported."[2] Large-scale agriculture seemed unfeasible, and, in turn, people's roots remained in eastern soil. Exemplified by what Royce called "the lynching habit," social instability abounded. Within a decade, however, a marked change occurred.

Although many prospectors rushed to California without intending to stay, significant numbers soon realized that they would in fact remain. Isolated from the East, these men and women decided "to create a community of which it was worthwhile to be a member."[3] Between 1860 and 1870, provincial California emerged—a place "self-conscious, independent, indisposed to take advice from without, very confident of the future of the state and of the boundless prosperity soon to be expected."[4] If that description continues to hold more than a grain of truth, it is far from the whole story, as Royce's third stage makes clear.

Isolation, which made provincialism unavoidable, gradually diminished. Spanned symbolically as well as physically by transcontinental railroads, West was linked with East. The uniqueness of California, concluded Royce, consisted of the attempt to blend "provincial independence . . . with the complex social influences derived from the East and from the world at large."[5] Nearly a century later, Royce's observation that "the California of today is still the theater of the struggle of these opposing forces" commends itself.[6] This ferment creates waves of the future.

Memories and Hopes: the Importance of Shared Commitment

As Royce well knew, waves of the future—especially those from Pacific shores—can storm away essential ties that bind families and friends, causes and commitments. Thus Royce summed up his prolific career in saying that "my deepest motives and problems have centered about the Idea of the Community."[7] The value of community first impressed him as he experienced the West's rugged ways. His appreciation for it grew with observation that progress increases when people faithfully pursue their best convictions and yet remain true to each other in exchanging, debating, and evaluating different points of view. A trust that God is ultimately faithful to creation in a healing and loving manner also played a role. Whatever the factors, Royce's thought did center on community, and thus it focused on loyalty and provincialism, too.

Royce believed that a community exists just to the degree that persons share memories and hopes, which include ethical commitments and collective responsibilities. Those memories and hopes typically contain elements that are broadly philosophical and even universalizing in their religious dimensions. Royce believed such elements were crucial, but he insisted that ethical commitment and collective responsibility are never abstract. Without commitment to a particular cause, which entails practical work at definite times and places, loyalty exists in word alone. The unavoidably particular nature of communal relationships, of course, may create as many problems as it solves. For many, commitments set up conflicts— internal and external—that cancel out the good. Hence, if human meaning depends on commitment, and if shared commitment is the basis of communal ties without which our existence is severely impoverished and perhaps ultimately incapable of survival, then those views of Royce's all suggest why provincialism rightly fascinated him.

Unsophisticated, narrow, countrified, those are just a few synonyms for the adjective "provincial." Usually we do not want the word applied to ourselves, although it serves well enough to disparage views or persons not to our liking. Royce, however, reconsidered whether "provincialism" is really a backward state for which only cosmopolitanism is the antidote. Provincialism, he believed, is certainly not an end in itself. In that guise it is dangerous. But provincialism can be virtuous, especially when it encompasses wisdom that recognizes how the particular and the universal should nurture each other. Royce was no oxymoron. To him, wise provincialism was precisely what the United States would need as the twentieth century unfolded. Any quick dismissal of that claim is unwarranted.

American Individualism: Asset or Liability?

To illustrate, consider the French statesman and philosopher Alexis de Tocqueville, whose tour of the country resulted in his classic *Democracy in America,* first published in 1835. For Tocqueville, nothing characterized Americans so much as their emphasis on equality. In a chapter entitled "Concerning the Philosophical Approach of the Americans," he observed, "Less attention is paid to philosophy in the United States than in any other country of the civilized world."[8] Nevertheless, continued Tocqueville, "of all the countries in the world, America is the one in which the precepts of Descartes are . . . best followed."[9] Prizing individualism so much, he explained, Americans are Cartesians in their propensity to display "a general distaste for accepting any man's word as proof of anything."[10] Instead, they rely on "individual effort and judgment" to determine what they believe.[11]

As with most of the American qualities he discussed, Tocqueville found the philosophical approach of Americans to possess both assets and liabilities. Skepticism might nurture a praiseworthy critical attitude; self-reliance could produce desirable innovation. But a cunning consequence was the undermining of authority, tradition, and communal loyalty. That result, in turn, could lead to other mischief. For where reliance on authority and tradition are severely undermined, people still seek confirmation in the judgments of others. The despotism of unthinking conformity, which is a long way from the public spirit that ensures real freedom and community, is not far behind. Tocqueville's uneasiness about American individualism was justified, and the consequences for our national well-being are enormous. In sum, while American individualism honed ingenuity and industry that led to positions of economic and political world leadership, the same spirit drew Americans further apart even as they lived closer together in conformity. Now giving self-fulfillment precedence over civic virtue and a publicly responsible loyalty, Americans care more for individual wealth than for their commonwealth.

Abundant evidence for these contentions can be found in the sociological survey conducted recently by Robert N. Bellah and his associates. Borrowing one of Tocqueville's phrases to title the study, they assayed "habits of the heart" in the powerful American middle class. There, Bellah found, "individualism may have grown cancerous—that it may be destroying those social integuments that Tocqueville saw as moderating its more destructive potentialities, that it may be threatening the survival of freedom itself."[12]

In brief, Bellah's study found that many Americans tend to be so obsessed with personal self-fulfillment that their capacity for commitment to the basic institutions of marriage, family, politics, and religion is dangerously impaired. Neither Tocqueville nor Royce after him would have found this surprising. They both understood that an overly individualistic democracy would unleash a sense of self-interest so dangerous as to starve civic obligation and impair communal health.

On the other hand, Bellah and his colleagues observed, contemporary Americans do not always practice the radical individualism they preach. Functionally, their lives are given meaning by familial, communal, and public ties—many of them provincial—that transcend the individual calculus of self-fulfillment and cost-benefit analysis at which Americans have become so verbally adept. If Americans express yearnings for autonomy and self-reliance better than they acknowledge the need for social commitment that sustains them, nevertheless they do sense that relationships of memory and hope are the substance of their lives. Such relationships become the American people well, moreover, just to the extent that Americans think of them less as the means to personal self-satisfaction and more as ingredients integral to personhood.[13] Their individualistic rhetoric notwithstanding, Bellah rightly contends, Americans "have never been, and still are not, a collection of private individuals who, except for a conscious contract to create a minimal government, have nothing in common.[14] Americans do need, however, to bring these elements to new levels of self-awareness, because for too long they have been living with "a thin political consensus, limited largely to procedural matters."[15] To those remarks Royce might have added that a wise provincialism could provide much that the United States needs.

Selfhood and Loyalty: Community Goals and Causes

Tocqueville wrote that "the Americans have no school of philosophy peculiar to themselves, and they pay very little attention to the rival European schools. Indeed they hardly know their names."[16] Like many of his other judgments, that one was not infallible. American thinkers have developed a variety of distinctive philosophical perspectives. Issues about individualism and community have often been their focal point. Royce, in particular, discerned what Americans and indeed persons everywhere needed when he spoke about the loyalty that a wise provincialism involves.

To set the stage for outlining that wise provincialism, recall that Royce understood human selfhood to be a temporal process.[17] If our existence is grounded in the ultimate purpose of God, our own concrete actualization depends on willing and choosing within a social context. According to Royce, the process of self-determination ultimately entails the giving of oneself to goals and causes. Persons become by acting, pursuing interests, and striving to achieve. The self will either be fragmented or unified in direct proportion to one's success in finding and actualizing a life pattern that can be consistently and harmoniously pursued through time.

Such a pattern entails a chance for the discovery, expression, and cultivation of talents and abilities. It also involves recognition that individuals who try to secure their own ways alone are far more likely to lose themselves than those who do their best individually

to help others. Just as coherent individualism requires caring relations that reach far and wide, interdependence is a condition that
makes independence possible. Personal initiative that does not serve
others impoverishes the communal spirit that gives it birth and
vitality.

In short, meaningfulness depends on loyalty, which Royce initially defined as "*the willing and practical and thoroughgoing devotion of a
person to a cause.*"[18] At this point, however, a serious problem arises.
Granted that loyalty is a necessary condition for a meaningful life,
how are we to cope with the fact that the causes to which one can be
loyal are not uniformly good? In fact, some causes are simply
destructive of the sense of community that Royce wanted people to
appreciate and make real. His awareness of this dilemma resulted in
his ultimate ethical principle: "*In choosing and in serving the cause to
which you are to be loyal, be, in any case, loyal to loyalty.*"[19]

According to Royce, the act of being loyal is a good wherever it
occurs. Even in cases where we disagree strongly with the cause for
which someone works, we may appreciate and recognize the value
of that person's dedication. As for "negative" causes, Royce believed
that their negativity consists primarily in the fact that such causes
are incomplete instances of loyalty. They arbitrarily or selfishly limit
or destroy other forms of loyalty.

Loyalty to any specific cause is not suitable to define the basic
principle of morality. That, Royce concluded, is best articulated in
terms of the general cause of *loyalty to loyalty*. But if our fundamental
moral responsibility involves being loyal to loyalty, is that idea
anything more than a formal principle that is essentially devoid of
content? Absolutely, said Royce.

One pursues loyalty to loyalty by discovering and developing his
or her particular talents and abilities, watching to find and imple-
ment the ways in which these gifts can best be used for communal
well-being. Royce's philosophy of loyalty aimed to remove any
ultimate opposition between authentic individuality and genuine
community. He constantly urged individuals to develop themselves
as far as possible, but argued at the same time that such development
is possible only in a social context and is fulfilled only in giving
oneself for others.

The concrete choices about the best ways in which to be loyal to
loyalty will always be finite and fallible, but even if a particular
project fails, persons who strive to be fully loyal will be worthy
examples. Often, in fact, the most vibrant instances of loyalty to

loyalty appear in human lives that are marked by defeat, tragedy, and great suffering. These instances radiate an integrity and significance that matter. Others will be inspired by them. Here Royce's philosophy of loyalty links up with his theory of good and evil. The greatest good, he believed, is vitally connected to devotion to ideals in the face of evil and to acts that overcome evil by creative action that sets right the wreckage left behind.

At the end of *The Philosophy of Loyalty*, Royce suggested that there is a basic relation between a life of loyalty and a life of religion. Briefly stated, this relation hinges on the fact that the religious life seeks to find and experience a basic communal dimension in all existence. In this community of being, the lives of individuals are to be unified, harmonized, and fulfilled in an altogether meaningful totality. Royce argued, therefore, that the genuinely religious life will be one of loyalty, because the religious person will recognize that he or she has a vital role to play in the establishment of such a community and that loyalty to loyalty is crucial for its actualization. On the other hand, although the loyal person may not be consciously or overtly religious, that individual's life pattern has an essentially religious aspect. Such persons also seek to find themselves in the reality of true community. Implicit in this devotion is the understanding that unless such community is ultimately real, the self is left in a fragmented condition, and negativity and death have the final words in life's drama.

Religious persons live in the faith that a fulfilling community of being is a reality. Royce felt such faith to be justified. Expressed through ritual, myth, and sacred writings, it could help to foster the life "we all in common need to live."[20] At the same time, the ultimate meaningfulness of the life of loyalty rests on the hope that a fundamentally religious vision of reality is true. The life of loyalty, then, both moves toward and can be sustained by a religious life style.

A Wise Provincialism: The Hope of the Future

The Philosophy of Loyalty explicitly devoted only a few pages to provincialism.[21] In 1902, however, Royce had prepared a substantial essay on the subject, which he read as a Phi Beta Kappa address at the Iowa State University. Recognizing that his theory of loyalty could become persuasive just to the extent that he illustrated its applicability to contemporary life, Royce included a version of the

1902 article in *Race Questions, Provincialism and Other American Problems.*

Delineating his topic, Royce called a province

> any one part of a national domain, which is, geographically and
> socially, sufficiently unified to have a true consciousness of its own
> unity, to feel a pride in its own ideals and customs, and to possess a
> sense of its distinction from other parts of the country.[22]

Provincialism, then, meant

> first, the tendency of such a province to possess its own customs and
> ideals; secondly, the totality of these customs and ideals themselves;
> and thirdly, the love and pride which leads the inhabitants of a
> province to cherish as their own these traditions, beliefs, and aspira-
> tions.[23]

Given these definitions, what most interested Royce was the question of provincialism's worth. He defended the thesis that

> in the present state of the world's civilization, and of the life of our
> own country, the time has come to emphasize, with a new meaning
> and intensity, the positive value, the absolute necessity for our wel-
> fare, of a wholesome provincialism, as a saving power to which the
> world in the near future will need more and more to appeal.[24]

That thesis did need defending. Throughout history, and not least
in the United States, the violence of sovereigns, sects, and sections
has produced a deplorable record that argues for movement beyond
the provincialism that spawned it. Precisely because of that record,
however, Royce believed that the world had been changed in ways
that defined "a new social mission which the province alone, but not
the nation, is able to fulfill."[25] Rightly practiced, enlightened provincialism would itself be a way beyond "narrowness of spirit [and]
jealousies between various communities."[26] It would, in fact, foster
loyalty to loyalty.

Again, Royce stressed, one cannot be loyal to "a mere abstraction
called humanity in general."[27] Loyalty to loyalty means commitment in a particular time and place and to specific causes. True, such
loyalty does enjoin attitudes that encompass a breadth of humanitarian concern, but Royce's point was that without a provincial base
this concern will have little substance. If a wise provincialism is
desirable, however, Royce denied that it could be taken for granted.
Modernity tends to erode it.

First, mobility makes us strangers much of the time, and where provincial ties do exist, such communities do not easily expand to make newcomers truly welcome. Second, a factor that both threatens provincialism and intensifies its importance is what Royce identified as "the levelling tendency of recent civilization."[28] Life becomes imitative to the point of homogenization. Not far behind is "a dead level of harassed mediocrity."[29] There are, of course, gains to be found in mobility, standardization, and uniformity. Provincialism itself requires its own conformities. As it confronts the leveling tendencies of modern civilization, provincial character nevertheless can be a countervailing force that nurtures both individual initiative and loyalty to loyalty. Third, at least where popular government is concerned, the leveling tendencies that worried Royce could develop into the spirit of a mob. That spirit is characterized by a lack of self-criticism and self-restraint. Those desirable qualities engendered by provincialism Royce found more likely to predominate when relatively small groups of persons interacted with each other. As he said prophetically,

> a nation composed of many millions of people may fall rapidly under the hypnotic influence of a few leaders, of a few fatal phrases . . . which tends to make the social order, under certain conditions, not only monotonous and unideal, but actively dangerous.[30]

Just because a wise provincialism accentuates local pride, loyalty to one's immediate community, and willingness to remember the best in particular traditions, the resulting contrasts with the larger leveling tendencies in society provide a fertile field for critical consciousness to sustain freedom against its enemies.

Apart from the benign influence of provincialism, contended Royce, "the nation by itself . . . is in danger of becoming an incomprehensible monster, in whose presence the individual loses his right, his self-consciousness, and his dignity. The province must save the individual."[31] To combat the danger, Royce drew attention to four elements that a wise provincialism incorporated. First, a wise provincialism is not so much boastful about local accomplishments, but instead is genuinely idealistic—it longs continuously for the community's improvement. Second, a wise provincialism is not closed to the values that other communities contain, but instead seeks to learn from them, interpreting and incorporating those insights in its own way to strengthen the provincial community.[32] Third, as a new generation is educated, the goal of a wise provincialism will be to arouse curiosity about other communities, but at the same time to foster a sense of responsibility for the welfare of the home community and then to ensure that opportunities for exercising responsibility are made available. Finally, urged Royce, a wise provincialism will not overlook the significance of sacrifice that aims "to put in the form of great institutions, of noble architecture, and of beautiful surroundings an expression of the worth that the community attaches to its own ideals."[33] Where such sacrifice accompanies the other traits he outlined, Royce believed there was little likelihood that provincialism would become too confined. On the contrary, by thus idealizing itself, provincialism would remind people that its major contribution is as a vital part that enriches the whole.

Provincialism and Religion: A Common Spirit

Noting that the root word for provincialism is "province," Royce emphasized that traditions associated with a state, city, or town are at the heart of a provincial spirit. His account of a wise provincialism says little explicitly about religion, but there is nothing in it to exclude loyalty to the local in diverse senses. For instance, much religious life involves membership in a specific congregation. Such a congregation will share concerns and activities that reach well beyond the local. Yet it will also reflect local ways and aspirations. Indeed, those particular elements will influence how it enacts more universal concerns. If we cultivate the loyalty that Royce urged, religion that is wisely provincial contributes a significant source of strength.

Religion and provincialism commonly go together, though not always wisely. That relationship exists because religion tends to retain elements of exclusivity that harbor narrowness. But religion's advantage, even where exclusivity and narrowness are found, is that this provincialism does include elements of the universal. Usually, for example, there is a vision of the good that is all-encompassing, and the particularity of a tradition is oriented toward its view of the whole. Granted, religion may be dogmatic about its claims to truth, and when that happens even its vision of the good becomes dangerously narrow. But the point here is as follows: If religion's provincialism can be made wise in the Roycean sense, then religion is a powerful base for fostering the ideals that Royce desired to encourage. For quite as natural to religion are wise provincialism's antidotes for the social ills of rootlessness, leveling mediocrity, and the conformity to mass politics.

To illustrate, consider some of religion's best forms, ones that in principle could characterize its practice in countless local situations. First, accompanying religious life that exists in communal form and in a particular location, there will be found a drive to keep improving and not to be satisfied, let alone merely boastful, about what has been accomplished in that place. Awareness that a tradition's memories and hopes must be enlivened in concrete settings will blend with conviction that loyalty to them requires a special giving, one recognizing that the right ideals are never totally fulfilled on earth and, yet, that effort toward them intensifies life's significance. Second, the effectiveness of such religious practices, it is recognized, does depend on openness to what others are doing and to what they have to teach. But the eye watching in those directions is also turned to perceive how the appropriate lessons can be interpreted locally to serve the ideal causes that religion extols. Third, religion at its best constantly seeks to educate the young to carry forward the memories and hopes that give it vitality. Again, the recognition is that this learning must extend far and wide, even to the point of risking loss of the young from the religious community. But that recognition also includes the insight that unless there is a match between breadth of training and opportunities for service within the tradition, the life of a religious community will be impoverished as one generation succeeds another. Finally, in its particular ways, religion does take seriously the notion that beauty resides in the service of the ideal. Form of expression may vary, but for those who care about a shared religious life, there is usually a concern to create places and moments of beauty that praise and honor what is good.

These qualities, which are natural to religion at its best, can help keep people armed against the social ills that Royce wanted a wise provincialism to combat. Indeed, unless we look to the religious life to provide this provincialism, we probably overlook provincialism's most promising source. For a wisely provincial religion understands that humankind is more than just the sum of its parts. They are relativized by power that transcends them for the good, and in whose service it is the proper task of the finite beings of the world to labor. At the same time, by putting those beliefs to work in particular times and places, religion can provide a home for those on the move. It can forestall the leveling Royce feared by supporting the conviction that individual persons and communities count and that they do so precisely because they can do good things that no one else can accomplish. Finally, through loyalty to its unique perspectives, religion can help to prevent the loss of freedom to tyrannical political authority.

Overarching all this is the essentially Roycean theme that full personhood is achieved neither atomistically nor in isolation, but through committed relationships. Robert Bellah's *Habits of the Heart* amplifies that awareness and takes it to be one of the things most needed to put in remission the cancerous individualism of contemporary American life. That prescription contains an irony, he realizes, because religion contributes much to America's individualistic self-understanding. Hence, the attachment of many Americans to religious groups is determined largely by the degree to which those groups meet their own personal needs. Nevertheless, within the American religious experience there are other strands, closer to the Roycean vision, that Bellah hopes we can renew and build upon. Significantly, he finds them not in the abstract, not in a sociological overview, but in the wisely provincial workings of local congregations.

In Christian life, for example, Bellah notes "an organic conception of the religious institution for which the defining metaphor is the Pauline image of the body of Christ."[34] He neither expects nor desires that this holistic image will eliminate the critical, reforming spirit of sectarian individualism or the propensity toward non-institutionalized mysticism that appeals to many Americans. But Bellah does resound Royce's sense of memory and hope when he urges that at present an overall understanding of religion would do well to capitalize on an organic metaphor. Bellah's findings fit well with what Royce had in mind when he spoke "as a native Californian," going beyond his own private experience to urge a wise provincialism, one that should and can be found especially in religious life.

NOTES

1. Josiah Royce, *Race Questions, Provincialism and Other American Problems* (New York: Macmillan Co., 1908), p. v.

2. Ibid., p. 211.

3. Ibid., p. 212.

4. Ibid.

5. Ibid., p. 214.

6. Ibid.

7. Josiah Royce, *The Hope of the Great Community* (New York: The Macmillan Company, 1916), p. 129.

8. Alexis de Tocqueville, *Democracy in America,* ed. J. P. Mayer and trans. George Lawrence (Garden City, N.Y.: Doubleday Anchor, 1969), p. 429.

9. Ibid., p. 429.

10. Ibid., p. 430.

11. Ibid., p. 429.

12. Robert N. Bellah et al., *Habits of the Heart: Individualism and Commitment in American Life* (Berkeley: University of California Press, 1985), p. viii.

13. Ibid., see especially pp. 20–2, 50–1, 81–4, 138–41, 146–7, 150–5, 277, 281–296.

14. Ibid., p. 282.

15. Ibid., p. 287.

16. Tocqueville, op. cit., p. 429.

17. In this section of the paper, I have borrowed from my Introduction to *The Philosophy of Josiah Royce,* ed. John K. Roth (Indianapolis: Hackett Publishing Company, 1982), pp. 22–5.

18. Josiah Royce, *The Philosophy of Loyalty* (New York: Macmillan Co., 1908), p. 16–17. Royce's italics.

19. Ibid., p. 121. Royce's italics.

20. Ibid., p. 5.

21. See Section VII of Chapter V, "Some American Problems in Their Relation to Loyalty," in *The Philosophy of Loyalty,* op. cit., pp. 244–8.

22. Josiah Royce, "Provincialism," in *Race Questions, Provincialism and Other American Problems,* op. cit., p. 61.

23. Ibid., p. 61.

24. Ibid., p. 62.

25. Ibid., p. 61.

26. Ibid., pp. 64–5.

27. Ibid., p. 67.

28. Ibid., p. 74.

29. Ibid.

30. Ibid., p. 95.

31. Ibid., p. 98.

32. In passages that retain a contemporary ring, Royce cites the Japanese as a people who are adept at learning from others and at adapting this learning to their distinctive ways. See ibid., pp. 103–7.

33. Ibid., p. 108.

34. Bellah et al., op. cit., p. 243.

5

Cognitive Styles or Hypocrisy? An Explanation of the Religiousness-Intolerance Relationship

RITA MATARAGNON PULLIUM

In the last few decades, survey research has repeatedly shown a relationship between various indices of religiousness such as church attendance and value for religion on the one hand, and negatively evaluated social tendencies such as prejudice, intolerance, and lack of social compassion on the other. As early as 1946, Allport and Kramer discovered that students who reported a strong religious (Protestant or Catholic) influence at home were higher in ethnic prejudice than students reporting only slight or no religious influence.[1] Several years later, Kirkpatrick found more punitive attitudes among religious people than among nonreligious people toward deviant groups such as criminals, homosexuals, and prostitutes.[2] As for nonconformist groups such as atheists, socialists, and Communists, Stouffer in 1955 also demonstrated that among a representative sample of church members, those who had attended church during the past month expressed more intolerance toward these groups than those who had not.[3] More recently, a carefully controlled study by Beatty and Walter in 1984 concluded that church attendance reduced political tolerance in all denominations studied with the level lower in some denominations than in others.[4]

A paradox has turned up, one that is at best thought provoking and, at worst, extremely disturbing to the religious and non-religious alike. Why should religious people show less tolerance and compassion for outgroups when all religious denominations essentially preach love for humankind? Is it all hypocrisy, as critics of religion like to point out?

One of the first reactions to such persistent but disturbing findings has been to check whether the relationship could actually be spurious or contrived. To this end, socioeconomic status and educational attainment were considered possibilities. However, Stouffer's study found that the tendency toward intolerance among church-goers existed even when educational level was held constant.[5] Beatty and Walter also found that levels of political intolerance remained after controlling for education and occupational prestige.[6] While demographic differences have failed to explain the relationship between religiousness and intolerance, some light has been shed on the matter by distinguishing between different types of religious individuals and exploring the personalities and cognitive styles of those who may find in religion a justification for prejudice, dogmatism, intolerance, and lack of compassion.

Extrinsic versus Intrinsic Religious Orientation

Gordon Allport offered an explanation for the association between religiousness and prejudice. He reasoned that the majority of churchgoers go to church for social support and/or for relief from personal problems. Such motivation, he suggested, would neither result in the most frequent church attendance nor an application of religion in all social dealings, that is, as a way of life. He used the term "extrinsic religious orientation" to describe the way religion fits into the lives of this group of people. These individuals who need social support and relief from personal problems and unwittingly use religion for such purposes might also be insecure enough to blame outgroups for their troubles or to feel threatened by social change.[7] They may be, in short, the ones who give religion a bad name.

On the other hand, Allport identified a subset of religious people who were the most frequent church attenders and who most seriously expended their energies on a truly religious life. Religion pervaded all their social dealings, and they exhibited great tolerance for others. Allport used the term "intrinsic religious orientation" to describe this kind of internally motivated approach to religion. Reviewing several studies, Allport and Ross concluded that a curvilinear relationship indeed exists between prejudice scores and church attendance. A U-shaped curve is obtained, with prejudice scores peaking for the moderate church attenders and lowest for nonattenders and frequent attenders (once a week or more often) alike.[8]

In view of the theoretical distinction between extrinsic and intrinsic religious orientations, a number of scales have been constructed which measure such religious orientations.[9] Preliminary work done using these scales has indicated that the extrinsic and intrinsic subscales are nearly independent, although each is related to bigotry in the predicted way. Interestingly, a number of people who were high on both scales, whom Allport and Ross labeled "indiscriminately proreligious" and described as having a confused religious orientation, turned out to be the most prejudiced of all.

Following the lead of Allport, several researchers have incorporated either frequency of church attendance or the extrinsic versus intrinsic orientation into their research on religiousness and prejudice, intolerance, and social compassion. Rokeach found that compared with nonchurchgoers, churchgoers were more bigoted and less compassionate regarding the death of Martin Luther King ("He brought it on himself.") *regardless* of frequency in church attendance.[10] On the other hand, Brannon reported that members of two southern churches which split from their parent church over the civil rights issue in the mid-1960s, showed significantly different scores on Allport's scales measuring extrinsic and intrinsic religious orientation.[11] In a second investigation done in a small, isolated southern town during the mid–1960s, Brannon wove Allport's extrinsic and intrinsic items into an interview about religion. He also presented five public issues (one of which was racial integration) and asked each subject to identify the issue he or she thought most about. Predictably, "not only did every person name integration as the topic he thought most about, he invariably launched into a heated discussion of this issue." Blind coding of the interviews yielded a score on religious orientation and one on overt racial prejudice; and correlation between these two scores yielded a significant coefficient as high as .55.[12]

More support for the validity of the extrinsic versus intrinsic distinction comes from a meta-analysis which reviewed a substantial number of studies using the typology.[13] Donahue concluded that an extrinsic religious orientation is positively correlated with negatively evaluated characteristics such as prejudice and dogmatism, whereas an intrinsic orientation is unrelated to such measures. Although unlike Allport, Donahue did not find intrinsically oriented religious people to be lower in prejudice and higher in tolerance and compassion; still, he found that being intrinsically religious did not increase prejudice, while being extrinsically religious did. It seems, therefore, that this subgroup accounts primarily for the paradoxical relationship between religiousness and intolerance.

The question that next confronts us is why? Why should a tendency to find personal comfort and social support in one's religion lead to prejudice, intolerance, and reduced compassion? What selection factors predispose prejudiced people to become "religious people," and what mechanisms within religion maintain such social attitudes? Is it simply hypocrisy, or could it be that, instead, genuine differences in personality and cognitive styles exist between nonbelievers and the majority of believers which explain their levels of tolerance and compassion?

The Just-World Belief

One of the major attractions of religion is the idea of a perfectly just and omnipotent Being who, despite the seeming injustices and vagaries of human existence, keeps some kind of score and eventually deals human beings their just due, either in this life or in the next. "Be not deceived; for whatsoever a man soweth, that shall he also reap." As Rubin and Peplau point out, the Book of Job sets forth both sides of the fundamental religious controversy.[14] God tests the faith of Job by inflicting tremendous suffering on him. Job's friends think that suffering is the result of sin, and that Job should repent. Although Job disagrees with them and eventually proves himself correct, nevertheless, Job's friends are typical of those who believe in a just world where the good are rewarded and the bad punished.

In recent decades, a concept has been developed within social psychology called the *just-world belief.* Belief in a just world can be high or low in an individual. Many people believe that the world is basically a place where good people are rewarded and bad people punished. In fact, we probably all developed some version of the just-world belief (Piaget's immanent justice) in early childhood that helped us graduate from the pleasure principle to the capacity to be moral and to delay gratification. Some people apparently cling to or even strengthen this just-world belief in the process of growing up; others reject it early, seeing life as largely arbitrary, random, and without justice. Regardless of the objective state of affairs, people vary in the degree to which they subscribe to the just-world belief.

Social psychologists have studied correlates and consequences of belief in a just world. To measure individual differences, a just-world scale was developed.[15] Just-world scores have been found to be correlated with a number of other individual differences. Religiosity is one such correlate. Rubin and Peplau found, for example, that scores on the just-world scale among college students were correlated with their reported frequency of church or synagogue attendance (r=.42). Since the belief in a just world also has much in common with the main tenets of the Protestant ethic, Lerner administered both the Protestant-ethic Scale of Mirels and Garrett and the just-world scale to a sample of undergraduates and found that the results were significantly correlated (r=.35).[16]

The belief in a just world does more than help an individual work hard and delay gratification. It has significant social and political consequences. If the world is perceived as just, then not only do people get what they deserve, but they also deserve what they get. Strong believers in a just world are therefore expected to admire and support people with success or power or good fortune, because privilege is associated with being deserving. On the other hand, strong believers in a just world are also expected to be more hostile and unsympathetic toward people who suffer personal misfortune or seeming social injustice, especially in cases where the situation can not be corrected. A related consequence is the tendency to derogate victims of social injustice and ascribe to them responsibility or their plight. Data from Peplau and Tyler indeed show UCLA students with high just-world scores to have more favorable attitudes toward established institutions and government officials.[17] Among Rubin and Peplau's respondents, belief in a just world was positively correlated with the belief that blacks and women were responsible for their inferior states. On the other hand, such belief correlated negatively with social and political activism such as demonstrating or donating money for causes.[18]

Overlooking Situational Attributions

Sorrentino found that while religious subjects were more likely to take the less lenient, less compassionate side of a social issue (e.g., immigration, free dental care), they did not derogate a specific and actual victim of innocent suffering more than a nonvictim.[19] This is apparently due to a tendency to ignore situational determinants of behavior and treat people alike. In fact, part of the reason why religious subjects take the unsympathetic side of social issues is because of their tendency to overlook situational factors and treat everyone according to the same rules.

When people consider an event, they can take either a situational or a dispositional position. For instance, consider illness. Why did X get sick? A situational approach would consider weather, contagion, and so forth; a dispositional approach would locate the cause within X—his negligent health habits, his hypochondria, and the like. Why are some people poor? A situational approach would focus on the social structure and lack of opportunities; a dispositional one would focus on individual traits such as laziness or incompetence.

While it is obvious that nobody makes exclusively situational or dispositional attributions all the time, individuals do differ in the general cognitive style by which they make attributions about causality of events. Some display a higher frequency of situational attributions, while others show a higher frequency of dispostional attributions. More work is needed in this area, but so far the evidence suggests that religious individuals are inclined toward dispositional attributions. The individual's character and intentions usually receive more attention than forces or pressures in the situation. By ignoring innocent suffering brought about by situational factors, individuals can protect their just-world belief from threat. In not considering situational determinants, religious persons can see no reason why those less fortunate should get special treatment.

The Authoritarian Personality

It has long been believed that the relation between religious orientation and prejudice is mediated by a personality variable called authoritarianism. In the 1950 book *The Authoritarian Personality*, it was found that ethnocentricism authoritarianism levels are significantly higher among church attenders than among nonattenders. Again, it should be noted that church attender here refers to the majority who tend to be casual members with an extrinsic religious orientation. A bell-shaped curve, as before, was obtained. Thus "regular" attenders (like nonattenders) were found to be less authoritarian and less prejudiced than "seldom" or "often" attenders.[20] Kirscht and Dillehay corroborated this high correlation between religiousness and authoritarianism.[21]

The authoritarian personality is characterized by an overwhelming concern with authority, power, and obedience. As children, authoritarians were taught, often by punitive methods, to fear authority and, indirectly, to covet it. Strong and powerful people are good, while weak and powerless people are bad. Authoritarianism is measured by the F (facism) scale. Authoritarian values and attitudes are marked by rigidity, inhibition, and oversimplification. One way to simplify the world is to divide people into ingroups and outgroups. Authoritarians therefore tend to be very ethnocentric; they consider only members of their own national, ethnic, or religious group acceptable. Their rigid and intolerant thinking also make them prone to dogmatism or closed-mindedness. Having low tolerance for cognitive inconsistency, authoritarians are unlikely to expose themselves to different points of view.[22]

An extrinsic religiosity is associated not only with authoritarianism but with the cluster of traits that go with it. It has already been mentioned that extrinsic religiosity is associated with ethnocentricism. In addition, several studies show that extrinsic (but not intrinsic) religiousness is positively correlated to dogmatism.[23] And since extrinsic religiousness is related to both the just-world belief and authoritarianism, it is not surprising to find authoritarianism correlated (r = .56) with just-world scores as well.[24] It seems logical that a respect for authority should follow from the belief that power is deserved. The concepts of authoritarianism and just-world belief are nevertheless distinct, in that authoritarians show negative attitudes toward all outgroups, whereas just-world believers show negative attitudes only toward unsuccessful outgroups.[25] Finally, several studies have suggested that in making judgments about behavior high authoritarians are more likely to attend to a person's character or attitudes, whereas low authoritarians are more likely to attend to situational factors as well.[26]

What in religion attracts and maintains authoritarianism? Religion offers absolute answers in a world where so much seems to be relative, and authoritarians have a strong need for definite answers. Most Western religions subscribe to one omnipotent deity; this is a strong symbol of authority. More fundamental denominations (generally but not always associated with higher intolerance scores) also emphasize an ingroup that possesses the truth.[27]

Locus of Control

The last concept that deserves mention as a possible intermediary mechanism between extrinsic religiosity and intolerance is the locus-of-control concept. Locus of control refers to a individual's expectancy that certain behaviors on his or her part will lead to certain outcomes. The perception that life is to a large extent controlled by fate and luck, random and uncontrollable outside forces, is known as an external locus of control. On the other hand, the perception that outcomes in life are mostly controlled by one's own actions is known as an internal locus of control. Individuals can veer toward either extreme on an internal or external (I-E) scale, such as the one devised by Rotter.[28]

How is locus of control related to the just-world belief? While the two concepts share a certain degree of overlap, they are conceptually distinct. An internal locus of control obviously requires the scaffolding of belief in a just world to support it. Correlational data offer strong support for the hypothesis that belief in a just world is associated with an internal locus of control. However, an external locus of control anchored on a just deity or even superstitions about retribution is also guided by a just-world belief. Indeed, just-world scores also correlate with belief in an active God.[29] The point is, locus of control may contribute to the social-intolerance pattern of the extrinsic religious believer through its relation to the just-world belief as well as through independent effects.

Among world religions, Western religions may generally be classified as "this worldly" rather than "other worldly." Western religions are typically not fatalistic; rather, they emphasize free will and human choice. They are not passive; rather they encourage the active notion that God works through people and that "God helps those who help themselves." Among Western religions, and more particularly among Protestant denominations, we find the epitome of such a worldly and active religious orientation in the Protestant ethic. Believers in the Protestant work ethic regard hard work as a value in its own right and as a key to success which glorifies God. Mirels and Garrett found scores on their Protestant ethic scale correlated positively with authoritarianism and internal control.[30] Garrett found that high scorers worked harder than low scorers on experimental task.[31] Such diligence, however, is what prompted them to expect the same from others, to agree that most people on welfare were lazy, and in general to derogate social victims.[32]

Probably more than any other factor, an internal locus of control is regarded to be beneficial and adaptive in religiousness. Individuals with an internal locus of control can better delay gratification, achieve more, give up less easily, and cope constructively with stress, moreover, they are more independent and resistant to persuasion. On the matter of social sympathy, although internal controlled individuals are more likely to be strict in attributing responsibility to social victims, *if and when convinced of a cause, they are also more active in working for it.* Thus students with high internality were more likely to volunteer for civil rights activities[33] or be involved with the women's movement.[34] Similarly, Staub and Midlarsky found that subjects high in internality engaged in more prosocial behavior.[35]

Hypocrisy or Cognitive Style?

It seems apparent from the foregoing studies that intolerance among religious individuals is connected with an extrinsic religious orientation. Inasmuch as the majority of religious people or churchgoers belong to the extrinsic-oriented group, it is not surprising that studies repeatedly show a relationship between religiousness generally and prejudice, intolerance, or lack of social compassion. On the other hand, a small minority of intrinsically religious people live in a way consistent with their religious teachings. As mentioned earlier, research has shown either higher tolerance scores for this group, or no relationship at all between this kind of religiousness and tolerance. *In fact, Gallup found that the highest percentage of those working with the poor, the infirm, or the elderly came from the group of Americans whom he classified as "highly spiritually committed."*[36]

The intrinsically religious provide us with a relatively comprehensible picture of what serious and selfless religion does to people. What is puzzling and more complicated is the majority, the extrinsically religious. While these people have often been accused of hypocrisy, my contention is that it is not hypocrisy but a cluster of cognitive styles that predispose them to act in a way that seems prejudiced, intolerant, and lacking in social compassion. If hypocrisy refers to "a feigning to be what one is not," then the extrinsically religious should not be considered hypocritical. They are not pretending to be something they are not. Their judgment, their prejudice and intolerance flow naturally and consistently from the cognitive styles they adopt.

Religious leaders seeking to overcome criticism of hypocrisy among their followers would do well to examine these cognitive styles and their implications. They could probably help their extrinsically religious congregations look at the world somewhat differently if they did the following: (1) Focus on brotherly love more than on retributive justice; (2) Attribute responsibility to situational factors as well as to character or personal choice; (3) Confront the reality of innocent and unexplainable suffering; (4) Question authority and power whenever necessary; (5) Adopt a searching rather than a dogmatic attitude; and (6) Apply an active approach toward helping behavior, whereby people see themselves as instrumental agents in relieving others' suffering. A change of cognitive styles may hopefully lead the average religious person to overcome intolerance and rekindle that spark of compassion and love that his or her religion preaches.

NOTES

1. G. W. Allport and B.M. Kramer, "Some Roots of Prejudice," *Journal of Psychology* 22 (1946): 9–39.

2. C. Kirkpatrick, "Religion and Humanitarianism: A study of institutional implications," *Psychological Monographs* 63, no. 304 (1949): 9.

3. S. A. Stouffer, *Communism, Civil Liberties, and Conformity* (New York: Doubleday, 1955).

4. K. M. Beatty and O. Walter, "Religious Preference and Practice: Reevaluating Their Impact on Political Tolerance," *Public Opinion Quarterly* 48 (1984): 318–329.

5. Cf. G. Allport and M. Ross, "Personal Religious Orientation and Prejudice," *Journal of Personality and Social Psychology* 5 (1967): 432–443.

6. Beatty and Walter, op. cit., 325–6.

7. G. Allport, *The Nature of Prejudice* (Massachusetts: Addison–Wesley, 1954).

8. Allport and Ross, op. cit. 433–4.

9. W. C. Wilson, "Extrinsic Religious Values Scale and Prejudice," *Journal of Abnormal and Social Psychology* 60 (1960): 286–8. Also see J. Feagin, "Prejudice and Religious Types: A Focused Study of Southern Fundamentalists," *Journal for the Scientific Study of Religion* 4 (1964): 3–13.

10. M. Rokeach, "Faith, Hope, and Bigotry," *Psychology Today* 11 (1970): 33–7.

11. R. C. L. Brannon, "Gimme That Old-Time Racism," *Psychology Today* 11 (1970): 42–4.

12. Brannon, op. cit., p. 44.

13. M. J. Donahue, "Intrinsic and Extrinsic Religiousness: Review and Meta-Analysis," *Journal of Personality and Social Psychology* 47 (1984): 1263–80.

14. Z. Rubin and L. Peplau, "Who Believes in a Just World?" *Journal of Social Issues* 31 (1975): 65–89.

15. Ibid.

16. M. J. Lerner, Belief in a Just World versus the Authoritarian Syndrome: But Nobody Liked the Indians. Unpublished manuscript, University of Waterloo, 1973. See also H. L. Mirels and J. B. Garrett, "The Protestant Ethic as a Personality Variable," *Journal of Consulting and Clinical Psychology* 36(1971): 40–4.

17. L. Peplau and T. Tyler, Belief in a Just World and Political Attitudes. Paper presented at the meeting of the Western Psychological Association, Sacramento, Ca, April 1975.

18. Z. Rubin and L. Peplau, "Belief in a Just World and Reactions to Another's Lot," *Journal of Social Issues* 29 (1973): 73–93.

19. R. M. Sorrentino, "Derogation of an Innocently Suffering Victim: So Who's the "Good Guy?" in *Altruism and Helping Behavior,* ed. J. P. Rushton and R. M. Sorrentino, 267–283.

20. T. W. Adorno, E. Frenkel-Brunswick, D. J. Levinson, and R. N. Sanford, *The Authoritarian Personality* (New York: Harper, 1950).

21. J. P. Kirscht and R. C. Dillehay, *Dimensions of Authoritarianism* (Lexington: University of Kentucky Press, 1967), pp. 67–72.

22. I. D. Steiner and H. H. Johnson, "Authoritarism and tolerance of trait inconsistency," *Journal of Abnormal and Social Psychology* 67 (1963): 388–391.

23. D. R. Hoge and J. W. Carroll, "Religiosity and Prejudice in Northern and Southern Churches," Journal for the Scientific Study of Religion 11 (1972): 369–76. See also R. D. Kahoe, "Personality and Achievement Correlates of Intrinsic and Extrinsic Religious Orientation," *Journal of Personality and Social Psychology* 29 (1974): 812–18.

24. Rubin and Peplau, op. cit., 1973.

25. Lerner op. cit., 1973.

26. K. S. Berg and N. Vidmar, "Authoritarianism and recall of evidence about criminal behavior," *Journal of Research in Personality* 9 (1975): 147–57. See also H. E. Mitchell and D. Byrne, "The Defendant's Dilemma: Effects of Jurors' Attitudes and Authoritarianism on Judicial Decisions," *Journal of Personality and Social Psychology* 25 (1973): 123–9.

27. Walter and Beatty, op. cit., 1984, pp. 323–4.

28. J. B. Rotter, "Generalized Expectancies for Internal versus External Locus of Control of Reinforcement," *Psychological Monographs* 80, no. 609 (1966).

29. Rubin and Peplau, op. cit., 1975, p. 79.

30. Mirels and Garrett, op. cit., 1971.

31. J. B. Garrett, *The Protestant Ethic Personality Variable and Work Behavior.* Paper presented at the meeting of the Eastern Psychological Association, Philadelphia, April 1974.

32. A. P. MacDonald, Jr., "More on the Protestant Ethic," *Journal of Consulting and Clinical Psychology* 39 (1972): 116–22.

33. H. M. Lefcourt, *Locus of Control: Current Trends in Theory and Research,* 2nd ed. (New Jersey: Erlbaum, 1982).

34. P. M. Gore and J. B. Rotter, "A Personality Correlate of Social Action," *Journal of Personality* 31 (1963): 58–64.

35. E. Midlarsky, "Aiding Responses: An Analytic Review, *Merrill-Palmer Quarterly* 14 (1968): 229–60.

36. G. G. Gallup, Jr., *Adventures in Immortality* (New York: McGraw-Hill, 1982).

6

Belief in God: Impetus for Social Action

IRENE KHIN KHIN JENSEN

*He hath showed thee, O Man, what is good; and what doth Jehovah require of thee, but
to do justly, and to love kindness, and to walk humbly with thy God? (Mic. 6: 8)*
American Revised Version

The above verse from the Old Testament holds a special place in the
lives of many people including my own family. If one shares in the
biblical faith that God has a claim upon his people—to "love kindness, do justly, walk humbly" with Him, then one has to understand and appreciate the impetus for social action among Christians
and all of society. There are scores of persons throughout the world
who affirm that a belief in God should generate social action. To
many who wish to abide by the Golden Rule, there is a conviction
that serving a neighbor in need is an act of worship. The meeting of
human needs is done in the name of Christ as well as for those
involved. This paper will focus on some selected examples in which
Belief in God has resulted in social action. Obviously, there are
many other examples which illustrate this theme.

The Family Metaphor

Throughout history, belief in God has resulted in a variety of responses from the believing community. If we use the family metaphor, accepting God as our father, then we should want to treat our
brothers and sisters throughout the world as equals. We should
want, for example, to help educate those who do not have those
opportunities, as many Christian denominations and missionaries
have done. The pioneering of such institutions amid great difficulties will be discussed later in the paper, with special focus on the
education for women in some countries.

Continuing the family metaphor, we can assume that as Christians we also have an interest in caring about the health and well-

being of the family. Hence, as Christians we need to be more sensitive to the medical needs of those less fortunate, those scores of persons who need medical facilities. Christian medical colleges and church-related hospitals have been established all over the world. If we consider Jesus Christ as Lord, the One who can salvage what is broken within us and restore wholeness to our lives then the establishment of medical colleges to provide training for doctors and nurses and health care for the needy is worthy of our financial support and concerned prayers.

India: Improving Medical Care

The Christian Medical College Hospital of Vellore stands as an example of response to medical needs in a poor community. Founded in India in the late nineteenth century by a dedicated medical missionary, Dr. Ida Scudder, it is today a special place with a 1,200-bed teaching hospital. Vellore is known throughout India and around the world. Its name, for those who know the work performed there, is synonymous with Christian mission, healing ministry, medical training, and health services for all of India. Vellore is today the largest Christian medical center in that part of Asia. Vellore also symbolizes the dream and work of its founder, Ida Scudder, who recognized the need to have trained Indian women doctors and nurses. Christians and non-Christians alike are welcomed within Vellore's hospital doors. There is also a chapel open twenty-four hours a day for people of all religions who wish to pray for their loved ones. The hospital prayer is a very appealing expression of hope:

> These buildings have a mission to fulfill
> They belong to God and to those in need,
> We bid the suffering and all who will,
> To COME and find the doors open and indeed
> We trust the Spirit of Christ may reign forever here:
> That anxious care may cease,
> That it may be a channel whereby pain long borne may end,
> And hearts may find release.
> God Grant that Christ may walk the wards today
> God grant He moves within these rooms at night,
> Heeding the cry of hurt hearts as they pray,
> Bringing them out of the darkness into light
> Come Lord, abide within this sacred place,
> And meet each need with Thy unfailing Grace.[1]

It has been my privilege to visit this medical complex twice, most recently in February 1986, and to observe the medical outreach of those who serve there. In 1948, the first mobile eye-care unit and community health service was started, by medical missionary Dr. Victor C. Rambo. This outreach model is today being copied in many parts of India. In addition to establishing mobile eye clinics and mobile hospitals, Dr. Rambo has personally performed more than 40,000 cataract operations. In the process, he has left a permanent imprint on the treatment of the blind in India. Thousands of villagers who would have been blind today, have had their eyesight restored through the outreach work of Vellore. Rambo has been called India's "Apostle of Sight." After more than fifty years of service in India, he writes that "God still calls men and women to service that may be difficult, even dangerous, but a service that brings the spiritual reward of joy beyond anything the secular world can offer."[2] Dr. Rambo is a firm believer in the following passage from the scripture: "I tell you the truth, whatever you did for one of the least of these brothers [and sisters] of mine, you did for me" (Mat. 25:40).

Vellore Medical College now has a New Life Center for the rehabilitation of those suffering from leprosy, persons still on the margin of Indian society. In addition it has research facilities for the study of chronic and life-threatening diseases. In 1977, the Rural Unit of Health and Social Affairs (RUHSA), comprehensive community health development and medical leadership training program, was established. This unit provides models for other parts of India. The motto of Vellore students and doctors is that our Lord came "not to be ministered unto, but to minister." Those who are familiar with Vellore's Christian medical college would affirm that its special fame is rooted in its ministry of service.

Church Care for the Needy

The New Testament reminds us that Christ provided for the needy with loaves and fishes. In this spirit, Christians individually and in groups have responded to unemployment, rural poverty, and unexpected natural disasters by donating food, clothing, and money to the needy all over the world. Although church denominations may function differently in their response to need, the significant common denominator is that all of them do respond when they hear of misfortune.

Spiritual Renewal

In Acts 18:28 we are reminded "For in him [God] we live, and move, and have our being. . . . For we are . . . his offspring." Today church leaders are very conscious of their congregation's need for spiritual renewal. Many provide workshops and retreats for families and individuals in church schools and other facilities. Prayer groups are now stronger than ever and intercessory prayer is important for many as an expression of caring and concern, a quiet form of social action. Workshops and retreats for spiritual renewal are particularly important because Christians often feel the need to be "refueled" with fellowship, and to interact with others who have similar concerns. In these experiences new insights are gained about social issues. Indeed, there is heightened consciousness among Christians today about many new social issues. For example, an issue discussed frequently at church retreats and workshops in the community is the environment and our need to protect the earth's precious resources.

Environmental Issues

The concern in the churches today about our environment is timely. This is a social action issue. Among the many books available concerning protecting our land, a recent and significant one is *Let the Earth Bless the Lord,* about land erosion and waste.[3] I had an opportunity to observe such erosion in 1986, in the mountains of Nepal, where local farmers had so carefully terraced their land on the steep mountainsides. For concerned Christians who are not content to sit back and just think about problems but want to grapple with them practically, *Let the Earth Bless the Lord* attempts to give a Christian perspective on land use. It points out that:

> Because the issues of land use and reform are key issues to the survival
> of humankind on earth, it seems necessary for the church to under-
> stand them—as it is important for the church to become engaged in
> all of the literally *vital* concerns of the earth's people.

This does not mean that members of the same denomination will always find themselves on the same side in environmental issues; what the study is advocating is that open debate in a Christian context is badly needed. Issues such as acid rain, appropriate technology in developing countries, and pollution are topics that need to be studied, and churches and concerned persons need to keep abreast of how to respond to these problems.

In the fall of 1985 Dr. and Mrs. Robert Carman, an American missionary couple serving in South India, wrote a letter to a co-worker, Dr. Daleep Mukarju, expressing concern about the depletion of the land resources in a section of Tamilnadu that would affect 100,000 people living in the area. This story was recorded in 1984, in *A Worldly Spirituality: The Call to Take Care of the Earth,* by Wesley Granberg-Michaelson. In it, Dr. Mukarji is quoted as saying:

> We must develop within our faith an understanding of God's creation and the stewardship role we have over its resources. . . . This is very much in keeping with the overall mission of healing, health and wholeness . . . which we as individuals and as Christians need to get involved in.

Dr. and Mrs. Carman, were conveying to their friends and supporting churches in the United States their concern for the unwise and uncaring use of God's earth. They agreed with Wesley Granberg-Michaelson that

> [s]ince creation is itself a recipient of God's salvation . . . our mission work must not take place simply in the whole earth, but must include the *whole* earth. The scope of Christ's redemption beckons mission work not only to soul-saving but also to earthkeeping.[4]

A byproduct of this concern, was the significant five-day symposium in November 1983, sponsored by the Rural Unit for Health and Social Affairs (RUHSA) of the Christian medical college of Vellore, with which Dr. Carman and Dr. Mukarji were closely associated. The theme of the symposium was Christian Perspectives in Stewardship of the Earth's Resources. One hundred and fifty delegates and resource people from various parts of India attended to discuss topics such as the biblical concept of man's relationship to creation, Christian concern for ecology and environment, water, forests, energy, health, and simpler life styles. A number of recommendations were made for the involvement of churches and voluntary organizations in the promotion of these concerns. There apparently is much more interest in India now about environmental issues, particularly since the Union Carbide gas-leak tragedy in Bhopal in December 1984, one of the largest industrial disasters in history. What is taking place halfway around the world is also of vital concern in the United States and merits further study on the part of all Christians interested in social action.

Currently, in my own church, we have study units drawing our attention to how we might learn more about caring for God's earth. Our women's organization is being alerted to literature that is current on what we are doing to our land and how we might become more knowledgable about water conservation.[5] It is obvious that interest at a grass-roots level in churches all over the United States is needed in order to protect our environment and leave a better heritage for our children and grandchildren.

Dealing with Stress

We will now focus on the concerns of the family, and how the church has responded to these needs. Church leaders realize more than ever that a belief in god means that there is a need to accept and help persons with problems, and to incorporate this aid within the church program as a social response to human needs. Many larger churches now have their own counseling centers, while smaller ones have part-time counselors on their staff. Churches now have marriage-enriching sessions, workshops for families with alcoholics, and blended-family group workshops for remarried couples. Churches and church-related groups are also involved in conflict-solving workshops, and many are hopeful that these models can be applied on an international level, thus bringing peace without violence to certain parts of the world.

Alternatives to Bearing Arms

Church groups such as Quakers accept the conviction that believing in God implies one does not bear arms even to defend one's own country. During this century, many believing Quakers chose to go to prison rather than serve in the army during war. Others chose alternate ways to remain true to their beliefs, for example, some taught in schools established in the war relocation centers for Japanese-Americans interned during World War II. Social action on many fronts in behalf of poor, defenseless, and deprived persons of all nations has been a special trademark of the Quakers. The American Friends Service Committee, a Quaker Organization, carries on its programs of social action as an expression of the belief in the dignity and worth of each person and in the faith that the power of love and nonviolence can bring about change.[6] This committee has received the Nobel peace prize for its role in promoting world peace.

The Quakers stand as a shining example of how belief in God can result in positive action to benefit mankind. Although people may not always agree with Quaker stands, the Quakers have often been on the cutting edge of social change, and they have always tried to do this in peaceful and constructive ways. They have provided a model for social-action groups of various denominations. They are considered on the forefront in the movement for peace and social justice on the international scene.

Racial Issues

Today there is an urgency to deal with racism throughout the world. As created beings and members of one family, it is important to treat everybody in that family, no matter what their color or race, with equality and human dignity. This is a goal that all Christians should strive for, and a belief in God certainly should be the impetus for preparing ourselves to treat others as we ourselves would like to be treated. I am reminded of the verse in Ephesians (4:6), which speaks of "One God and Father of all, who is over all, and through all, and in all."

In this century, we are mindful of a courageous man, the late Dr. Martin Luther King, Jr. who was assassinated because he championed racial justice. As a Christian minister and a human being Dr. King did not feel he had the rights of a free man in the United States. Today, his protest marches are a part of history of America and of the Christian church as well. No one will ever forget his famous words: "I have a dream, that one day, my little children will be judged on the content of their character and not the color of their skins." As Christians, there is an urgency to fulfill this dream of Martin Luther King, Jr., and of the many others who died risking their lives for social issues. Racism is an issue on which churches do not always agree, yet it is a compelling subject for social and economic justice. In this regard, certain denominations have adopted a "Charter for Racial Justice," which they hope to see implemented in their local churches across the nation.[7]

Education for Women

In the last two decades of the nineteenth century, two American women, Isabella Thoburn and Ida Scudder, challenged social norms of Indian society by offering to educate Indian women in both the liberal arts and the field of nursing and medicine. It was a slow and difficult process, but the torch was lighted for Indian women, and they have proved equal to tasks provided for them by these two pioneering missionaries. Institutions established by Thoburn and Scudder stand as monuments to their success. Renowned national educators, nurses, and medical doctors have emerged from these institutions, and their work has touched many lives in many parts of the world. Vellore Christian medical college, as discussed earlier, has provided medical help to Hindu and Muslim women who, prior to its founding, would have received no medical help. Both Isabella Thoburn and Ida Scudder were dedicated Christians, and their belief in God was certainly an impetus for social action.

Gaining equal access to education for Korean women in the late nineteenth century was the work of several American women. It took the vision of Methodist missionary Mary F. Scranton to found the first Korean school for women. What began as a one-room one-pupil, one-teacher school in Seoul, Korea, in 1886, is now Ewha University, the world's largest university for women. The vision of others like Lulu E. Frey and Dr. Alice R. Appenzeller from Pennsylvania have continued to light the torch for women's education, and Korean educators like Dr. Helen Kim and Dr. Okgill Kim have helped to develop Ewha University to its present size—almost 18,000 students. Today Ewha produces graduates in medicine, law, finance, liberal arts, education, social work and the sciences. It took much courage in a male-dominated society like Korea's to begin this undertaking, but the dream of these women pioneers was to take the spirit that they had been exposed to in their homeland and to transplant it in another land halfway around the world. This spirit is exemplified in the motto of Ewha University: "Not to be ministered unto, but to minister!"

A belief in God can and must lead to social action in various directions and dimensions. Each person is capable of implementing this in a small way. Much has been accomplished by persons in the past with a strong belief that to be Christian one must impact on society in a positive way. Examples cited in this paper have merely touched on the surface. If we all keep in mind that we have standards set for us in the Scriptures and in the actions of those who have done so much for society, we can also accomplish our goals.

Conclusion

In closing, I would like to quote here a prayer often used by pioneer women doctors who established one of the great medical centers in Asia.

Father whose life is within me and
Whose love is ever about me,
Grant that thy life may be maintained
In my life today and every day
That with gladness of heart, without haste or
Confusion of thought, I may go about my daily tasks,
Conscious of ability to meet every rightful demand,
Seeing the larger meaning of little things,
And finding beauty and love everywhere,
And in the sense of Thy Presence
May I walk through the hours
Breathing the atmosphere of love.[8]

Belief in God has created an impetus for social action in other arenas not covered in this paper. Christians and non-Christians alike are involved in issues national and international, such as nuclear arms build-up, the rights of refugees, child molestation, prison reform, and drunk driving. Many are currently involved in raising our nation's consciousness about the need for legislators who will make the right decisions not just for their constituents but for the nation and the world. Being good stewards involves a concern for everyone. If we cannot give time and talent to some of these causes, perhaps we can give our prayers to those who do work for the social good which we believe in and support, all in the name of the Creator.

NOTES

1 Dorothy Clark Wilson, *Dr. Ida, Passing on the Torch of Life* (New York: Friendship Press, 1976), p. 367.

2. Dorothy Clark Wilson, *Apostle of Sight* (New York: Christian Herald Book, 1980), p. 255.

3. C.A. Cesaretti and Stephen Commins, eds., *Let the Earth Bless the Lord, A Christian Perspective on Land Use* (New York: The Seabury Press, 1981), p. ix.

4. Robert and Lucille Carman, Newsletter #29 of Overseas Mission News, India-American Baptist International Ministries (Valley Forge, PA., 1985), p. 2.

5. Geralding Heilman, "Caring for God's Earth," in *Response-United Methodist Women* (March 1986): 40.

6. American Friends Service Committee, *Quaker Service Bulletin* 153, vol. 67, no. 1 (Winter, 1986): 8.

7. *Faithful Witness on Today's Issues—Racial Justice,* AO. C597 (Washington D.C.: The General Board of Church and Society of the United Methodist Church, 1985): 13.

8. Dorothy C. Wilson, *Dr. Ida,* op. cit., p. 367.

Part III

SOCIAL CONSEQUENCES OF BELIEF ON THE MACRO LEVEL

Macro-level analysis of religion tends to focus more explicitly on the impact religious forces exert on culture, societal systems, and large-scale organizations within a wider social context. The range of concerns investigated under this heading is not so much committed to obscuring the place of individual participants in religious collectivities as it is to highlighting the global significance of theological ideas and ecclesiastical organizations.

The seven chapters that comprise this segment of the volume represent quite diverse subject matters and interpretive approaches, encompassing a somewhat more cross-cultural concentration than was evidenced in Part II. The first contribution, by Richard L. Rubenstein, for instance, analyzes the relation between religion and the rise of Japanese capitalism to its current place of international prominence. Richard Quebedeaux returns us to American society by examining the role of conservative Protestants here in the contemporary dynamics of religio-political controversy. He raises the question of whether conservatives are really fighting against "the world" or having their agenda defined by it.

The following three chapters define in separate contexts a struggle of religious against societal forces. Franz Feige turns to his native Germany to provide an interpretation of the church struggle against Nazism, a struggle at once noble and woefully inadequate to counteract the demonic forces of the Fascist regime. Also reflecting on circumstances in his native land, South African Willem Nicol considers the problems of justifying a belief in one God with apartheid practices in that country today. And Rabbi Dan Cohn-Sherbok rounds out this trilogy by comparing issues of liberation theology with those of the exodus tradition in Judaism.

The final two chapters in this section are written by one author, Frederick J. Maher. None of the other papers in this volume deal with important changes taking place within contemporary Catholicism. Maher's contributions are designed to fill in some of the details on this issue. His point of focus is the Pastoral Letter of the American Bishops on the economy. Employing basically a symbolic interactionist approach—long regarded as an essentially micro-level investigative strategy—Maher provides a macro-level analysis from the vantage points of economic morality and political language. What becomes clear from this analysis is the difficulty which religiously motivated functionaries encounter when they attempt to devise policies for secular polities relative to both economic and political affairs. Good intentions do not, unfortunately, always translate into sound social policy devoid of ideological distortion. Churches of all denominational persuasions can learn a great deal from these critiques.

7

Japan and Biblical Religion: The Religious Significance of the Japanese Economic Challenge[1]

Few if any developments in the Post-World War II era possess as great a potential for historical significance as the reemergence of Japan as a world power. Normally, Japan's rise is discussed in economic or political terms. Its religious significance, especially for a nation such as the United States whose cultural inheritance is so deeply rooted in Christianity, is seldom discussed, much less understood. Japan is the world's most successful nation with non-Christian roots. Even the Soviet Union has Christian roots. Marxist atheism is grounded in the very biblical tradition which Marxism negates. Moreover, the apparent conflict in the West between religious and a secular ethics takes on the appearance of a family quarrel when seen against the horizon of Japanese religion and culture. Far from being the antithesis of biblical religion, the secular spirit which pervades so much of Western life is its unintended consequence.[2] Wherever the biblical faith in a unique, exclusive, extramundane God penetrated, it has been utterly destructive of indigenous gods and traditions. Sooner or later, this polemic, desacralizing faith was bound to give birth to a consciousness that would not rest until *all* the gods, without exception, were dethroned. Under the circumstances, it is hardly surprising that a civilization as determined to preserve its own integrity as Japan, would marshall all its forces to resist both the believing in and the secular manifestations of biblical religion.

The Japanese have created a thoroughly modern, high-technology civilization whose religious foundations rest upon animistic and polytheistic traditions that adherents of biblical religions normally assume to be primitive and idolatrous, a remnant of a far earlier stage of religious "evolution." From the Japanese perspective, such views are, of course, utterly without substance.

The Protestant Ethic: The Rise of Modern Capitalism

We can perhaps best understand the long-range significance of the Japanese religious challenge—and it is a challenge—if we consider the role of religion in fostering the modernization of both Japan and the nations of the West. In the case of the West, no attempt to understand the role of religion in the formation of the modern world can ignore the work of the German sociologist Max Weber. As is well known, Weber set forth the thesis that the modern, Western, bourgeois-capitalist world is an unintended consequence of the rise of ascetic Protestantism in the aftermath of the Reformation.[3]

Weber did not hold that religion by itself was the cause of modern capitalism. He regarded religion as a necessary but not sufficient factor in the origin of modern economic rationalism. Weber stressed that material conditions alone could not have produced the peculiar form of economic rationalism in which the impulse to accumulate was combined with disciplined restraints upon consumption. Nor could capitalism by itself have produced the kind of economic ethic needed for its development. For Weber, the economic ethic which fostered the development of capitalism was an unintended consequence of the work of the great reformers and their followers, especially John Calvin.

According to Weber, Calvin's doctrine of double predestination was of crucial importance for the development of modern capitalism. By insisting that the issue of personal salvation had been settled at the very first moment of creation, Calvinism had the effect of radically devaluing the religious significance of all earthly institutions, including the Church. The believer was thus thrust back upon himself or herself with no assurance of where he or she stood before an awesome, inscrutable, and utterly sovereign God. The believer's situation was further aggravated by the fact that there was no longer any credible mediating agency authorized to prescribe the conditions under which an individual, aided by God's grace, might merit salvation. Concerning the impact of predestination, Weber observes: "In its extreme inhumanity this doctrine must above all have had one consequence to the generation that surrendered to its magnificent consistency. That was a feeling of unprecedented inner loneliness of the single individual."[4] Under the circumstances, it was inevitable that the believer seek for some hint of where he or she stood in the divine order. According to Weber, at this point economic activity took on a new meaning for the believing Protestant.

Service in one's worldly calling, even if it involved deriving profit from money itself, soon came to be regarded as offering the believer a sign of where he or she stood before the Creator.[5] Believers who had prospered in their callings could reasonably assume that the God who had predestined all things from the beginning had been the ultimate cause of their well-being. The sober, methodical accumulation of wealth took on a religious meaning it had never before possessed. Thus methodical work within the profane world became the path to spiritual ease which prayer, ritual, and mystical contemplation had been in other traditions.

The radical devaluation of religious redemption by ascetic Protestantism was part of a process identified by Weber as the "disenchantment of the world," by which he meant that "there are no mysterious incalculable forces that come into play, but rather one can, in principle, master all things by calculation."[6] According to Weber, the roots of this disenchantment, which was indispensable to the development of the distinctive rationalism of the modern world, were to be found in the monotheistic exclusivism of biblical Judaism.[7] By affirming a unique, supramundane, creator God, biblical Judaism denied any inherent sacrality to the natural world or to the political order. God alone was regarded sacred. No longer were there divine spirits inherent in nature to be appeased, supplicated, or magically manipulated. Nor was there anything inherently sacred about the political order. Of particular relevance is the fact that biblical religion is especially vehement in its rejection of the institution of divine kingship. The biblical injunction "Thou shalt have no other gods before me" (Ex. 20:3), was as much a political statement rejecting the divine kings of Egypt and the ancient Near East as it was a rejection of animism, magic, and polytheism.[8] The Bible's radical desacralization of both the natural and the political order was thus an enormously significant step toward the rational mastery of the world.

Nevertheless, before the rationalizing activities of the modern era such as creation of an impersonal market economy, scientific investigation, bureaucratic organization, and technology, could become culturally predominant, these activities had to be given a religiously legitimated, positive valence. Weber argued that this only became possible after ascetic Protestantism had redefined worldly activity, including the changing of interest, as a way of serving God. Neither rationalization nor Protestantism's interpretation of worldly activity as a sacred calling could by itself have brought about modern capitalism. Only the strange combination of the two could have provided the "take-off" energy that made capitalism possible in the West.

Biblical Religion: The Father-Son Conflict

The development toward a purely secular, rationalized society can thus be seen as an unintended sociological consequence of biblical Judaism's "disenchantment of the world." However, Judaism's marginal position in the Christian West limited its ability to influence the latter's development. The full force of biblical disenchantment was only felt after Protestantism elevated the authority of the Bible over that of the Church.

From a social psychological perspective, Protestantism's rejection of the authority of the Church can be seen as a revolt of the sons against the fathers. A similar revolt was indispensable for the successful displacement of traditional society by modern civilization. According to sociologist Robert Bellah, biblical religion provided the legitimation that made these revolts ethically and psychologically acceptable. Bellah's argument takes as its starting point a comparison of the father-son symbolism in Christianity and Confucianism.[9] According to Bellah, although the father-son symbolism plays a decisive role in Christianity, the natural family has little or no religious significance. By contrast, the father-son symbolism is inapplicable to the Ultimate in Confucianism, whereas the natural family has overwhelming religious significance.

Contrary to both popular and Freudian belief, the biblical God was not originally a father God but the ultimate suzerain of a political association. The Bible does not depict the God of Israel as the head of a natural family or as an originating ancestor. His relation takes the form of a political treaty between a suzerain and his vassal. In the ancient Near East, this type of treaty was known as a *b'rith* or covenant. In such a pact, the superior party stipulates the conditions under which he will protect the inferior party, and the penalties to be incurred if the treaty is violated. Indeed, contemporary scholars have come to see the biblical covenant as modeled after Hittite treaties of the fourteenth and thirteenth centuries B.C.[10]

Isaiah ben-Dasan, a perceptive Japanese writer who uses an Israeli pseudonym, has also argued that the divine-human relation in biblical religion is not analogous to that between a natural parent and child. Ben-Dasan does not stress the political character of the relationship. Instead, he argues that the relation is that "between adopted child and adoptive parent," God being the adoptive parent and Israel the adopted child.[11] According to ben-Dasan, by thus depicting the divine-human relationship, biblical religion introduced an element of insecurity and anxiety into Western religious life. Unlike the unconditional relationship between a natural parent and child, that between an adoptive parent and child is likely to be conditional upon the fulfillment of contractual obligations involved in the adoption process. As ben-Dasan reminds us, adoption is a relationship established by contract. That is, of course, how the Bible depicts God's relationship with Israel. The conditional character of the relationship is repeatedly stated. For example, Moses solemnly warns the Children of Israel lest they fail to observe God's commandments: "But if you do not obey the Lord your God by diligently observing all his commandments and statutes which I lay upon you this day, then all these maledictions shall come to you and light upon you." (Deut. 28:15) This admonition is followed by the terrible list of chastisements which await those who disobey Israel's God.

Both Judaism and Roman Catholicism, each in its own way, sought to mitigate the potential harshness of the divine-human relationship. By insisting upon the unadorned, literal reading of Scripture, however, ascetic Protestantism rejected all such mitigations. By contrast, there is no sovereign, personal Creator God in Confucianism. Instead, the Tao refers to the cosmic harmony of Heaven, earth, and man. Nor is there anything comparable to Christianity's use of the father-son metaphor. Nevertheless, insofar as religious life is founded upon the family and the ancestor cult in Confucianism, there is a coincidence between the sphere of the family and that of religion which is absent from biblical religion. Ben-Dasan points out that the Japanese find the biblical idea of God as an adoptive parent distasteful. They regard their relationships to their deities to be blood ties. It is traditionally assumed, for example, that the emperor is descended from the sun goddess, Amaterasu-omi-kami.

In the biblical tradition, religion and the family are represented by a common set of symbols yet they are institutionally differentiated. Both Christianity and Judaism tend to devalue filial piety when it conflicts with the imperatives of religion. The case of Christianity is the more obvious. Baptism, the rite by which one is initiated into the Christian church, is in principle destructive of filial piety. In baptism one dies to one's old natural self and to one's old familial relations and is reborn a new being in Christ. Thus Paul writes,

> Are you ignorant of that when we were baptized in Christ Jesus we were baptized in his death? In other words, when we were baptized we went into the tomb with him and joined him in death, so that as Christ was raised from the dead by the Father's glory, we too might live a new life. [Rom. 6:3,4][12]

Similarly, Jesus is depicted as admonishing his followers to "hate father and mother, wife and children, brothers and sisters" as an indispensable condition of becoming his disciple (Luke 14:26). Fundamental to the Christian ethic is the injunction to obey God rather than man. Before the Reformation, only the celibate clergy and monastic orders were in theory expected to harken to the injunction in its full severity. The Reformation radicalized and universalized the injunction with its doctrine of the priesthood of all believers. Without realizing it, the Reformers had unleashed the full revolutionary force of biblical religion's subordination of the natural spheres of human activity, namely, both the nuclear family and the extended family we know as the nation, to a supramundane principal. However, the seeds of the subordination were already present in biblical Judaism. No commandment is more central to Jewish tradition and experience than that of honoring one's parents (Ex. 20:12; Deut. 5:16). Nevertheless, in Judaism filial piety is legitimated *ab extra* by the supramundane God who is the source of the commandments. When filial piety conflicts with obedience to God's commandments, the latter must take precedence, as is evident in the Akedah (Gen. 22:1–19). Ultimately, there is only one offense in biblical religion, namely, want of conformity with the will of God as expressed in the covenant between God and Israel.

In general, traditional societies can be understood as more or less autonomous, religiously legitimated, extended kinship groups. In such groups far greater emphasis is accorded to collective than to individual interests. As we shall see, in spite of its modernization, Japan remains such a society. An enormous psychic effort is required to reject traditional society for the individualistic, depersonalized professionalism of the modern West. The effort may have involved the most radical value transformation in all of human history. Weber believed, correctly in our opinion, that only a religiously legitimated redefinition of the sacred could have fostered the transformation. The Reformation's assertion that all things hu-

man are to be subordinated to the sovereign Creator God gave
Protestants the moral and emotional leverage with which to turn
away from old ways and old authorities and to begin anew, not once
but continually. It was psychologically possible for Luther to reject
the authority of the pope in the name of God, as indeed he had
rejected the authority of his own father when he vehemently opposed Martin's choice of a religious vocation; it would have been
impossible for Luther to oppose the authority of either father or
pope on the basis of his personal authority alone. The modern world
could only have come into being when it became possible for men to
cast aside the emotional ties with which they were bound to the
traditional order. This capacity to reject tradition became the source
of the permanent revolution we call capitalism. As the German
sociologist Wolfgang Schluchter has observed, "ascetic Protestantism . . . enabled a group of religious virtuosi . . . to overcome the
psychological barriers which the guiding principles of personal
loyalty put in the way of depersonalizing man's relation to the
natural and social world."[13]

The Rise of Modern Japan: Preserving Old Traditions

By contrast, filial piety is at the heart of the Confucian ethic. Unlike
biblical religion, the Confucian system has no point of leverage by
means of which disobedience to parents can be justified. Without
this ethical loophole, modernization within a Confucian civilization
seems virtually impossible. Nevertheless, not only has East Asia
modernized, but it has done so with far greater success than Africa,
the Middle East, or Latin America. Moreover, if present trends
continue, Asia is likely to outstrip Western Europe and the United
States in economic development. Hence, the question arises
whether the Weber's Protestant-ethic hypothesis has been dis-
proven. In reality, Weber did not hold that the non-Western nations
were incapable of modernization. He did, however, believe that the
process could only have been *initiated* in the Protestant West. Weber
argued that the material factors necessary for capitalist development
were at least as favorable in China and India as in the West. Since
both East and West shared more or less comparable material conditions, these could not account for the difference in development.
Weber found that difference in religion.[14]

Perhaps the most fundamental insight offered by Weber is that, in
addition to appropriate material conditions, *traditional societies can*

only be transformed into modern societies by a radical redefinition of the sacred.[15] The case of Japan would appear to confirm this insight. According to Marius B. Jensen, "The intellectual history of Japan in the first half of the nineteenth century is dominated by the consciousness of domestic weakness and foreign threat."[16] Even before the appearance of Commodore Perry and his Black Ships in 1853, word of China's 1842 humiliation at the hands of Great Britain had reached Japan. Shortly after China's defeat, a questionnaire was addressed by an official of the shogunate to one of the Hollanders living in Nagasaki. The European was asked, "Why have the Tartars lost, since they are said to be brave enough?" The Hollander replied, "Bravery alone is not sufficient, the art of war demands something more. No outlandish power can compete with a European one, as can be seen by the great realm of China which has been conquered by only four thousand men."[17] Given the Chinese foundation of much of Japanese civilization, China's defeat shocked many thoughtful Japanese. It was also an event that Japanese administrators could hardly ignore. When China's humiliation was followed by the forcible opening of Japan by Perry in 1853 and the unfair commercial treaties forced upon Japan between 1858 and 1866, Japan had the choice of either radically restructuring its society or suffering defeat and humiliation by the predatory Western powers. Moreover, Japan was threatened economically as well as militarily. Commercial treaties exposed Japan's premodern, agrarian economy to destructive competition from industrialized nations of the West. With tariffs on imported goods set by foreigners and its handicraft industries incapable of competing with Western factories, Japan soon found itself flooded with foreign goods. This had the effect of ruining much of its domestic handicraft industries at a time when its currency was rapidly depreciating and high inflation was dangerously distorting its domestic economy.[18]

As we know, the foreign threat was met speedily and successfully by perhaps the most radical restructuring of a society the world has ever known. One of the most remarkable aspects of Japanese modernization is that it was carried out with relatively little bloodshed. The samurai elite responsible for the Meiji restoration of 1868 were genuine revolutionaries who had largely emerged out of a group of dissidents from the lower strata of their class. Crucial to the success of their revolution was the transformation wrought in the imperial office, whose sacred charismatic character is deeply rooted in Japan's earliest history. Just as religion had played a crucial role in the modernization of the West, so too a very different kind of religion, one that rested upon the archaic institution of divine kingship, played an equally important role in Japan's modernization.

For our purposes, it will suffice to take brief note of the character of the imperial office during the *sengoku jidai,* Tokugawa, and Meiji eras.[19] In the *sengoku jidai* period, the "period of the warring states" that preceded the Tokugawa shogunate, the emperors were often bitterly impoverished, yet their office symbolized sacralized, legitimate authority. The emperors were rulers who could influence politics but could not rule. The Tokugawa shogunate brought to an end whatever overt political authority the emperors possessed. The shogun assumed almost all the political prerogatives of the imperial office, such as the bestowal of titles of nobility, the right to veto the appointment of court officials, and the right to govern those Buddhist monasteries formerly controlled by the imperial court. At the same time, the material conditions of the imperial court were greatly improved and the imperial office was treated with genuine reverence. Scholars responsible for formulating loyalist ideas concerning the throne in the late eighteenth century even discerned a causal connection between the Tokugawa shogunate's ability to pacify the country and its respectful attitude toward the emperor.[20] During this period, the emperor was the head of state and the shogun the functioning head of government.

It was fortunate for Japan that this division of authority existed in the period immediately preceding modernization. Had the supreme sovereign been the functioning head of government in the 1850s, his policies rather than the shogun's might have been discredited.[21] As a result, there might not have been any institution to guarantee the continuity of legitimate authority from the premodern to the modern period, and the Japanese would have been far less able to withstand the deterioration of their indigenous institutions in the face of the Western challenge. As it was, the period between 1860 and 1880 witnessed a tendency among Japanese leaders to overestimate Western culture and institutions and to denigrate their own indigenous institutions.

The role of the monarchy changed in the Bakumatsu or late-Tokugawa period. When it became apparent that the shogunate was unable to cope with the challenges confronting Japan, there were occasions on which expressions of political preference were enunciated in the name of the Emperor Komei, such as the refusal to ratify the treaty of 1858. However, even in this period, reverence to the throne did not normally involve direct imperial rule.

The final step in bringing the shogunate to an end was taken with

the Meiji restoration and the proclamation of the sacred character of
the imperial office. The first article of the Constitution of 1889
reads: "The Empire of Japan shall be reigned over and governed by a
line of Emperors unbroken for ages eternal." The third article reads:
"The Emperor is sacred and inviolable." There is an element of
vagueness in the third article which invites interpretation. Perhaps
the most important interpreter of the Meiji era was Prince Ito, who
was largely responsible for drafting the written constitution. His
Commentaries on the Constitution appeared in 1889, and his comment
on the imperial office is instructive:

> The Sacred Throne was established at the time when the heavens and
> earth were separated. The Emperor is Heaven descended, divine and
> sacred; He is preeminent above all his subjects. He must be reverenced
> and is inviolable. He has indeed to pay due respect to the law, but the
> law has no power to hold him accountable to it. Not only shall there
> be no irreverence for the Emperor's person, but also He shall not be
> made a topic of derogatory comment nor one of discussion. [22]

As in the early Tokugawa period, the emperor's position was once
again exalted. In addition, the policies of government were now
depicted as representing the imperial will. At the same time, the
emperor's residence was transferred from Kyoto to Edo, and he lost
the ability to speak independently of his counselors. He spoke, if at
all, through the oligarchs who governed in his name. No longer
could dissidents claim to speak on his behalf in opposing the policies
of government. In effect, the ceremonial aspects of the imperial
institution were exalted, but the emperor was isolated from dissidents and power was exercised in his name.

In spite of the loss of an active political role, the imperial institution gained an overwhelming new importance. As a direct descendant of the sun goddess Amaterasu-omi-kami, the emperor
symbolized national continuity, identity, and sovereignty at a time
when foreigners threatened these values more profoundly than at
any other time in Japan's history. The emperor also symbolized
national unity and the harmony between the rulers and the ruled.
According to Herschel Webb, the Meiji oligarchs were thus able to
utilize the imperial institution first "to give unprecedented policies
the color of great antiquity," and second "to make it appear that
what was in fact an administration by relatively lowly placed new
men proceeded instead from the most highly pedigreed and unquestionably legitimate of all possible sources." [23]

When we compare the extreme social and political disorder which accompanied the development of modern societies in the Christian West with the relatively bloodless transformation which took place in non-Christian Japan, the Japanese achievement appears truly impressive. Unlike their modernizing counterparts in the English Revolution of the seventeenth century and the French Revolution of the late eighteenth century, who purchased change with regicide and civil war, the modernizing elite of Japan succeeded in rationalizing the economy and society of their nation with a minimum of domestic violence or alienation of elite classes and institutions. Modernization and political centralization were carried out under conditions of far greater social cohesiveness and stability. By utilizing a seemingly conservative doctrine, that of the emperor's divinity, to legitimate a radical social and political revolution, the elite was able to create a strong central government, abolish all estate distinctions, eliminate warrior privileges, open military service to commoners hitherto forbidden to possess arms, establish a system of universal public education, and facilitate the entry of members of the samurai class—in general the best educated class—into the world of business and commerce. All this was done without turning the elite classes into embittered enemies of the new social order, as was so often the case in Europe.

The doctrine of the emperor's divinity, his status as a "living kami," was crucial to the expeditious creation of a strong, centralized government, which could replace the shogunate and establish an effective modern economy. By subordinating all other loyalties to loyalty to the emperor, the samurai were enabled to transfer their allegiance from local leaders, who in many cases could no longer support them, to the leader of the new centralized state and, perhaps of greater importance, to the oligarchs and bureaucrats who claimed to speak on his behalf. This was a precondition of successful modernization in an era of heavy industry requiring large-scale capital investment. Japanese modernization involved the blending of the most archaic traditions, albeit renovated under the pressure of new dangers, with the imperatives of economic, political and industrial rationalization.

Modern East and Modern West: A Study in Contrasts

We have already noted that a precondition of modernization in the West was the weakening of the value of filial piety. No such rejection was necessary for Japanese modernization. Apart from religion, filial piety had to be breached in the modernizing West in the relations between sovereign and subject. Normally, the Western "carriers" of modernization were the urbanized commercial classes rather than absolutist monarchs. The latter facilitated the modernization of the polity by bureaucratic rationalization of the state administration, but they were seldom inclined to set social hierarchies in disarray by favoring these carriers over the nobility, whose roots were largely agrarian. Class warfare, often religiously legitimated, was an almost endemic by-product of Western modernization. By contrast, the social transformations necessary for modernization in Japan were initiated from the top down rather than from the middle up. Filial piety was not abrogated, but instead became an indispensable component of Japanese modernization.

That thoughtful Japanese leaders of the Meiji era were concerned lest too great a reliance on Western ways lead to the destruction of the value of filial piety is evident in the "Imperial Rescript: The Great Principles of Education, 1879," written by Motoda Eifu, the Confucian lecturer to the emperor. The rescript reads in part:

> Although we set out to take in the best features of the West and bring in new things in order to achieve the high aims of the Meiji restoration . . . this procedure had a serious defect: It reduced benevolence, justice, loyalty, and filial piety to a secondary position. The danger of indiscriminate emulation of western ways is that in the end our people will forget the great principles governing the relations between ruler and subject, and father and son. Our aim, based on our ancestral teachings, is solely the clarification of benevolence, justice, loyalty, and filial piety.[24]

Men like Motoda saw the need for modernization. Nevertheless, they also understood one of the principal dangers of Western-style modernization—destruction of the historic continuity of civilization—and this the leaders of Japan were determined to resist. The Imperial Rescript of Eifu gives expression to the determination of Japan's leaders to preserve the historic continuity of Japanese civilization and its values at a time of the most revolutionary socioeconomic transformations in all of Japanese history. Few if any other documents are as instructive in exhibiting the contrast between the Japanese and Western responses to modernization. Whereas the West initiated modernization with a rejection of the highest religious and political authorities, not excluding regicide, and tended to equate modernization with secularization, Japan undertook modernization under the authority of its supreme religio-political authority and in defense of the values of its traditional civilization. Writes Eifu:

> Know ye, our Subjects!
> Our Imperial ancestors have founded our empire on a basis broad and everlasting and have deeply and firmly implanted virtue; our subjects, ever united in loyalty and filial piety, have from generation to generation illustrated the beauty thereof. This is the fundamental character of our empire, and herein also lies the source of our education. Ye, our subjects, be filial to your parents . . . pursue learning and cultivate arts, and thereby develop your intellectual facilities and perfect your moral powers; furthermore, advance the public good and promote common interests; always respect the constitution and observe the laws; *should any emergency arise, offer yourselves courageously to the state; and thus guard and maintain the prosperity of our Imperial throne, coeval with heaven and earth.*[25]

The religious traditions fostering modernization in Japan and the West can thus be seen as polar opposites. Whether one is Jewish, Christian or Moslem, it is impossible to worship the God of Abraham without rejecting the gods of one's earliest ancestors. When Joshua assembled the Israelite tribes at Shechem to swear fealty to the Lord, he reminded them: "Long ago your forefathers Terah and his sons Abraham and Nahor, lived beside the Euphrates and they worshipped other gods" (Joshua 24:2). In order to worship the God of the Bible, somewhere in history a drastic uprooting process had to take place. The old pagan gods had to be foresworn and the ways of humankind's oldest ancestors abandoned. Here again, Catholicism sometimes mitigated the harshness of the process by identifying local deities with Christian saints. Not surprisingly, the young Hegel, although Lutheran by tradition, expressed his bitterness at this alienation from his own archaic religious inheritance:

> Every nation has its own imagery, its gods, angels, devils or saints who live on in the nation's traditions. . . . Christianity has emptied Valhalla, felled the sacred groves, extirpated the national imagery as a shameful superstition, as a devilish poison, and given us instead the imagery of a nation whose climate, laws, culture, and interests are strange to us and whose history has no connection whatever with our own. A David or a Solomon lives in our popular imagination, but our country's own heroes slumber in learned history books. . . . Thus we are without any religious imagery which is homegrown or linked

with our history . . . all that we have is the remains of an imagery of our own, lurking amid the common people under the name of superstition.[26]

Hegel concludes his complaint by asking: "Is Judaea, then, the Teutons' fatherland?"[27]

Hegel understood the profoundly destabilizing character of the uprooting involved in converting Germany to biblical religion. He also appears to have grasped the fact that biblical religion is inherently uprooting, at least in the first generation. Biblical religion effectively begins when God commands, "Get thee out of thine own country, and from thy kinsmen, and from thy fathers house, and go unto a land that I will show you" (Gen. 12:1). It is instructive to recall Hegel's bitter condemnation of Abraham's voluntary departure:

> Abram, born in Chaldea, had in youth already left a fatherland in his father's company. Now, in the plains of Mesopotamia, he tore himself free altogether from his family as well, in order to be a wholly self-subsistent, independent man, to be an overlord himself. He did this without having been injured or disowned, without the grief which after a wrong or an outrage signifies love's enduring need, when love, injured indeed but not lost, goes in quest of a new fatherland in order to flourish and enjoy itself there. The first act which made Abraham the progenitor of a nation is a disseverance which snaps the bonds of communal life and love. The entirety of the relationships in which he had hitherto lived with men and nature, these beautiful relationships of his youth (Joshua 24:2), he spurned.[28]

As noted, Abraham's departure from his native land entailed unconditional rejection of the gods of that land. All Jews, Christians, and Moslems are the heirs of that spiritual uprooting.

The contrast with earthbound, non-nomadic Japan, a nation that has never foresworn her most ancient gods nor thought of these spirits as separate from nature, could not be greater. Japan's modernization was predicated upon unconditional reaffirmation of the sacred connection between the modern state and its most archaic roots. One of National Socialism's long-range objectives was to eradicate the biblical heritage in Germany and regain Germany's archaic inheritance. The Japanese did not require the social and political violence inherent in National Socialism to remain in touch with their roots. Unlike every nation of Judaeo-Christian inheritance, the Japanese remain in contact with their oldest sources of

religious and cultural values. Moreover, the Japanese have so structured their society and their economy that they will have no motive
to abandon their most ancient traditions.

There are important similarities between the way the emperor
functioned in Japanese society, at least until 1946, and the way the
pharaohs functioned in ancient Egypt. Both Japan and Egypt were
sacralized kingdoms, with dynasties of extremely long and stable
duration. The following description by Henri Frankfort of the role
of the ancient Egyptian monarchy is reminiscent of Prince Ito's
comments concerning the emperor:

> The Egyptian state was not a man-made alternative to other forms of
> political organization. It was god-given, established when the world
> was created; and it continued to form part of the universal order. In
> the person of Pharaoh a superhuman being had taken charge of the
> affairs of man. And this great blessing, which ensured the well-being
> of the nation, was not due to a fortunate accident but had been
> foreseen in the divine plan. The monarchy then was as old as the
> world, for the creator himself had assumed kingly office on the day of
> creation. Pharaoh was his descendant and his successor.[29]

When in 1945 the victorious Americans used their political leverage to secure the emperor's denial of his divinity, they were
responding to the institution of divine kingship in a way which
accorded with their age-old biblical tradition. Because of the cultural predominance of sectarian Protestantism in the United States
and the absence of a feudal inheritance, American culture has been
more strongly influenced by biblical religion than any other Western
country. According to William P. Woodard, who served as an adviser on religion to General MacArthur's occupation administration, MacArthur was conscious of being called by the biblical God
for the hour, and regarded himself as the leader of the Protestant
world "as the Pope was the leader of the Catholic world."[30] Although he later moderated the tone of his remarks, in the early years
of the occupation, MacArthur made unfavorable comments about
both Buddhism and Shinto.[31] He favored the return of Christian
missionaries in large numbers to Japan and saw the occupation as an
unparalleled opportunity for the conversion of the Japanese to
Christianity.[32] MacArthur saw himself as called by the God of the
Bible to lead the Japanese out of what he, as a believing Christian,
regarded as their spiritual ignorance.

In spite of apparently favorable circumstances, the postwar mis-

sionaries who came to Japan quickly discovered that few, if any, free
countries offer less promise to Christian missions than Japan. After
more than a century of strenuous efforts, with one of the world's
largest concentrations of foreign missionaries (almost 5,200 in number), Japan remains more resistant to Christianity than any other
developed country. Less than 1 percent of the population is Christian and the numbers are declining.[33] By contrast, many observers
anticipate that neighboring South Korea, whose Christian population comprises almost 25 percent of the whole, will have a Christian
majority by the year 2000.[34] Apart from the fact that Christianity is
rejected as "un-Japanese" by a population with a very strong sense
of group identity and a strong distrust of anything foreign that
cannot be readily assimilated, the Japanese find the biblical conceptions of an omnipotent, extramundane Creator who establishes a
covenant with a non-Japanese group utterly lacking in credibility.
Japanese believe themselves to be descendants of a race of gods and
their emperor a direct descendant of the sun-goddess, but, as we
have seen, descent is an organic rather than a conditional relationship, as in the case of the covenantal relationship with the transcendent Creator God.

Another respect in which the paths to modernization taken by
Japan and the United States have diverged profoundly has been in
the "disenchantment of the world." Biblical monotheism, with its
affirmation of one sovereign Creator God and its persistent tendency to desacralize both the natural and political orders, led to the
disenchantment, that is, rejection of animism, polytheism, and
magic in the civilizations that derived from biblical religion. Contemporary sociologists of religion tend to concur in Weber's judgment that biblical disenchantment of the world was an indispensable
precondition of the rationalization of the economy and society characteristic of Western capitalism.[35] It is precisely that which a disen-
chanting religion rejects, namely, animism and polytheism, that
Shinto affirms. Here again, indigenous Japanese religion is the polar
opposite of the biblical tradition. Moreover, it should be noted that,
in spite of its animism and polytheism, Shinto plays a significant
role in contemporary Japanese business, science, and technology.[36]

Biblical religion and indigenous Japanese religious tradition have
thus provided alternative paths to the modern world. Biblical religion alone, with its denigration of filial piety and its tradition of
relativizing human institutions in the light of the ideal of service to a
sovereign Creator God, possessed the psychic mechanism to begin

the monumental breach with the past implied in modernization. It alone had a value system which legitimated the break with the past as service to an ultimate principal. Furthermore, by eliminating the necessity to appease any spirits or divinities thought to inhere in the natural or political order, biblical disenchantment fostered the functional rationality in finance, scientific experimentation, bureaucratic organization, and the processes of production which was indispensable to the creation of the bourgeois capitalist world.[37] One can without exaggeration say that the modern Western world is largely an unintended consequence of the cultural triumph of a biblical understanding of the nature of things.

Nevertheless, if Japan did not have a value system capable of initiating a fundamental breach with the past, it did have the religious and cultural resources necessary to *defend* its civilization against the West. And, that it has done with astonishing success. As noted, *modernization in Japan was essentially a defensive strategy.* Its first objective was to secure Japan against Western military aggression, its second was to defend Japan against Western economic aggression. Its ultimate purpose was to defend Japanese civilization against the destruction of its historic values, which would most assuredly have ensued if Japan as a nation had been converted to any form of biblical religion. Japan would have been compelled to abandon the gods and ways of its ancestors as surely as had Abraham's progeny in Judaism, Christianity, and Islam.

If Japan is not yet the world's richest nation, it soon will be. Its extraordinary achievements have a meaning, both for Japan and for the rest of the world, which transcends economic success. There is, for example, the question of whether Japan will become the world's greatest military power in the twenty-first century. This writer has discussed that issue elsewhere.[38] Here, we are interested in the cultural and religious consequences of Japan's transformation. One consequence is already apparent: A majority of Japanese have interpreted their postwar economic and technological achievements as confirming the superiority of their civilization over that of their trading partners and competitors.[39] If ever the Japanese were amenable to conversion to a biblical religion, that time has passed. In his last year in office, Prime Minister Yasuhiro Nakasone's office published a translation of a conversation between the prime minister and Professor Takeshi Umehara, one of the leading Japanologists. The prime minister offered the following comment on Japanese religion:

The Japanese tend toward polytheism rather than monotheism. We believe in many Gods and consider ourselves part of nature's unending cycle. There is broad and general acceptance of the idea that a man's fate is inseparable from that of every animal, tree, and blade of grass.

Side by side with this is the Indian concept that each man is the whole of nature unto himself—as is evident in Zen philosophy as well. The Japanese combine both of these concepts, oneness with nature and the individual as the whole of nature, within their being. It is my belief, however, that our sense of oneness with nature is indigenous and goes back to our Jomon roots. Japan's ancestor worship is thus quite different from Christianity's contract between man and his monotheistic god. In the process of honoring our forefathers, we create the harmony which is such an integral part of our lifestyle.[40]

According to Umehara, Japan's "Jomon roots" cover a period which preceded the introduction of agriculture and lasted almost ten thousand years, coming to an end about 300 B.C. The prime minister thus asserts that Japan's religious culture goes back to her earliest roots. This is not a heritage he or any other Japanese is likely to abandon. Nor do all Japanese regard the emperor's postwar denial of his divinity as having really changed his status. In a document prepared for the Ninth International Congress for the History of Religions in 1958, the Shinto Publications Committee declared,

Since the change was merely a change in outward treatment, it is only natural that the Shinto of the Imperial House and Shrine Shinto should still be considered orthodox. It is one of the noteworthy peculiarities of Shinto as a religion that, since these types of Shinto are not bound by dogmas and scriptures but preserve their life in traditional form, in so long as there is no great impediment in the continuation of the religious rituals, the wounds inflicted by this change are not too deep.[41]

The divinity of the emperor was never considered comparable to that of Jesus in Christianity or God in biblical Judaism. The emperor was thought of as *ikigami,* "a living human *kami.*" The term refers to outstanding servants of the nation who might be enshrined and worshiped while still alive. Imperial princes, national heroes, Shinto priests, and the emperor can all be reverenced as *ikigami.* To the Japanese, the emperor remains the supreme living *kami.* At present, his status is somewhat ambiguous. As Japan's power continues to grow, however, there is every likelihood that the ambiguity will be clarified in favor of the traditional understanding of the emperor's divine status.

Unlike most "primitive" indigenous religions, Japanese religion has demonstrated its power to inspire a civilization capable of competing successfully with the West in almost every significant sphere of human activity. Seldom, if ever, has the monotheistic exclusivism of biblical religion been challenged as successfully as it has by modern Japan.

Conclusion: Can Japan Retain its Position and Continue to Rise?

It should be obvious that this writer has a very profound respect for the achievements of Japanese civilization, especially in the Meiji and post-World War II periods. Nevertheless, he feels constrained to conclude by raising an issue which may prove to be of considerable importance in the years ahead. Those who fault biblical religion for its exclusivism tend to overlook one of its principal strengths, namely, its ability to unite men and women hitherto strangers to each other in a new community of worship and moral obligation. Indeed, the covenant at Sinai served that function when it transformed a "mixed multitude" of escaped fugitives into a community united in worship of the God who redeemed them from Egypt. Enlarging on an impulse already present in Scripture, Christianity was able to create a community of moral obligation which transcended old religio-communal boundaries of ethnicity and common descent.[42] It is perhaps no accident that the United States is the modern nation most committed both to biblical religion and to the absorption of an immigrant population that includes every race, color, and creed. If, as ben-Dasan asserts, the relation between Israel and God is "artificial" rather than organic, then the bonds the Founding Fathers created to unite Americans were also a matter of human invention, and were potent nonetheless. By contrast, while Japan has been most successful in defending the integrity, continuity, and organic character of its civilization, its indigenous traditions offer little basis for a wider base of community than that which rests on kinship and common descent. Apart from the obvious constraints Japan's limited space imposes upon the size of her population, Japan is of all modern nations, the least able culturally and psychologically to absorb new immigrants, even those physically indistinguishable from themselves. Here again, Japan and the United States are polar opposites.

In view of the overwhelming international importance of Japan, one must ask whether it can any longer ignore the problem of

finding a more universal basis for community than is offered by its indigenous traditions. Were Japan a minor provincial power, this issue might be of little consequence. However, Japan is not a minor power but a world leader, and there is a profound conflict between the traditions which have enabled Japan to achieve its current position and the universal responsibilities that position demands. Whatever shortcomings can be discerned in biblical religion, it has repeatedly demonstrated its capacity to enlarge humanity's sense of community. The question of whether Japan has the indigenous spiritual resources to enlarge its sense of community may be the most important confronting her in the coming era.

NOTES

1. This essay is a revision of "Religion and the Rise of Capitalism: The Case of Japan," *The World and I* (February 1987).

2. This assessment of the relationship between biblical religion and the secular spirit rests upon the view that it has been the destiny of biblical religion to negate itself in ever-widening domains of human activity. See Peter Berger, *The Sacred Canopy: Elements of Sociological Theory of Religion* (Garden City: Anchor Books, 1969), pp. 105–26. However, long before contemporary sociologists of religion came to interpret the secularization process as a dialectical consequence of Christianity, the secular consciousness was thus understood by Hegel and a number of nineteenth-century German philosophical critics of the Christian religion. Karl Lowith has observed: "Philosophical criticism of the Christian religion began in the nineteenth century and reached its climax with Nietzsche. It is a Protestant movement, and therefore specifically German. This holds true both of the criticism and the religion at which it was directed. Our critical philosophers were all theologically educated Protestants, and their criticism of Christianity presupposes its Protestant manifestations." Lowith, *From Hegel to Nietzsche: The Revolution in Nineteen-Century Thought* (New York: Holt, Rhinehart and Winston, 1964), p. 327. According to Lowith, Hegel "translates" the forms of religion, which belong to the imagination, into the conceptualization of reason. Lowith observes that "the historical consequence of Hegel's ambigous 'translation' was an absolute destruction of Christian philosophy and of the Christian religion," a development that became fully manifest in the work of Friedrich Nietzsche. *From Hegel to Nietzsche,* op. cit., p. 333.

3. The Weber hypothesis was first stated in Max Weber, *The Protestant Ethic and the Spirit of Capitalism* (1904), trans. Talcott Parsons (New York: Charles Scribner's Sons, 1958). The Parsons translation is of the revised version of the essay published in Weber, *Gesammelte Aufsatze zur Religionssoziologie* (Tubingen: J.C.B. Mohr, 1920).

4. Weber, *Protestant Ethic,* op. cit., p. 104.

5. On the sanctioning of the taking of interest, see Benjamin Nelson, *The Idea of Usury: From Tribal Brotherhood to Universal Otherhood* (Chicago: University of Chicago Press, 1969), pp. 73–83.

6. Max Weber, "Science as a Vocation" *From Max Weber: Essays in Sociology* ed. H.H. Gerth and C. Wright Mills (New York: Oxford University Press, 1946), p. 139.

7. See Peter Berger, *The Sacred Canopy: Elements of a Sociological Theory of Religion* (Garden City: Anchor Books, 1969), pp. 111–25.

8. See article, "Covenant" in *Encyclopedia Judaica,* vol. V (Jerusalem: 1972), 1012–22, and George Mendenhall, *The Tenth Generation: The Origins of the Biblical Tradition* (Baltimore: Johns Hopkins University Press, 1973), pp. 64–6.

9. Robert Bellah, "Father and Son in Christianity and Confucianism," in Bellah, *Beyond Belief: Essays on Religion in a Post Traditional World* (New York: Harper and Row, 1970), pp. 76–99.

10. Article, "Covenant" in *Encyclopedia Judaica,* op. cit.

11. Isaiah ben-Dasan, *The Japanese and the Jews,* trans. Richard L. Gage (Tokyo: Weatherhill, 1985), pp. 134 ff.

12. For a discussion of the subordination of the natural family to the imperatives of faith in Pauline Christianity, see Richard L. Rubenstein, *My Brother Paul* (New York: Harper and Row, 1972), pp. 54–77.

13. Wolfgang Schluchter, *The Rise of Western Rationalism: Max Weber's Developmental History,* trans. Guenther Roth (Berkeley: University of California Press, 1981), p. 173.

14. See Talcott Parsons, *The Structure of Social Action: A Study in Social Theory with Special Reference to a Group of Recent European Writers,* vol. II (New York: Free Press, 1968) pp. 539–78.

15. See Robert Bellah, *Tokugawa Religion: The Values of Pre-Industrial Japan* (Glencoe, Ill.: Free Press, 1957), p. 8.

16. Marius B. Jensen, "Changing Japanese Attitudes toward Modernization," in *Changing Japanese Attitudes Toward Modernization,* ed. Marius B. Jensen (Princeton: Princeton University Press, 1965), p. 54.

17. C. R. Boxer, *Jan Compagnie in Japan* (The Hague, 1950), App. v, pp. 185–7. Cited by Jensen, op. cit., p. 57.

18. See T. C. Smith, *Political Change and Industrial Development in Japan* (Stanford: Stanford University Press, 1955), pp. 25–41.

19. For an informed analysis of the transformations in the role of the emperor from the period known as *sengoku jidai* "the period of the warring states," through the Tokugawa, Bakumatsu, and Meiji eras, see Herschel Webb, "The Development of an Orthodox Attitude toward the Imperial Institution in the Nineteenth Century," in Jensen, op. cit.

20. For example, Fujita Yukoku (1774–1826) wrote, "What qualities enable the shogunate to unite the country? Above, its reverent attitude toward the em-

peror, and below, its protective treatment of the feudal lords. Its rule, however, is nothing more than the exercise of the emperor's sovereignty. Kikuchi Kenjiro, ed., *Yukoku zenshu* (Tokyo: 1935), p. 229, cited by Webb, op. cit., p. 177.

21. It is also likely that Christianity would have made far greater inroads in Japan had the imperial office been discredited. We shall return to this issue shortly.

22. Hirobumi Ito, *Commentaries on the Constitution of the Empire of Japan,* trans. Miyoji Ito (Tokyo: Government Printing House, 1899); cited by D.C. Holtom, *Modern Japan and Shinto Nationalism* (Chicago: University of Chicago Press, 1947), p. 9.

23. Webb, op. cit., p. 167.

24. "Imperial Rescript: The Great Principles of Education, 1879" in *The Japan Reader: Imperial Japan: 1800–1945* ed. Jon Livingston et. al. (New York: Pantheon Books, 1973), p. 150.

25. "Imperial Rescript on Education, 1890" in Livingston, op. cit.

26. G.W.F. Hegel, "The Positivity of Christianity," in Hegel, *Early Theological Writings,* trans. T.M. Knox (Chicago: University of Chicago Press: 1948), pp. 145–48.

27. Ibid.

28. Hegel, "The Spirit of Christianity and its Fate," in *Early Theological Writings,* pp. 185–6.

29. Henri Frankfort, *Ancient Egyptian Religion* (New York: Columbia University Press, 1948), pp. 30–1.

30. William P. Woodard, *The Allied Occupation of Japan 1945–1952 and Japanese Religions* (Leiden: E. J. Brill, 1972), p. 241.

31. Woodard, op. cit, pp. 241–5.

32. Douglas MacArthur, Letter to Dr. Louis D. Newton of Atlanta, December 13, 1945. Cited by Woodard, op. cit., p. 244.

33. Bernard Wysocki, Jr., "Christian Missions Convert Few in Japan," in *Asian Wall Street Journal,* July 16, 1978.

34. See cover story, "Korea: The Cross as Catalyst," *Far Eastern Economic Review* 19 (April 1984): 44–54.

35. See, for example, Berger, op. cit., pp. 105–25.

36. See for details, Honda Soichiro, "Shinto in Japanese Culture," *Nanzan Bulletin* 8 (1984) 24–30. (The *Bulletin* is published by the Nanzan Institute of Religion and Culture, Nanzan University, Nagoya, Japan. This article originally appeared in Japanese as "*Bunka no naka no Shinto,*" in *Shukyo Shinbun,* February 1 and March 1, 1984. Honda Soichiro is the founder of the Honda Motor Company.)

37. See Richard L. Rubenstein, *The Age of Triage* (Boston: Beacon Press, 1983), pp. 2ff; David Landes, *The Unbound Prometheus: Technological Change and Industrial Development in Western Europe from 1750 to the Present* (Cambridge: Cambridge University Press, 1969), pp. 21–4.

38. See Richard L. Rubenstein, "Will Japan Be the World's No. 1 Superpower in the 21st Century?" in *The Academician*, vol. III (Autumn/Winter, 1985): 14–18.

39. See, for example, Susan Chira, "New Pride Changes Japan's View of U.S.," *The New York Times,* June 30, 1988.

40. "The Flow of World Civilization and Japan's Role in the 21st Century: A dialogue between Prime Minister Yasuhiro Nakasone and Professor Takeshi Umehara," Tokyo: Prime Minister's Office, April 1986, p. 11. I am indebted to Dr. John Tepper Marlin of New York City for this reference.

41. Cited in Stuart D. B. Picken, *Shinto: Japan's Spiritual Roots* (Tokyo: Kodansha, 1980), p. 40.

42. This point was effectively made in 1964 by Fustel de Coulanges, *The Ancient City: A Study on the Religion, Laws, and Institutions of Greece and Rome* (1864) (Garden City: Doubleday Anchor Books, 1956), pp. 389–96.

8

Conservative Protestants in Modern American Society: Who's Influencing Whom?

RICHARD A. QUEBEDEAUX

Although Billy Graham had achieved visibility and notoriety in the American mass media already by 1949, it was not until the mid-1970s that conservative Protestants as a whole came to the media's attention. This had to do largely with the election of Jimmy Carter, the born-again Christian, to the presidency in 1976. With that event, conservative Protestantism symbolically entered the mainstream of American society, and it appeared as a force to be reckoned with. The nature of this force and its impact—or lack of impact—on modern society is the focus of this essay.

Conservative Protestantism, as understood in the mid-1980s, consists of those American Christians who identify themselves as fundamentalists or evangelicals. George Gallup defines the latter as persons who (1) say they have had a born-again experience; (2) have encouraged others to believe in Jesus Christ; and (3) believe in a literal interpretation of the Bible. Although generally thought of as even more conservative than evangelicals, fundamentalists meet Gallup's criteria just as well, if not better. Together they made up 22 percent of the adult population in the United States—35 million people—in 1984.[1]

Who exactly are these conservative Protestants? According to recent survey research findings, they are predominantly white, and disproportionately female. Their overall population is generally older than that of other religious groupings, and the clear majority of them are married. The largest concentrations of conservative Protestants are found in rural, small-town areas of the South, West, and mid-Atlantic regions, and in the medium-size cities of the South and Midwest. They are grossly underrepresented in the large cities. Conservative Protestants are most often found among the less educated and poor. And despite their large numbers, they remain a minority in mainline Protestant denominations, the only exceptions being the conservative Southern Baptist Convention and the small, sectarian Baptist, Presbyterian, and holiness-pentocostal denominations. In the Missouri Synod Lutheran and Disciples of Christ denominations, they make up about half the membership.[2]

Considering the foregoing, it may seem strange that the media have given so much attention to this religious group in recent years. The reason, however, is simple. Although, by and large, conservative Protestantism is really a white "underclass"—a marginalized Christian population as a whole,—its leaders have become enough like the mainstream in terms of financial resources, constituency, and potential influence, to warrant that attention. Evangelical and fundamentalist elites have changed dramatically since the 1970s, and that change has a lot to do with how the public now views them. They and their churches have become extremely upwardly mobile of late, but that upward social mobility occurred over a long period of time. A close look at the course of change among conservative Protestants will help illuminate their present and potential impact on American society in general.

The Origins of Conservative Protestantism

With the rise in elite academic circles of Darwinism, higher biblical criticism, and what became known as the social-scientific study of religion during the late nineteenth and early twentieth centuries, Protestantism in America divided into two opposing camps. The first *accommodated* its religion to worldly circumstances, meeting these new intellectual trends, which were all concomitants of modernity, with every available resource. This camp comprised the liberals or modernists. The second camp tried to resist the use of critical scholarship to study the Bible and Christianity and the relativism inherent in modernity more generally. They sought to hold firm to the inherited religious convictions of classical orthodoxy, insisting that worldly changes do not alter supernatural truths. These were the conservatives. In the second decade of the twentieth century, some of the latter's best spokesmen wrote a twelve-volume series of pamphlets to oppose the spread of modernism in the established Protestant denominations. These "fundamentals," as they were called, covered doctrinal issues related to biblical infallibility; archeological confirmation of biblical stories; apologetics for orthodox teaching on the existence of God, the deity of Christ and his personal, visible, premillennial return; commentary on the need for evangelism and foreign missions; and a repudiation

of other religious systems (including Roman Catholicism). Ultimately, the then nonaccommodating conservative Protestants took
on the label "fundamentalist," which has persisted until the present
day.

In the early nineteenth century, evangelical Christianity, boosted
by the Second Great Awakening, was the mainline expression of
Protestantism in America. It was not conservative then, but was
rather a new development, a departure from Puritan orthodoxy. In
its zeal to evangelize America, it kept pace with culture and took
bold steps to found hospitals, publishing firms, newspapers, magazines, and colleges. Evangelicalism sent missionaries abroad to convert the heathen, build schools, cover native breasts. It constructed
factories and encouraged capitalists to be philanthropists, while it
exalted rural and small-town ideals. It championed abolitionism.
But with the rapid social and intellectual changes of the later nineteenth and early twentieth centuries, evangelicalism became conservative, resisting modernity, fighting cultural change, and engaging
in a warfare with the ascendant Protestant liberalism over control of
the churches and seminaries. The war was symbolically won by the
modernists with the 1925 Scopes trial in defense of Darwinism,
after which the fundamentalists either grew silent and disaffected in
the pews of the mainline churches (which gradually became predominantly liberal), or left those institutions to found their own.
This they did in a sectarian fashion—establishing not only churches
and denominations, but Bible schools, colleges, radio and then
television ministries, publishing houses, journals, and foreign mission boards. As American society around them changed and became more liberal from the late 1920s to the 1940s and as liberal
Protestantism followed suit, the fundamentalists lost credibility and
visibility in that society.[3]

Modern Evangelicalism

But by the early 1940s, conservative Protestantism had taken a
major step toward acceptance within the wider Christian community. A handful of highly educated, younger fundamentalist theologians began to reject the *extreme* sectarianism of conservative
Protestantism—its total separatism from the rest of Christendom,
its "bad manners," obscurantism, antiintellectualism, and lack of
social concern—but not its essential theology and its strong belief in
biblical inerrancy. In 1942, under the leadership of Harold John

Ockenga, the National Association of Evangelicals (NAE) was formed to bring together the forces of moderate fundamentalism in a common cause—to penetrate the major liberal denominations from within, rather than just criticizing them from the outside. A good number of the small sectarian denominations born with fundamentalism's rise joined together with holiness and pentecostal churches for united action, in the same way that the liberal denominations had come together in the Federal Council of Churches (later the National Council of Churches). Ockenga coined the word "neo-evangelicalism" to designate the new movement of upwardly mobile fundamentalists, many of whom still belonged to the large, increasingly liberal denominations. The new evangelicals wanted to identify with the culture-affirming "mainline evangelicalism" of the early nineteenth century, before world-denying fundamentalism emerged. In so doing, however, they caused the more conservative fundamentalist leaders to repudiate the new movement. This resulted in a division within conservative Protestant ranks—with the self-identified fundamentalists still on the separatist Right and the evangelicals moving closer to the middle.

To accommodate the interests of the new evangelicalism's growing number of theologians and other scholars in the late forties and fifties, Fuller Theological Seminary in Pasadena, California, was founded in 1947 as an interdenominational graduate school of theology. The Evangelical Theological Society (ETS) was established in 1949; and *Christianity Today,* a sophisticated biweekly journal for ministers and educated laity, emerged in 1956. After his first revival that caught the mass media's attention, in Los Angeles in 1949, the young fundamentalist evangelist Billy Graham aligned himself solidly with the evangelicals, and was denounced by most of the still hard-core fundamentalist leaders for doing so.

Evangelical theology, based largely on Reformed orthodoxy and premillennialism—and centered on the doctrine of biblical inerrancy—was not all that different from its fundamentalist predecessor and counterpart. It retained the essential conservative spirituality, characteristic lifestyle, and social stance of fundamentalism; and its values also were rooted in those popularized by revivalism and based upon rural and small-town ideals. Even the white pentecostal and holiness churches, with Wesleyan and perfectionist origins and a lack of interest in doctrinal scholasticism, came into line with the Reformed position of the NAE and other evangelical organizations in which orthodoxy and biblical inerrancy remained pivotal. But the seeds of change had been sown already, in the early forties and by the fifties, evangelicalism was ripe for further transformation.[4]

As evangelicals emerged from the margins of society in the post–World War II years, their long-time tendency to withdraw from the world and wait for Christ's premillennial Second Coming gradually shifted to a desire to *change* the world in anticipation of that event. In order to change the world, however, the evangelical elites, consciously and unconsciously, adjusted to the world system which earlier had been to them hopelessly satanic. And, more specifically, they also accommodated their theological studies to the critical methodologies and broad cultural analysis which had become dominant in the mainline liberal denominations. To change the world, the evangelicals felt they had to be recognized and accepted by it. Like their liberal Protestant counterparts, they, too, had to become "relevant" to the needs of modern man; thus from the 1950s to the present, subtle but highly significant transformations have occurred among the evangelicals in their theology and ecclesiology; politics and social attitudes, and acceptance of a more permissive morality. (The public resurgence of fundamentalism since the late 1970s was outwardly a repudiation of the liberalization of evangelicalism, but it was also, as we shall see, evidence that fundamentalists were becoming modern, too. They, no less than the more liberal evangelicals, now wanted to change the world rather than withdraw from it—but in very different ways.)

The New Evangelical Theology

With respect to academic theology, the most important adjustment among evangelical intellectual elites was the gradual erosion of the fundamentalist doctrine of biblical inerrancy, affirming, in a scholastic way, that Scripture is "free from error in the whole and in the part." The demise of this doctrine was first noticed at the December 1962 faculty-trustee retreat of the Fuller Theological Seminary. (Fuller's faculty, several with Harvard doctorates in religion, were well educated in higher biblical criticism.) The final outcome of this retreat was the removal, in 1972, of the inerrancy clause from the seminary's statement of faith, signed by all faculty members, and its replacement with a less specific affirmation of biblical authority. This followed shortly after the elimination of belief in premillennialism as an article of the creed as well. (Premillennialism, with its doctrine of a hopelessly corrupt and sinful world until Christ's return, mitigated against social and political action to change the world, to make it better.) Since the 1970s, most of the other faculties of evangelical seminaries and colleges have followed the spirit of Fuller's example, though they have stopped short of altering their own statements of faith. Only the ETS and a few theological schools enforced adherence to their inerrancy clause. And it was well known that numerous theological scholars signed statements of the evangelical faith with serious mental reservations.[5]

Inerrancy had been the doctrine which made theological dialogue between evangelical and liberal theologians impossible. With its demise, however, evangelicals began, in the 1970s, to play a more prominent role in mainline liberal theological societies such as the American Academy of Religion (AAR), which now includes a well-attended evangelical "theme group" at its annual meetings. Evangelical theologians and ministers contribute regularly to the standard Protestant and Catholic journals. Their scholarship in these articles, moreover, is not very different from that of the more liberal scholars and clergy.

In terms of ecclesiology, the doctrine of the pure, completely orthodox, evangelical church or denomination waned considerably especially after the "charismatic renewal" or neopentecostal movement emerged in 1960. In this movement, mainline denominational Christians (e.g., Episcopalians, Lutherans, Presbyterians, and, later, Catholics) received the pentecostal "gifts of the Spirit" outlined in I Corinthians 12–14—including "speaking in tongues" and divine healing, practiced them in their own churches, and accommodated them to the nonsectarian religious style of mainline liberal Christendom. When white fundamentalist pentecostals, most notably those of the Assemblies of God (an NAE charter member), began praying and worshipping with mainline Christian ministers and laity during the 1960s, they could no longer easily condemn them for their denial of inerrancy, their sacramental liturgies, their espousal of baptismal regeneration, and the like—beliefs and practices once publicly repudiated by evangelical theologians. Their basic unity now, rather, was in the renewed pentecostal *experience,* not in other shared doctrines. In this movement, white pentecostals shed much of their ecclesiastical exclusiveness, which they learned from fundamentalism, and replaced it with the original black pentecostal insistence on the priority of experience and testimony over doctrinal formulation. In so doing, pentecostal elites led their non-pentecostal evangelical counterparts in the same direction.[6]

Although most evident in the charismatic renewal movement, the

roots of nonsectarian cooperation between evangelicals and non-
evangelicals actually extend all the way back to the establishment of
the NAE in 1942, which allowed member congregations with ties
to the liberal National Council of Churches, to keep them. Later, in
the 1950s, Billy Graham began insisting that his city crusades be
supported by at least *some* of the local, mainline Protestant clergy
and denominational leaders.

At the level of popular religiosity, there were also changes among
the evangelicals suggesting further accommodation to the larger
Christian community and the wider society. Beginning with the
rapprochement of Billy Graham and Norman Vincent Peale during
Graham's New York City crusade in 1957, there has been a growing
trend to join evangelical Christianity with the long tradition of
New Thought, represented by Peale's "power of positive thinking."
When the world seems out of control in almost every other respect,
accepting Christ as one's personal savior may provide not only a
certain comfort, but also a warrant for not worrying about whether
or not the world, too, is still redeemable.[7]

In addition to New Thought, psychology, once a "tool of Satan,"
became popular among evangelicals as they sought personal integration. Evangelical theology was in large measure psychologized
in popular bestsellers (notably those of James Dobson) and mental-
ized in the books by Peale's disciple, Robert H. Schuller, who
formulated a new positive mental technique for salvation, "possibility thinking." Fuller Theological Seminary opened a graduate
school of psychology in 1965, and evangelical elites followed their
liberal peers by engaging in "group therapy" and "sensitivity training." Lay theologians Keith Miller and Bruce Larson developed a
"relational theology" which existentialized and relativised evangelical doctrine by insisting that theology is *not* conceptual but relational (e.g., "Any law of God that destroys people is not a law of
God."). Such thinking, of course, further weakened the once pivotal
evangelical belief in the absolute authority of "propositional revelation" as expressed in the Bible.[8]

The New Evangelical Politics

The changes in evangelical theology and ecclesiology among elites
during the sixties and seventies marked a significant shift from
transcendence to immanence, from a focus on the hope of heaven
and avoidance of hell to an emphasis on building a just society on

earth. Traditionally, fundamentalism and its evangelical derivative had maintained a pretty uniform alliance with the conservative wing of the Republican party. But from about 1966 to 1976, many of the evangelical intellectuals moved to the left politically. Senator Mark Hatfield of Oregon was a forerunner of this trend, which emerged largely among young people from the countercultural Jesus People movement of the late 1960s as a protest against the political and social conservatism of the evangelical establishment. These young evangelicals were a small, highly literate elite—moderate Republicans to radical pacifists and near Marxists—whose spokespersons helped formulate the "Chicago Declaration of Evangelical Social Concern" in 1973. This document—signed by evangelical elder statesmen as well—promised a more immanent concern with the world and its social problems than evangelicals had previously shown, and a much more liberal political and social stance as well.[9]

As the young evangelicals adjusted further, they became more worldly with upward mobility by the late seventies, and the New Left radicalism of many of them turned into a more liberal Democratic position, which made an appearance, now and then, even in the pages of *Christianity Today* and *Eternity,* two of evangelicalism's leading conservative journals. And young evangelical magazines like *The Other Side, The Reformed Journal, Sojourners,* and *The Wittenburg Door,* became increasingly sophisticated, attracting the attention and subscriptions not only of evangelicals themselves but also of mainline, liberal Protestants and Catholics. In many ways, the political liberalization of the evangelical elite was epitomized by the election in 1976 ("the year of the evangelical") of Jimmy Carter. With that event, as we have said at the outset, evangelicals entered the mainstream of American society. But later that decade, media attention would turn away from them and toward the more visible resurgence of fundamentalism and reassertion of conservative politics by its leaders, so much so that the leftward trend of evangelicalism during the seventies has by now been all but forgotten.[10]

The New Evangelical Morality

The secular counterculture influenced the Jesus People movement politically. It legitimated protest in the evangelical ranks. In addition, the social, cultural, and moral permissiveness of the secular counterculture also gradually seeped into that movement—with

long-term effects on the whole of evangelicalism. In the Jesus People movement, communal and alternative lifestyles emerged, replacing the fundamentalist and conservative evangelical stress on the priority of the nuclear family. An emphasis on "simple living," for a time, repudiated the material upward mobility of traditional Protestant conservatism. The fundamentalist taboos against social dancing, alcohol, and tobacco were rejected by the young evangelicals, and there was even some experimenting with recreational drugs. Most notably, the Jesus People legitimated "satanic rock 'n' roll" (as the fundamentalists saw it) by creating a new genre of Christian rock music. At first, the eroticism inherent in secular rock music was subdued, but as it moved from suggestive to explicit in its erotic character, Christian rock and its performers became suggestive. To the core, rock is a form of music that made its way by outrage against taboo. In accepting this modern expressive mode, evangelicals accommodated further to the world.

By the early 1970s, even feminism became acceptable among most of the young evangelicals. The Evangelical Women's Caucus (EWC) was established in 1975, and the sophistication of its current newsletter, *Update,* now rivals that of secular feminist publications. This is not hard to understand when we discover that, for example, more than 70 percent of the readers of Daughters of Sarah have been to graduate school. [11]

A measure of sexual permissiveness also became apparent among the young evangelicals. Books appeared, like Letha Scanzoni and Virginia Mollenkott's *Is the Homosexual My Neighbor?,* which affirmed the possibility of moral homosexual relationships. Ralph Blair, an evangelical psychotherapist, founded Evangelicals Concerned (about homosexuality) in 1976, as a support community for practicing homosexuals in the larger evangelical subculture, and he began publishing another sophisticated newsletter, *Record.*

The acceptability of divorce has increased rapidly in the *whole* evangelical movement since the 1970s. Even conservative evangelical celebrities were talking publicly about their experience of divorce and remarriage (in the past, such action would have caused any evangelical to lose his or her credibility). Singleness thus was implicitly affirmed, and singles ministries emerged even in conservative evangelical churches. The trend toward sexual permissiveness within the larger American evangelical community had been hinted at since the late 1960s, but it began to be documented in 1979, when *Christianity Today* published an article surveying the

sexual behavior of divorced men and women in a representative singles group of a large evangelical church in California (all identified themselves as born-again Christians). Of the 203 participants in the survey, only 9 percent of the men and 22 percent of the women had been celibate during the previous year, and 18 percent of the men and 8 percent of the women had had intercourse more than 50 times during the same period.[12] The new participation of divorced persons in evangelical singles groups also liberalized the sexual behavior of never marrieds, who had been more likely to observe celibacy than formerly marrieds.

From the 1940s to the present, evangelicalism became increasingly like mainline, liberal Protestantism in its theological, political, social, and cultural concerns, with a small, highly educated elite leading the way. The larger American society showed its acceptance of the culturally accommodated evangelicals by electing one of them to the presidency in 1976. And by 1983, it became clear that even the liberal theological academy had begun to accept them, when Harvard University's divinity school, which had educated a number of the most prominent evangelical scholars, announced plans to seek endowment for a professorship of evangelical Christianity.[13]

Modern Fundamentalism

As the evangelical intelligentsia moved toward modernism and modernity in the 1970s, giving up the older commitment to traditional, rural, and small-town values, its fundamentalist counterparts reacted against this trend. Conservative, usually older, fundamentalists repudiated the new evangelical use of higher biblical criticism by reasserting the inerrancy of Scripture as the watershed of conservative Protestantism. They insisted, moreover, that political liberalism and radicalism are un-Christian phenomena, incompatible with true Christian teaching. And they denounced vigorously the new evangelical tendencies toward increased social and moral permissiveness—reasserting the older dictums against premarital sex, homosexuality, and abortion—while they condemned feminism as destructive of traditional family values.

The growing visibility of fundamentalist leaders since the late 1970s emerges on the heels of the wider trend toward political conservatism in the United States during the same period of time. The early demise of Jimmy Carter's popularity and his defeat by

Ronald Reagan in 1980 turned the mass media away from the evangelical liberalism, which it liked, and toward the new threat of status-quo fundamentalism, which it did *not* like. This New Christian Right, led by television evangelists like Jerry Falwell, Jimmy Swaggart, Jim Bakker, and Pat Robertson, fought what it considered to be modernism—not only within evangelical Christendom, but more importantly, in secular society itself—in the schools, the marketplace, government, and the entertainment industry. Yet, there was an irony in this reaction, because the New Christian Right had also become modern in *its* approach, a fact that brought fundamentalism widespread secular recognition for the first time since the 1920s.

The so-called reactionary fundamentalists (like Falwell, Swaggart, and Bakker) and conservative evangelicals (like Robertson) became modern with the use of advanced technology in their religious broadcasting systems. Their television shows utilized Hollywood styles, sets, and mannerisms, and they developed sophisticated fund-raising techniques, with toll-free telephone numbers and computers to engage viewers in a long-term personal correspondence with the celebrity evangelist. They used satellites to spread their message to millions of viewers—conservative Christians who reaped not only inspiration from the programs, but entertainment as well.[14] These conservative Protestant celebrities were also modern in their building of large communications networks and teaching institutions—like Pat Robertson's Christian Broadcasting Network (CBN) and Jerry Falwell's Liberty University and Robertson's CBN University—to perpetuate their ministries. And they showed modernity by creating sophisticated political lobbying organizations (like Falwell's "Moral Majority") to give their conservatism more clout in Washington.

Now fundamentalism, which had always prided itself in separation from the world, was suddenly willing to work with others in common political and social concerns—even with Mormons, Moonies, and outright nonbelievers (whom its forbears had consigned to hell—from the pulpit). In their willingness to align themselves with heretics and the unsaved in this way, fundamentalist leaders, no less than the evangelicals they now condemn had done earlier, also accepted the principles of accommodation—of revisability—and pluralism so inherent in modernity. These changes in attitude and practice are clearly documented in Jerry Falwell's *The Fundamentalist Phenomenon*. With increasing upward social mobility and higher education, the once clear lines of demarcation between fundamentalists and the less conservative evangelicals are mostly gone. The differences today are simply a matter of the degree to which modernity has been accepted, consciously or unconsciously.

There are other ways in which conservative Protestants have adjusted to modernity. At one level, concessions have been made to modern rationality by the widespread tendency among them to codify the religious components of the evangelical or fundamentalist worldview into standardized doctrine on how to become a Christian, how to mature in one's faith through prayer, how to read the Bible, how to do evangelism, and so on. Packaging spirituality in this way provides a uniform product as well as an easy means for marketing the faith in modern society. At another level, concessions have been made to the modern privatization of religion. Although conservative Protestantism does have a public face in its social and political pronouncements and action, it has also taken on subtle aspects of privatization by embracing a new subjectivism in its attempt to solve common psychological problems and emotional difficulties, just like the upwardly mobile members of the wider culture around it, but in a distinctively *Christian* way. [15]

Social Implications

The point to be made here is that in the course of conservative Protestantism's endeavor to fight *against* the world (i.e., modernity), to change it, it has made so many concessions *to* the world that one wonders who's influencing whom? Both evangelicalism and fundamentalism have been influenced profoundly by the wider culture and have, therefore, become worldly. But to what degree have these subcultures, in so doing, been able to sway the world around them? How effective has conservative Protestantism been in carrying out *its* transformative agenda?

The young evangelical elite wanted to change the world by liberalizing or radicalizing it along the lines of the New Left of the 1960s, with evangelical Christian symbolism. But that goal did not get very far in a society which, by the late seventies, was tired of the well-worn rhetoric of the Left. Nevertheless, the new evangelicals did gain attention and stature in the secular media and among "burned-out," overly secularized Protestant and Catholic liberals, who welcomed their fervor as they "took the Bible seriously, but not literally."

Fundamentalists and conservative evangelicals desired to change the world by improved evangelism techniques designed to reap more conversions and gain more new church members. And they wanted to counter the modernism of secular humanism by creating *activist* political and social conservatives who could influence Washington and even run for office. But the mass revival crusades and the evangelistic Christian rock concerts of the last two decades reached very few nonbelievers. Ninety percent or more of those in attendance were Christians already.[16] And, although conservative churches have grown appreciably since the early 1970s, survey research has shown that they did *not* grow as the result of successful proselytization of large numbers of nonbelievers, but rather, through (1) the reaffiliation of a highly mobile population (switching from other similar churches), and (2) the natural matriculation of the offspring of church members.

Television ministries, as well, have been shown to reach only those who are *already* in theological (and sociopolitical) agreement with the evangelists—the very people who are at the same time active members of conservative evangelical and fundamentalist churches. Likewise, fundamentalist political lobbies like the former Moral Majority and Robert Grant's Christian Voice have had far less social and political impact than they had hoped for (in part, because of the advanced state of secularization in the whole public sphere—a process which leaves little opportunity for religious organization to wield influence). Even if one of the leading televangelists, like Pat Robertson, were elected President of the United States, his evangelical faith and personal religious associations would probably have no more impact on his administration than did the faith of Jimmy Carter on his.[17]

James Davison Hunter, however, does point out that even if the New Christian Right is truly a "vanguard reactionary movement," it still has made a political impact in the United States, if only because its opposition has overestimated its magnitude, in effect giving it more credibility than its actual power base warrants.[18] Nevertheless, given all of the foregoing, it should now be clear that conservative Protestantism—in all its forms—has been influenced far more by the wider society around it than vice versa. Thus it has lost its war against modernity, and failed in its once-overarching attempt to be "in the world, but not of it."

NOTES

1. George Gallup, Jr., *Religion in America—50 Years: 1935–1985* (*The Gallup Report,* No. 236, May 1985), p. 38. See also Richard Quebedeaux's definition of evangelicalism in *The Young Evangelicals* (New York: Harper & Row, 1974), pp. 3–4.

2. James Davison Hunter, *American Evangelicalism: Conservative Religion and the Quandary of Modernity* (New Brunswick, N.J.: Rutgers University Press, 1983), pp. 56–9.

3. Phillip E. Hammond, "The Curious Path of Conservative Protestantism," *The Annals of the American Academy of Political and Social Science* (July 1985): 54–6.

4. For the history of the development of modern evangelicalism as a whole, see Quebedeaux, *The Young Evangelicals; The Worldly Evangelicals* (San Francisco: Harper & Row, 1978); *By What Authority: The Rise of Personality Cults in American Christianity* (San Francisco: Harper & Row, 1982); and "Conservative and Charismatic Developments of the Later Twentieth Century," in *Encyclopedia of Religion in America,* ed. Charles H. Lippy and Peter W. Williams (New York: Scribners, 1987).

5. See Harold Lindsell, *The Battle for the Bible* (Grand Rapids, MI.: Zondervan, 1976), pp. 106–21; and Quebedeaux, *The Worldly Evangelicals,* op. cit., pp. 84–96.

6. See Quebedeaux, *The New Charismatics II* (San Francisco: Harper & Row, 1983).

7. Hammond, op. cit., p. 59.

8. See Quebedeaux, *The Worldly Evangelicals,* op. cit., pp. 96–7; and *By What Authority,* op. cit., pp. 60–75.

9. See Ronald J. Sider, ed., *The Chicago Declaration* (Carol Stream, IL.: Creation House, 1974); and Quebedeaux, *The Young Evangelicals,* op. cit., pp. 118–23.

10. See Robert Booth Fowler, *A New Engagement: Evangelical Political Thought, 1966–1976* (Grand Rapids, MI: Eerdmans, 1982).

11. "Survey Results," in *Daughters of Sarah* (March–April 1981): 20.

12. Harold Ivan Smith, "Sex and Singleness the Second Time Around," in *Christianity Today* (May 25, 1979): 16–22.

13. On the "evangelical connection" at Harvard, see the relevant articles in *Christianity Today* (February 4, 1983): 14–20.

14. See Jeffrey K. Hadden and Charles E. Swann, *Prime Time Preachers* (Reading, MA.: Addison-Wesley, 1981).

15. Hunter, "Conservative Protestantism on the American Scene," in *Social Compass* XXXII/2–3 (1985): 239–40. See also his *American Evangelicalism;* Frank J. Lechner, "Fundamentalism and Sociocultural Revitalization in America," in *Sociological Analysis* (Fall 1985): 257; and Quebedeaux, *By What Authority,* op. cit.

16. John W. Styll, "Why Are We Doing This, Anyway?," in *The Wittenburg Door* (October–November 1984): 4. This statistic has circulated widely over the years in reference to Billy Graham's crusades as well, which depended on the "success" local conservative churches had getting their own members to the meetings.

17. Hunter, "Conservative Protestantism on the American Scene," op. cit., pp. 236–8.

18. Ibid., p. 239.

9

Social Consequences of the German Church Struggle

FRANZ G. FEIGE

The challenge posed to the German Protestant church by National Socialism provides a supreme test case for the question of the relevance of religion in politics. This is one vantage point from which the theme of this volume—the social consequences of belief in God—may be reviewed. The lessons to be learned from the German church struggle far exceed the narrow bounds of Germany and the Christian religion. This explains, for example, the continuing strong interest in the life and thought of the theologian Dietrich Bonhoeffer.

A great deal has been written about the German church struggle, especially in Germany. In my opinion, though, most scholars have treated the struggle too narrowly. They have tended to focus on the relationship between the institutional church and the state, on the fighting factions within the church, or on purely theological elements of the church struggle. This has resulted in a preoccupation with church-political and theological questions. It is my intention here to broaden the perspective contextually and methodologically by looking at the whole spectrum of the relationship between Protestant theology and National Socialism, of which the church struggle was only one albeit major part. More specifically, I am attempting to outline the theopolitical responses of German Protestantism to National Socialism.

In regard to the overarching theme of this volume, my primary interest is not to *proove,* in the narrow sense of the word, the political significance or relevance of some belief or theology at the time of Hitler's takeover in Germany. No doubt, all theopolitical factions within the Protestant church at one point or another proved to be relevant to the ongoing political scene in a positive or negative sense—that is, either sanctioning, accommodating, or confrontational.

The aim of this paper is more modest. It is to recount the story of the confrontation between National Socialism and Protestantism from the above-mentioned broader perspective. The German church struggle, then, stands out as an intriguing example of the social consequences of belief in God. It shows that the most narrowly conceived theological stance, that is, a purely confessional attitude, may lead to social consequences that even defy the political attitude of those confessing. The German church struggle establishes this in terms of the unavoidability of passive resistance under certain circumstances, and it also testifies to the importance of the active execution of responsibility in the civic arena.

I will proceed by outlining the theopolitical factions within the church during the closing years of the Weimar republic, that is, in the first three years of the 1930s. On the whole, the responses to National Socialism initially fell within these factions. With Hitler's takeover, most of the public criticism of National Socialism disappeared. What essentially remained was the church struggle, an indirect Protestant response to National Socialism—which is addressed in the second part of this paper.

Protestant Responses to National Socialism Until 1933

Throughout its short duration, the Weimar republic was severely shaken by political, social, and economic crises. The psychological aftermath of the war was a very destabilizing factor. The German people felt betrayed by the Peace Treaty of Versailles and oppressed by the continuous demands of the victorious powers. Finally, with the onset of the world economic crisis, the republic entered its death throes. It was then that National Socialism suddenly rose to become a major contender for state power.

Protestantism was very much affected by the crises and the prevailing nationalist *Zeitgeist*. Threatened by the new socialist and democratic state and the general decline of churchliness and morality, it was not able to forget its privileged and secure status as a state church during the monarchy. It lacked the strong unitary hierarchical structure of the Catholic church. Similarly, it did not have a political home, such as the Catholic Center party provided for Catholicism.

The effects of World War I and the general crisis also helped to spawn new theological developments. Beside the theologically liberal and the orthodox conservative traditions, which had long standing, there appeared now the religious socialists, the Lutheran neoconservatives, and the dialectical theologians. All these also had a decidedly political emphasis. [The exception was dialectical theology which opposed all combinations of theology with isms.] Though the official church had tried to remain neutral toward political parties, it very often betrayed a conservative nationalist bias.[1] This was because the majority of its clergy remained conservative nationalists.

A sudden politicization of the Protestant church occurred at the beginning of the thirties with the rise of the right-wing national liberation movement, of which National Socialism was the driving factor. Hitler's strategic political decision to cut his party off from its Germanic religious origins and to commit it to a vague stance for "positive Christianity" made it possible for the party to appeal to Christians. The patriotic slogans and national promises of the Nazis, their fierce stance against Marxism, materialism, and the decline of morality, made them palatable to the nationally leaning and conservative parts of the Protestant church.

The Protestant response was somewhat complicated by the ambiguities within National Socialism itself and by the Nazi's opportunism and deceptive tactics. At first, the official Protestant church avoided a formal position toward National Socialism, thus continuing its course of neutrality. In contrast, the Catholic church started out by rejecting the Nazis uniformly. It would have been hardly possible for the Protestant church to take such a stance, if for no other reason than its lack of hierarchical structure and unity and its corresponding lack of strong political representation (such as the Catholic church had in its Center Party). Therefore, the situation within the church made the Protestant response to National Socialism variegated. It took place at the level of church groups, church parties, and Protestant movements.

The first Protestant appraisals of National Socialism began to appear when, surprisingly, it became the second largest party in the Reich in the fall elections of 1930. The majority of the voices then still rejected National Socialism, but a large part seemed undecided, weighing the positive and negative aspects of the movement.[2] On the whole, until Hitler's seizure of power, the argumentation for or against National Socialism conformed to the political and theological landscape of Protestantism.

In keeping with this landscape metaphor, the various streams of political Protestantism in the waning years of the Weimar Republic may be described thusly. There are the two major rivers on the right—conservatism and the German Christians (the Nazis in the church)—which, fed by contemporary tributaries (fascism and nationalism) and the cataclysmic downpourings (social, economic, and political crises), were to flood the political landscape of Protestantism. There was the once-mighty stream of liberal Protestantism that, after entering the democratic age, shrunk to a minor rivulet. There was the still-young political countercurrent of religious socialism that attracted attention through its thundering waterfalls, rapids, and riffles.[3]

Thus four major theopolitical factions may be distinguished: (1) the German Christians; (2) the Protestant conservatives and neo-conservatives; (3) the religious socialists; and (4) the Protestant democratic liberals. Their responses shall be described briefly.

The Faith Movement

The National Socialist's official policy of neutrality toward the dissident Confessing church (which opposed the intermingling and politics) had obstructed the development of a strong organization of National Socialists within the larger Protestant church. Finally, however, because of the party's grievances about the church's obstinacy, the Faith Movement of German Christians was called into being. It was to serve the Nazis in the conquering of the church.[4]

Points seven to ten of its official program identified the Faith Movement clearly with National Socialism. It called for the purification of the German race, protection from the feckless and the inferior, and prohibition of marriage between Germans and Jews.[5] The program's lack of theological acumen revealed the church-political and opportunistic nature of the Faith Movement, that is, to serve the tactical interests of the NSDAP. This became clear when the party threw its apparatus behind the German Christians in the church election campaign in the fall of 1932. This obvious political invasion of church politics by the Nazis politicized the church in an unforeseeable manner.[6] The German Christians were able to gain about a third of the total seats, and their organizational machine kept gaining momentum after Hitler's takeover until the fall of 1933.

Members' enthusiasm and will to change the church according to the ideas of National Socialism, and the possibility of representing the interests of the church in the party, served as integrating forces to gather under the German Christian umbrella a number of sym-

pathetic groups, movements, and organizations of varied theological persuasions. Among the groups that merged with the German
Christians were the Thuringian German Christians (Kirchenbewegung Deutsche Christen). Though relatively small, they deserve mention because they differed noticeably from the largely
opportunistic German Christians. The Thuringians began as a
grass root effort in 1927, under the leadership of close friends
Siegfried Leffler and Julius Leutheuser. Since their work as Nazi
speakers and German Christian organizers was strongly interre-
lated, their religious and political beliefs formed an integrated
whole. It was their sincerely held but naive religious interpretation
of history which differentiated them from other groups. It also gave
them strength and made them the most lasting of any group. Following are just a couple of passages from one of the pages of Leffler's
Christus im Dritten Reich der Deutschen, which demonstrate the
group's idolatrous religious glorification of National Socialism:

> We see in the person of the leader the one sent by God who calls
> Germany to face the Lord of history. . . . But it is a fact that in the
> pitch-dark night of the history of the Christian church Hitler became
> for our time, in a way, the wonderful transparency, the window
> through which the light shines on Christianity. It is through him that
> we are able to see the Savior in the history of the Germans. . . . Those
> wanting life in the future must center on him [Hitler].[7]

Hitler's takeover at the beginning of 1933 gave new impetus to the
German Christians movement. As well-known, more moderate
Christians began to join, a new, more conservatively dressed program was aired that avoided the stark racism of its previous program [8] The national church election, in which the German
Christians secured three fourths of all votes, pointed toward a
complete regimentation of the church in line with the Nazi party
and the new Germany.

It may be concluded that while the majority of the German
Christians favored a "Constantinian arrangement" between National Socialism and Christianity, the underlying German Christian
interests in that union were diverse. Though among many, political
and professional opportunism abounded, there were also religious
motivations at play, such as the chance to missionize within the
National Socialist state. Thus not all who interpreted the Nazi
events religiously did it opportunistically. The Thuringians, for
example, tended to be sincere. Emanuel Hirsch, too, who unlike

Leffler and Leutheuser, belonged to the most erudite and influential among the young German theologians, was utterly persuaded by the affinity of the Third Reich with Christianity. If one can speak of the social consequences of the German Christians' belief in God, then their theologies took the role of a conscious religious sanctioning of the Third Reich. Whether the apprehension of the political events as religious experiences was genuine, is a question not to be pursued here. What is clear in my opinion, though, is that not everybody's assent to National Socialism may be reduced to political interest alone.

Protestant Conservativism

The young conservatives, also called neoconservatives, were the first to respond to the new nationalist thinking in Germany, of which National Socialism was only one part. They made it their task to incorporate the concerns of the nationalist movement into their theologies, especially the concept of the nation (*Volk*). Most of them, however, tried to avoid the more radical racist overtones. Paul Althaus, for example, one of their well-known representatives, incorporated the concept of nation into his theology of the orders of creation, where it was given paramount importance.[9] His acceptance of the nationalist concerns went hand in hand with typical right-wing complaints about the republic and its peace treaty, democracy and parliamentarism, Marxism and socialism, materialism and immorality, to name only a few. The similarity to the Nazi rhetoric is apparent.

The Christian German movement (Christlich-deutsche Bewegung), founded in 1930, best exemplified this stance with its vague differentiation between conservative and neoconservative concerns. While some of its members came to reject National Socialism and the more radical German Christian groups, others joined them: thus the group as a whole was marked by a fluctuating or mediating attitude. For example, the Christian Germans wholeheartedly affirmed the more broadly conceived national movement, yet voiced reservations toward the more radical racial demands, made by the Nazis.

Because of their more moderate and rather conservative position, and because of the renown of some of their spokesmen (such as Hirsch, Althaus, and Rendtorff), the Christian Germans had considerable effect on both conservative and radical factions in the

Protestant church.[10] It is true that while the German Christians were the most undiscerning about the dangers of National Socialism, they were likewise blinded by their exaggerated national concerns and their aristocratic and antidemocratic resentments. Thus while it is easy in hindsight to pass judgment on a phenomenon that had not yet revealed its real face, it must be admitted that the neoconservatives' influence on undecided Christians at the crucial time between 1932 and 1933 can hardly be overestimated. While most of them did not outrightly sanction every aspect of the new regime, many neoconservative theologians contributed, at least indirectly, to its tacit affirmation.

Religious Socialism

In one point neoconservative theology differed markedly from the liberal and conservative tradition. It elevated political ethics, that is, the national mission of the German people, to a key position. Thus it may be called a modern political theology. In this latter sense, it was similar to religious socialism, a movement which began in Germany after World War I. Instead of placing the mission of the German nation in central position, religious socialism placed the mission of the proletariat in the key position, thus coming close to identifying the latter with the kingdom of God. In fact, its early naivete and enthusiasm concerning the relationship between politics and religion compares with that of the German Christians. Consider, for example, the words of one of its outstanding representatives, Paul Tillich, in an early leaflet:

> A new age of unity is arising. Socialism will form its economic and social foundation. And Christianity stands before the task to convey to this development its moral and religious powers and thereby to initiate a great new synthesis of religion and social structure.[11]

The similarity becomes apparent when we exchange "socialism" for "National Socialism."

The parallel in theological structure, however, did not translate into an approval of National Socialism or the German Christians. On the whole, the religious socialists were fiercely opposed to both of them. For one, they stood on opposite political grounds. The socialists and the Nazis considered each other as political enemies. Consequently, the religious socialists were among the first to unveil the political dangers the Nazis posed to Germany and Europe: "In the effort to realize the impossible by force, they could bring the physical downfall upon the nation. The fight against them is the fight for the preservation of the nation."[12] Thus, not surprisingly, there are a number of religious socialists among the exiles and political martyrs.

The political element was so strongly part and parcel of religious socialist rhetoric that their opposition to National Socialism could easily be dismissed by the Nazis and their sympathizers as being merely political.[13] Even to many neutral observers, the religious socialists were just another politicized group that did not offer a real alternative to the politicized German Christians. Because of this, and because of the minority status of the religious socialists, their stance had hardly any influence on the general response to National Socialism.

Protestant Liberalism

The liberal democratic tradition within German Protestantism found most of its advocates among the liberal theologians. The journal *Christliche Welt* probably best represented that tradition. It was extremely open and tolerant toward a wide array of theological as well as political opinions. Martin Rade had made this journal a forum for the most dissident voices in Protestantism. Its commitment to democracy, ecumenism, the relative separation of church and state, humanistic values, and the individual made it an early critic of the Nazis and the German Christians. The liberals seemed to be especially disconcerted by the cultural and ethical menace the Nazis posed, that is, their vulgarities and brutalities.[14] This explains their alertness to the Nazi treatment of the Jews, which they spoke openly about from very early on.[15] Undoubtedly, though, they underestimated the dangers of National Socialism.[16]

Though liberals connected the Reformation call for freedom of conscience theologically to democratic civil liberties, they avoided open political confrontation with the Nazis, especially after 1933. The shifting theological currents after World War I had marginalized the democratic liberals in the church. Thus at the time of Hitler's rise to power, their voice was hardly heard.

The German Church Struggle

Hitler's seizure of power was a watershed for society at large, political Protestantism, and the German church. The plurality of perspectives gave way to a broad conformity with the new state. By the end of 1933 Hitler had eliminated most opposition. Organized religious socialism disappeared and so did the Friends of the Christliche Welt, the liberal organization affiliated with the journal of the same name. No concerted political opposition within Protestantism prevailed. Free political Protestantism vanished because the Nazis eliminated the conditions for a free political society.

What openly endured was a church-political and purely theological response—not to National Socialism as such, but to the activities and views of the German Christians within the Protestant church. And yet, what appeared in most part to be an internecine theological and church-political fight proved in the end to be the most consequential response to National Socialism because it was, at least in intention, limited to church politics and theology.

Thus the National Socialist party as such did not lead to the church struggle. Rather it was the German Christians that provoked it. The opposition began in the spring of 1933, when the German Christians most actively propagated their church reforms with the help of the Nazi party. It was then on the occasion of church elections, that a group of mostly young theologians and pastors formed the Young Reformation movement (Jungreformatorische Bewegung). Under the leadership of Martin Niemoeller, it developed into the Pastors Emergency League. The Young Reformers' position was marked by a paradox. While they joyously affirmed the new National Socialist state and the importance of church reforms, they attacked the German Christians on two major points— the intermingling of Gospel and politics and the exclusion of non-Aryans from the church.[17]

Much to the credit of Karl Barth and dialectical theology, the opposition reached greater theological clarity and developed a confessional stance. At the beginning of 1934, it began to take shape as a grassroots synodical movement. Its central theological insight consisted in the conviction that the German Christian's appropriation of National Socialism was heretical to the true Christian creed. It conveyed to Reformers the religious fervor to fight the German Christians" within the church under the threat of great personal risk and sacrifice.

The so-called German church struggle began with the acceleration of the confessional movement in late 1933 and early 1934 and the sudden break-up of the German Christians. It was to last until the end of World War II. The change occurred at the time when the German Christians seemed to have conquered the church and almost fully aligned it with the new state. The German Christian disaster, however, was not merely the work of the opposition alone. Other factors contributed, such as Hitler's official withdrawal of support from the group, its own factionalization and radicalization, the foreign and domestic controversy concerning the introduction of the Aryan clause into the Protestant church, the ruthless regimentation of the church, and, not insignificantly the lack of leadership among the German Christians. The victory of the opposition was never to become complete though, for most of the church reforms initiated by the German Christians could not be reversed, nor could all the positions in the church be regained. For example, Hitler's confidant Ludwig Mueller survived in his position as Reich bishop, insuring the influence of the state, the party, and the German Christians within the Protestant church.[18]

But the confessing front had managed to organize itself into the Confessing church at its national Synod of Barmen, issuing the famous Barmen Declaration in May 1934.[19] By virtue of its confession, it claimed to be the true representative of the Protestant church in Germany, thus locking itself into a struggle against the entrenched, state-aligned church. To avoid dealing with the complicated course of the Confessing church's struggle, it suffices to point out that the struggle may be divided into three principle periods: (1) 1933–1935: The struggle was understood solely as a church struggle, with the opportunity for nonconformism; (2) 1935–1938: The church struggle became an unwanted political struggle, pressure being exerted toward disobedience; and (3) 1938–1945: The church struggle disintegrated into a mismanaged political struggle; the alternatives became secret resistance or truce.[20]

The struggle eventually took on a political edge because the Nazi state exerted more and more direct pressure on the church to conform, while at the same time revealing anti-Christian feelings by intermittently bursting into hostile actions. In other words, Nazism began to unveil its true totalitarian face. The fifth point of the Barmen Declaration, which sought to define the relationship between state and church, forestalled such an attitude by the state. It clearly stated: "We reject the false doctrine, as though the State, over and beyond its special commission, should and could become the single and totalitarian order of human life, thus fulfilling the Church's vocation as well."[21]

Yet from the very start, the Confessing church (even initially, the political opponent Karl Barth) had difficulty identifying the Nazis as the real culprits in the situation. The Confessing church spent its energies on an internecine fight, while losing almost complete sight of the atrocities committed by National Socialism. While it defended the participation of Jewish Christians within the church, it failed to defend their rights as citizens within the state. It had no idea of how to use resistance to defend humanistic or liberal values. This weakness persisted also through its second and third stage, when the political implications of the confession became obvious in the face of an oppressive and hostile state. The steps from nonconformism to disobedience to active resistance were followed by fewer and fewer people.

Most definitely, then, the story of the German church struggle reveals ambiguity. In terms of its results, it may be judged as a great success because the Confessing church was the only organization able to prevent the complete Nazi regimentation of a significant organization within Germany, that is, the Protestant church; or as a failure because of the little difference it made outside the church walls or in the overall development of Germany.

The success of the Confessing church, no matter how small one may judge it, was attained through the issuing of a contemporary confession which discerned true from false belief. The lesson relevant here is that a confession may indeed require civil disobedience and active resistance, as seen in the second and third stages of the Confessing church struggle. That it happened because of National Socialism does not make it obsolete today; the world still knows totalitarianism, segregation, and racism.

It is important to note that because there were issues of faith at stake, resistance to the German Christians, and even later to National Socialism, did developed. It was not political convictions, but the narrow theological concentration that made resistance possible and defensible within an oppressive state. Its confessional convictions internally fortified most Confessing church members, and to some yielded the strength to risk imprisonment and even death.

The case of Dietrich Bonhoeffer embodies perhaps the best example of the strength and the shortcomings of the Confessing church. As a political and theological opponent of the Nazis and the German Christians, the Confessing Church provided a home for Bonhoeffer's nonconformism. Here he could excel as a leader. His biographer, Eberhard Bethge, captures this nonconformist environment in the following passage:

And this purely confession- and church-oriented opposition in its totalitarian surroundings became not only a witness for but even an

organized stronghold of freedom. It was in fact an island of nonconformism. Parts of the population understood this at once. People who
had forgotten that there was such a thing as "pure preaching of the
gospel and confession" came to Church. Every Sunday morning
liberals, artists, politicians, and others came, and church collections
in Dahlem and other places suddenly increased at a previously unknown rate.[22]

Bonhoeffer eventually left the Confessing church behind, dedicat-
ing himself secretly to the destruction of Hitler. An assassination
plot failed on March 23, 1943; thereafter, Bonhoeffer and others
were imprisoned and executed by the Nazis.[23]

This is not to say that most Confessing church members were
assassins, rebels, or even nonconformists. Conversely, most members of the Confessing church sympathized with the new state—
some were even members of the National Socialist party.[24] This
is the most intriguing feature of the Confessing church: the
Barmen Confession eventually revealed a political dimension that
was contrary to most members' initial political convictions. It
became apparent that National Socialism—and, for that matter,
totalitarianism—and the Christian faith were incompatible.

Conclusion

The most important lesson the German church conflict teaches is
that it failed in the civil and political area. The supreme example is
the church's acquiescence toward the crimes committed against the
Jews, an unspeakable irresponsibility.

This raises the question of the place of humanistic values in
church and theology. It was only a small minority of liberals and
socialists who appreciated the importance of political rights and the
discussion of political forms of state. One of the failures of the
church's conservative majority during the Weimar republic was its
disregard for the relative importance of Enlightenment values, such
as the rights of individuals and democratic process. The reason for
this lay basically in the church's embrace of monarchic, aristocratic,
antidemocratic, and nationalist principles. There is no doubt that
the state-church tradition of Lutheranism was greatly responsible
for the church's lack of political awareness, acumen, and transformative power. Dialectical theology, also, undercut the importance
of these positions, with its radical concentration on theology per

se.[25] The Protestant response to National Socialism, then, reveals the weakness of both a reactionary German church and a narrow, too antiliberal dialectical theology. The role of the liberals and religious socialists had become too diminished to be able to figure significantly in the controversies.

It was only the Confessing church which made a difference in the end. Though the results were weaker than one would have wished, they did come about in large part because of the convictions of the Confessing Church members. It is telling that the theological basis of the political views of both liberals and socialists in the church was generally rather weak. In line with this reasoning, it is interesting to note that those German Christians whose stance toward the Nazis was religiously motivated were most persistent in their support. Therefore, in this sense, belief in God does matter in terms of social consequences. Yet, the variegated responses of Protestantism to National Socialism prove that one should not expect the consequences to be uniform. The consequences vary as much as do the beliefs.

NOTES

1. For a short overview in English of the situation of the Protestant church, see Robert P. Ericksen, *Theologians under Hitler: Gerhard Kittel, Paul Althaus and Emanuel Hirsch* (New Haven: Yale University Press, 1985), pp. 1–27.

2. C.f., Leonore Siegele-Wenschkewitz, *Nationalsozialismus und Kirchen. Religionspolitik von Partei und Staat bis 1935* (Duesseldorf: Droste Verlag, 1974), p. 27.

3. For a thorough delineation of the various facets of German political Protestantism and its members response to National Socialism, see my dissertation: Franz Feige, Responses of German Protestant Theology to National Socialism: Background, Typology, and Evaluation, Ph.D. dissertation, Drew University, 1988.

4. James A. Zabel gives a detailed account of the main groups of the "German Christians" in his *Nazism and the Pastors: A Study of the Ideas of Three "Deutsche Christen" Groups* (Missoula, Mn.: Scholars Press, 1976).

5. The program is available in English language in several versions, e.g., Arthur C. Cochrane, *The Church's Confession under Hitler* (Pittsburgh: Pickwick Press, 1976), pp. 222–3.

6. The uncharacteristic call by the Social Democrats for a similar organization against the German Christians is an indication of the rippling effects of this

politicization. Klaus Scholder, *Die Kirchen und das Dritte Reich,* vol. 1: *Vorgeschichte und Zeit der Illusionen 1918–1934* (Frankfurt: Propylaeen Verlag, 1977), p. 271.

7. Siegfried Leffler, *Christus im Dritten Reich der Deutschen. Wesen, Weg und Ziel der Kirchenbewegung "Deutsche Christen"* (Verlag "Deutsche Christen": Weimar, 1935, p. 29.

8. For a reprint, see Peter Matheson, ed., *The Third Reich and the Christian Churches* (Grand Rapids, Mi.: Eerdmans, 1981), pp. 21–3.

9. See Paul Althaus, e.g., *Religioeser Sozialismus. Grundfragen der christlichen Sozialethik* (Guetersloh: C. Bertelsmann, 1921), p. 79.

10. Kurt Nowak, *Evangelische Kirche und Weimarer Republik. Zum politischen Weg des deutschen Protestantismus zwischen 1918 und 1932* (Goettingen: Vandenhoeck & Ruprecht, 1981), p. 221.

11. Cited by John R. Stumme in his introduction to Paul Tillich, *The Socialist Decision,* trans. Franklin Sherman, (New York: Harper & Row, 1977), p. xiii.

12. Eduard Heimann, "Was will der Nationalsozialismus. Ein Beitrag zur soziologischen Analyse," *Neue Blaetter fuer den Sozialismus* 2 (April 1931): 148.

13. Therefore, it is not by accident that the religious socialist Paul Tillich felt such a strong need to set himself theologically apart from his friend Emanuel Hirsch, who had joined the cause of the German Christians.

14. See, e.g., Rade's concern about the behavior of National Socialists in "Verschiedenes," *Christliche Welt* 44 (1930): 1162.

15. Otto Baumgarten, *Kreuz und Hakenkreuz* (Gotha: Leopold Klotz Verlag, 1926), p. 30.

16. See, e.g., Hans E. Friedrich's evaluation: "Nationalsozialismus," *Christliche Welt* 45 (1931): 407.

17. See the theses of the Young Reformation Movement in *Der deutsche Protestantismus im Jahr der nationalsozialistischen Machtergreifung,* ed. Guenther van Norden (Guetersloh: Guetersloher Verlagshaus Gerd Mohn, 1979), pp. 245–6.

18. See, e.g., one of the most thorough and recent works in English on the German church struggle: Ernst Christian Helmreich, *The German Churches under Hitler: Background, Struggle, and Epilogue* (Detroit: Wayne State University Press, 1979).

19. For an English translation, see Franklin Hamlin Littell, *The German Phoenix: Man and Movements in the Church in Germany* (Garden City, N. Y.: Doubleday 1960), pp. 184–8.

20. Eberhard Bethge, "Troubled Self-Interpretation and Uncertain Reception in the Church Struggle," ed. Franklin H. Littell and Hubert G. Locke (Detroit: Wayne State University Press, 1974), p. 168.

21. Cochrane, op. cit. p. 241.

22. Bethge, "Troubled Self-Interpretation," op. cit., pp. 171–2.

23. Eberhard Bethge, *Dietrich Bonhoeffer: Man of Vision, Man of Courage,* trans. Eric Mosbacher et al. (New York: Harper & Row 1970), p. 830.

24. Friedrich Baumgarten, *Wider die Kirchenkampf-Legenden* (Neuendettelsau: Freimund-Verlag, 1976), pp. 24–37.

25. See especially Klaus Scholder, "Neuere deutsche Geschichte und protestantische Theologie," *Evangelische Theologie* 23 (1963): 510–36.

10

The Interaction Between Social Structures and Belief in God in South Africa

WILLEM NICOL

Those who wish to study the social consequences of belief in God and inversely the theological consequences of social structures will find South Africa a useful laboratory. In 1980, 74.1 percent of all South Africans claimed to be Christians.[1] In the current situation, with social tensions in South Africa running extremely high, leaders on both sides of the power struggle are using Christianity to legitimize their cause and motivate their followers.

The Theoretical Approach

Do people's beliefs and convictions structure their society, or conversely, does their location within their society structure their beliefs and convictions? The debate concerning the relation between the material and the cognitive world is a very old one in the West: examples include Platonism versus Aristotelism, realism versus nominalism, rationalism versus empiricism, idealism versus materialism, sociology of knowledge versus Marxism and neo-Marxism versus positivism. The development of thorough scientific methods for the study of society has largely outdated this debate. What is needed today is a comprehensive systems-analytical model in which the complicated interaction between the cognitive and the material aspects of human life can be analyzed.[2]

To get a mental picture of the basic patterns of this interaction, we must be aware of the flow of influence from the top and bottom and the power struggle in between.

Humankind wants to make sense of the world it lives in. Therefore, it always creates an overarching system of meaning. This system of meaning derives its relative stability from nonnegotiables or axioms which may be referred to as ultimates. From this system of meaning, a normative system is derived. So at the top end, we have *convictions* comprising ultimates, meanings, and norms.

On the opposite end, we have the factor of position in the overall societal power structure. This position determines the material and sociopsychological needs of the people concerned, which leads to what can be called a mental predisposition, that is a general mood of acquiescence, ambition, revolt, or resistance to change. When these predispositions materialize into concrete and specific wants or demands, we call them *vital interests*. These are not the same as needs, because they are needs already interpreted, evaluated, and arranged according to priorities. Convictions, therefore, have a definite influence on the formation of vital interests. The manner in which needs are conceptualized, evaluated, and prioritized to become vital interests is always guided to some degree by convictions.

But since needs usually have stronger influence on the formation of vital interests, a conflict between vital interests and convictions often arises. Normally, people are unable to live with such conflict, so that intense interaction takes place in order to restore at least a superficial harmony. Vital interests have to be justified in terms of convictions. This means that the pursuit of self-interest is justified. Psychologists refer to such a system of self-justification as rationalization. Radical sociology calls it ideology. In institutional terms, we speak of legitimation.

Three basic methods are used to make vital interests seem acceptable:

(1) *The system of convictions* (including meaning and norms) is reinterpreted in such a way that the vital interests appear to be covered. An example of this is the way the notion that Anglo-Saxons were the ten lost tribes of Israel was used to justify the building of the British Empire. Traditional convictions can be manipulated in subtle or massive ways to legitimize vital interests.

If a group of people is religious, what happens to their God? A religious group tends to hold its basic ideas about God as ultimates, so that these ideas normally remain fairly stable even though the related systems of meaning and norms change. The result is that the basic ideas about God are, as it were, wrapped up in a blanket of reinterpreted convictions which are not really in harmony with the former. Such a group will still be able to repeat its basic ideas about God, but these ideas will be inoperative, isolated from the real life of the group. The result is that the religion of this group will become formalized and dead. The system of meaning will, to some extent, also influence the image of God, so that it will be adopted to suit the pursuit of vital interests even though some of the words describing this image may remain the same. The operative image of God may change to such as extent that believers of the same tradition, but belonging to other groups, may experience the religion in question of the group as idolatry.

(2) The perception and interpretation of the society concerned may be twisted in such a way that the pursuit of vital interests can be presented as acceptable. A person's entire perception of his or her society then becomes narrowed by the group he or she belongs to, so that location in society determines what is seen and how it is interpreted. Those aspects of society that seem to legitimize the position and actions of the group are emphasized, and those questioning the group overlooked. One can say that the actual result of religion then is to lead a group into dishonesty. Religion intensifies the group's blindness to the full reality of its society.

(3) It may be maintained that the particular area in which the vital interests operate, for instance business or politics, falls outside the jurisdiction of the prevailing system of convictions. For a religious group, the actual result will be disobedience to its God. Members are dishonest with themselves in the sense that they profess to have a God, but keep Him out of the areas that are vital to them, because other interests are reigning there.[3]

People who utilize such a process of deceptive self-justification live in a climate which is spiritually and psychologically unhealthy. There is no real integration between convictions and actions. The dualism is not admitted, but hidden behind rationalizations.

Our main interest, therefore, should be directed toward the question of how we can restore the reign of God in this entire process. Before we try to formulate positive answers, we must describe the various ways in which this process is functioning in South Africa. So far, I have merely given an impressionistic description of how the process may work in general. Now I shall attempt to give a phenomenological interpretation of the process in that society.

The Oppressive System

Although, at present, whites form only 16 percent of the total population of South Africa, they dominate the rest. The dominant group among these ruling whites are the Afrikaners. A very religious ethnic group, they have always actively justified their politics in terms of Calvinist Christianity.

The Cape of Good Hope was colonized in 1652 by Dutch and German settlers from the lower strata of European society. Most of their descendants took to farming, subjecting the indigenous population as they took over the land. During the nineteenth century, colonial rulers in the cape, especially the British, began to be influenced by the dynamic liberal spirit that prevailed in Europe and to disagree with the feudal-patriarchal mentality of the settlers. The settlers, for their part, saw the British authorities as siding with the subjugated indigenous population, as well as with the hostile black tribes along the eastern border. These experiences led to the formation of the typical Afrikaner *laager* (ethnic-fortress) mentality before 1835.

At this time, a significant part of this settler population decided to emigrate from the cape colony to the interior, beyond British rule. This was done in the faith that God would lead and protect them, as he had the Israelites during their exodus from Egypt. In the long run, however, the Afrikaner community could not escape—the British followed them and colonized the areas to which they had moved. The Afrikaners waged two wars against the colonizers, but were subjugated in 1902. By 1930 the Depression and drought had immersed many of them in dire poverty. However, the biblical message that God aids the weak heartened them, and they clung to the faith that He would liberate them.

At this stage the Afrikaners became aware of the threat of black power. A strong unity was forged, and the underprivileged Afrikaner was uplifted. In 1948 their political party won the general election, and the policy of apartheid was implemented. The Afrikaner party is still in power, and the way in which it has ruled the country during the last decades has been generally harsh, unjust, and un-Christian. Its rationalization for apartheid practices has always been a Christian one. How did the Afrikaners manage to combine such convictions with such oppressive practices?

It is clear that all three basic methods of justification of vital interest have been functioning. It is also interesting to note that the course of history forced the justification process to take different forms from decade to decade. Four types of ideology emerged.[4]

(1) *Lordship.* Since the seventeenth century, a basic idea has been that the whites must rule over other races. Canaan "will be a slave to his brothers" (Gen. 9:25) has been misinterpreted to legitimize this attitude.

(2) *Guardianship.* As it became increasingly difficult to hold the former position in the light of Christian teaching about the basic equality of all human beings, the ideology was slightly shifted to maintain that

the whites had to lead the blacks like parents until they became
mature enough to care for themselves. The task of the church to
spread Christianity, as well as many other Christian convictions,
was used to support this.

(3) *Separate development.* As soon as it became clear that blacks in South
Africa and throughout the world were demanding equal treatment,
the rationalization had to make a huge leap. To accept that blacks had
"grown up" and were entitled to equal rights, would mean that a
small minority of whites would have to surrender their power to the
black majority. To avoid this, the theory was then evolved that
blacks had to be helped to develop to their full potential, but that
they should achieve this in their own little states.

The justification process became more intricate. Whereas in ideology one and two, the reinterpretation of convictions more or less
sufficed, in this case the perception of reality also had to be twisted.
Convictions were reinterpreted by alleging that the Bible demanded
racial purity. An impossible idea was broadcast, namely that the
millions of blacks already engaged in the cities could be induced to
move back to their homelands, where they would be able to develop. The fact that these homelands comprised only 13 percent of
the land, while the people expected to live there comprised about
two-thirds of the total population, was generally overlooked. That
these homelands included some of the best farming land in the
country and did not include the large semi desert areas, however,
was constantly emphasized.

(4) *State Security.* History shattered the ideology of separate development. The number of blacks in the cities continually increased.
Because of the uneven distribution of political power and economic
privilege, a revolutionary climate gradually developed. The white
government suppressed it. At the same time, the whites accepted the
permanency of the blacks in the white-dominated parts of the country, and slowly induced some reforms to appease black demands.

The justification process began to function to make vital interests
acceptable. Christianity was used to combat communism and revolutionary chaos. The Christian God was the god of law and order,
the One on the side of the South African government in its defense
against a total onslaught. Social reality was also reinterpreted. Small
reforms were portrayed as giant concessions so that the growing
dissatisfaction among blacks could be seen as an extremely radical,
revolutionary spirit designed to destroy the entire country. The
widespread dissatisfaction of the blacks was portrayed as the work

of a small number of agitators. To defend against growing religious criticism of white domination, religion and politics were separated—and religious leaders were warned to keep out of politics.

Lately, the reforms of the government have been closely connected to religion. Internal and external political and economic pressure on the government has increased immensely, accelerating the reform process. The conservative part of the white electorate tends to oppose reform, but Christian convictions concerning justice and love are used to support it. The problem is the reforms are generally "too little, too late." Their strong Christian justification, however, makes their rejection by the Left seem un-Christian.

If one asks whether influence in the opposite direction, from convictions to actions, can also be discerned, the answer is more difficult. Actions can always be interpreted in many ways. Some of the churches at the heart of Afrikanerdom have been very active in evangelizing the blacks, even after the emerging black churches began to oppose the government. Church and state have spent large amounts of money to alleviate all kinds of suffering. On the personal level, whites have frequently tried to be very good to blacks, albeit in a paternalistic manner. Of course, all these actions have also served selfish vital interests, but it seems impossible to deny that convictions also played a role in motivating them.

On the whole, however, religion functioned in this historical process to intensify racial problems. Selfish vital interests modified religion so that it in turn strengthened the pursuit of vital interests and heightened selfishness. Because of the religious legitimation of apartheid policies, the ruling group has become self-righteous, so that they are unwilling to see the damage their policies has wrought. Instead, they remain rigid and harsh. Religion has simply aggravated the blindness of the Afrikaners. While it becomes clearer and clearer that their policies are simply not producing the results they planned for, many have persisted in believing that these policies will eventually work. All men have a tendency to be blind to their own failures, and if they also believe that what they are attempting is God's will and that God will let them succeed in the end, they become even blinder. In this way religious ideology has tempted the Afrikaners to "take-off" from social reality and to live in a false dream.

One is tempted to ask whether it would have been better if the Afrikaners had had no religion and had therefore been more in touch with worldly and human realities? This question has a catch in it, however, because all human beings have a desire to make sense of their world, and create a system of meaning based on certain ultimates. Would the Afrikaners have been closer to reality and more humane if they had had another set of ultimates? Where do we find ultimates that will truly sensitize us to the world? Are there other ultimates which are more resistant to manipulation than Christian ultimates? Or does the true God always leave humans the freedom to choose whether they will manipulate his image or submit to his gentle voice?

The Revolutionary System.

The spirit of revolution has become widespread among the blacks of South Africa in the last three decades. It is striking that their religious leaders play an important role in the revolutionary movement. By this I do not mean that they preach or practice violence, but that they function as leaders in the black movements that pressure society to change its power structure.

Although many blacks are still moderate, a radical black theology has also arisen since the seventies, and it is not difficult to understand its historical context. The black experience has been not only one of oppression but one of oppression by a state professing to be Christian! For the non-Christians, this need not have caused a problem, but to the 74.1 percent who claimed to be Christian in the 1980 census, it must have caused distress![5] It is not surprising then that blacks have tended to construct a theology which is the antithesis of that preached in the Afrikaner churches.

Another factor that has alienated blacks from orthodox Christianity is its emphasis on reconciliation between the races rather than social justice. Church leaders tell blacks that they should be reconciled to their oppressor and should remain calm about their grievances, trust in that justice will be restored in the long run. This is not a true Christian message, since the Bible teaches that reconciliation must inevitably lead to justice. This false, cheap imitation has functioned as part of the repressive system, and blacks have sensed it. It is completely understandable that they feel a need for a different kind of theology.

The black theology that has arisen out of this has many nuances. Here, I concentrate on its more radical side. From the black perspective, it seems very clear that the Afrikaner churches had reconstructed their religious convictions in such a way as to support their un–Christian, oppressive policies. Black Christians were very sensitive to the fact that the image of God had been tarnished, and they accused the Afrikaner church leaders of heresy, idolatry, and even diabolism.[6] The Afrikaner could not understand this accusation at all, but this is not surprising. A group is usually unconscious of how its vital interests influence its convictions, with the result that the dialogue about convictions between two groups with opposing vital interests is like the dialogue of the deaf. If we keep in mind that the system of meaning by which people live is always influenced by their vital interests, accusations of idolatry and diabolism at least seem to be exaggerated. If, on the other hand, the pain of oppression that is justified by twisted systems of meaning is remembered, these exaggerated accusations can be understood.

Black theology went further than rejecting the God of the oppressor: it also clarified its own convictions about God. It reacted against the mild, reconciling God of the mainline churches and proclaimed a God of justice, judgment, and anger. Because of the demonic character of the present political system, no compromise with it whatsoever can be acceptable to this God. His judgment is that it must be replaced. Revolutionary violence against it is thusly legitimized. God sides with the oppressed in their struggle for liberation, and the church is challenged not to be a third force, but to cooperate with the people.[7]

Is there a conflict between convictions and vital interests in black theology, and by what process is it resolved? Black Theologians know that they have developed a new theological method. They continually stress that they are involved in contextual theology. By this they mean that theology should consciously be practiced within a social context, that the primary point of departure should not be a holy look or certain abstract principles, but the social circumstances of the group. This means that the influence of vital interests on religious convictions is openly accepted. This is an honest stand, and much better than one in which vital interests operate without acknowledgment. The question is, however, does this open the door to selfish vital interests which determine theology and reduce it again to a mere process of self-justification?

The first two methods by which vital interests are legitimized can be discerned in the current radical black theology in South Africa. The traditional Christian system of meaning has clearly been adapted. The biblical Exodus motif is strongly emphasized, while the biblical message about the sinfulness of all human actions is only rarely applied to the liberation movements. The biblical invitation to the poor to believe that God is standing with them in their suffering is carried further. Now the poor and oppressed *are* the people of God even before they believe it.

Social realities are also reinterpreted to suit the pursuit of vital interests. Society is uncritically analyzed according to Marxian dogma. It is, for instance, accepted that justice can only come from the underdog.[8] In light of the distribution of power in South Africa, the strong international, political, and economic pressure on the government, and the extent to which human suffering has already in some ways been alleviated by those in power, this surely is a one-sided social analysis.

There need be no doubt that Christian convictions are also influenced by radical blacks. Their patience and self-control in the face of adversity is astonishing. Their strength in demanding justice is reminiscent of the Old Testament prophets. Again, however, there exists the uneasy feeling that religion is playing a harmful role in the whole process. Isn't it drawing black theologians away from self-criticism and realism? By connecting the devil to their opponents and God to their own cause, they fail to see the flaws in their own struggle and the possibilities of more justice in the present social system. That religion should motivate the struggle for more justice is good, but where do we find ultimates that will at the same time help people to be more sensitive to human realities?

Conclusions

We have compared the oppressive and revolutionary theology in South Africa and have seen that in both cases the influence of vital interests on convictions is strong. Our study of the process by which vital interests are justified in terms of convictions left us with the uneasy impression that the availability of religious concepts to assist this process may be harmful for the humanization of South Africa. Vital interests manipulate religion, and it in turn strengthens vital interests, with the result that group-centeredness and selfishness is enhanced, while the perception of reality is blurred.

Convictions about God are drawn into ever-new syncretisms in the sense that they are integrated with conceptual systems in which vital interests are justified. By this justification process, God is coopted as a partner in the struggle. Gods with opposing characteristics result within the same religious tradition. It is clear that, if there is a living God, these twisted and coopted gods must be far removed from Him. These false gods function as a wall between believers and the true God. If man can have any kind of contact with a living God, the spirituality in which these coopted gods function must, in comparison, be eliminated.

How can these problems be solved? We have already seen that trying to do away with religion will be of no avail, because people without religion have other ultimates which may also be made to function in harmful ways. What is needed for a solution is (a) ultimates that will really inspire the humanization of society and (b) ultimates that function in such a way that their influence on people is stronger than the manipulative influence of people on them. These needs will be simultaneously fulfilled if we can come in contact with the living God. If He lives, the direct contact with Him will bring us under his power, and keep us from manipulating Him. I believe that the true God will always direct us toward real humanization.

The question is, therefore, how contact with the true God can be experienced? In truth, God reaches out to us, so we need not go to Him. He is so powerful that He can liberate us from the bondage of our vital interests, so that we can allow Him to purify them and bring them into harmony with Himself. Then we shall be liberated from contorting our convictions and our perceptions of reality in order to justify our vital interests. We shall be freed from the frightful obligation to justify ourselves before God, because He comes to us to accept and renew us. As a Christian, I believe that He sent his son and his spirit to us to justify us. This is the power that expels the smokescreen. As soon as I realize that I need not justify myself, I am liberated from myself in order to be renewed.

The different aspects of the process by which a believer is liberated from self-justification and ideology can be seen. Free grace enables him or her to accept other believers, directs him or her toward people and moves him or her to solidarity with the poor.

Free grace means the unconditional acceptance of the unacceptable. I receive it from God and give it to other people, beginning with those who are my brothers and sisters in Christ. The whites did not really show the blacks grace in South Africa, and therefore many of the churches split up into factions. At present, however, grace is enabling some of the churches to begin restoring the unity of the body of Christ. Therefore, an impossible community will ensue. Those who start functioning as one will have to find out in church that they are not fully one, as they are one another's opponents in the social struggle. If the unity functions in the right way, reconciliation should be accompanied by confrontation. In this way, ideologies are filtered out. Through the eyes of my oppressed brother, I, as oppressor, can begin to see how I have twisted my convictions and my perception of society in order to justify myself. I see how selfish my vital interests have been, and my brother helps me to broaden them so that I develop vital interests that are to the advantage of my country and the world as a whole. Whereas racial identity dominates the actions of many South Africans, the experience of the unity of the church helps some others to broaden their experience of their identity in order to incorporate wider aspects, like being South Africans *and* world citizens.

That this is not mere theory can be clearly seen in the present South African scene. There are whites who oppose the oppressive system by standing in solidarity with the oppressed, and blacks who are not overpowered by the natural tendency simply to mirror white theology in black theology. What enabled them to swim against such strong streams? One of the answers usually is that they have had open contact with Christians.

Free grace does not only direct us toward cobelievers, but also toward people in general, and the realities of their circumstances. Free grace means that God loves me unconditionally. To know God means in the first place not to cling to convictions and concepts, but to be filled by his love. This has one unavoidable result, namely that one wants to love others, which means to serve them in order to enable them to live a more human life. Serving means taking reality seriously and discerning the best possibilities for improving circumstances among the needy. Therefore, the true God drives me out of my concepts and ideologies toward real people. I cannot live without a system of meaning, but when I experience God's presence, I am liberated from making my own meaning through concepts, to finding meaning in free service. I will always have my ideas and convictions, but the living God helps me to realize how relative and preliminary they are, so that I can continually adapt them to the demands of service rather than sacrificing people on their altar.

The Bible guides us out of spirituality in the unworldly sense toward a worldly realism. Paul's first letter to the Corinthians is a striking example. High spirituality caused them to act unlovingly and without realism about the limited possibilities of the world. Converted men, for example, wanted to divorce their wives when they did not accept the Christian message. Paul warns these Christians that they should have a realistic respect for social institutions like marriage, as rejecting such institutions may cause more suffering. He stresses that the main task of the Christian is to love others as they are. (I Cor. 13).

In stressing realism, I do not mean to exclude the spiritual. People have real spiritual needs which are just as important as their physical needs, and in our service we should take this into account.

Free grace also moves us toward solidarity with the poor. The love of God is all-encompassing love, reaching down to the lowest sinners and poor people. The Bible assures us that God is not only a God of light, giving blessings to us, but also a God of darkness who is very close to those suffering. Just as He stretched out his hand to the slaves in Egypt, He moves close to all who are in need now. This sheds light on what the loyalty of Christians should be like. Their loyalty to the weakest in their society should always be stronger than their loyalty to their own natural groups. This does not mean that they must take sides with any liberation movement. As we have seen, liberation movements are also in danger of forgetting the true needs of humanization. Attaining political power frequently becomes more important to them than the real needs of the poorest people. Ideas about liberation can also become an altar on which the weakest are sacrificed.[9] But solidarity with the oppressed means that Christians should completely break away from the strategy of the oppressor and stand as close as possible to the oppressed in working and struggling for more justice. Christians have to identify with the cause of the oppressed in so far as it is a righteous cause.

All this will happen when we are open toward the living God and are guided by Him. We who are considering this should realize that this openness is the central challenge. God is "shy," He is not obtrusive, He does not impose Himself on us. Convictions about Him can be manipulated as easily as any other convictions. Human selfishness is so strong that religion is in any case usually manipulated for the sake of vital interests. How can we escape? We cannot: only God can set us free. How? We cannot give the answer, as He has his own methods. As soon as we realize that we do not know, and cannot give saving ideas and formulations to one another, we are at the point of opening up to the real God.

NOTES

1. G.C. Oosthuizen et. al., *Religion, Intergroup Relations and Social Change in S.A.* (Work committee: Religion of Human Sciences Research Council Investigation into Intergroup Relations, Pretoria, 1985), p. 19.

2. Cf. Klaus Nurnberger, *Power, Beliefs and Equity; Economic Potency Structures in S.A. and Their Interaction with Patterns of Conviction in the Light of a Christian Ethic* (Research report on 04/P017 submitted to the Human Sciences Research Council, Pretoria, 1984), pp. 113–25.

   I am deeply indebted to Professor Nurnberger for many of my insights concerning a systems-analytical model. The new ERA leaflet explaining the theme for Group VI of this conference seems to be biased toward an idealist position in that it stresses "the social consequences of belief in God" and only leaves room for the possibility that these consequences "may be inhibited or facilitated by social structures." What about the possibility that social structures do more, namely form or reform the belief in God itself?

3. Nurnberger, op. cit., pp. 119 ff.

4. Ibid., pp. 142 ff.

5. Oosthuizen et. al., p. 22.

6. Cf. John de Gruchy and Charles Villa-Vicencio, *Apartheid Is a Heresy* (Guildford: Lutterworth, 1983), p. 179.

   Leaders of the Dutch Reformed Mission Church, a daughter church of the largest Afrikaner church, spoke about heresy and idolatry. The Kairos Document, issued by a number of radical theologians in September 1985, referred to the worshiping of the devil (cf. *Journal of Theology for Southern Africa* 53 [December 1985]: 66 ff.).

7. This is a very short interpretation of the Kairos Document (*Journal THSA* 53:61–81)

8. Ibid., p. 70.

9. Cf. Peter Berger, *Pyramids of Sacrifice* (Middlesex, England: Pelican Books, 1977).

11

Liberation Theology, Judaism, and the Kingdom of God

DANIEL COHN-SHERBOK

Recently Reform rabbis have been in the forefront of Jewish-Christian relations. Such writers as Samuel Sandmel, Jacob Petuchowski, Eugene Borowitz, and Walter Jacob have in different ways stressed that Jews and Christians must learn from one another about their respective faiths. In such an interfaith encounter, a number of vital issues have been put on the agenda, among them: New Testament anti-Semitism, Christian theology and the Jewish covenant; Jewish views of Christianity; Jesus and the Pharisaic tradition; and theology and the Holocaust.[1] Yet there is one aspect of current Christian theology that has been neglected in this discussion. In South America, as well as in other countries of the Third World, a new Christian theological development has been taking place in the last few decades. Liberation theology, as it is often called, has captured the imagination of Roman Catholics and Protestants. Combining theory with practice, this movement attempts to forge a new vision of the Christian message. Most importantly for Jewish-Christian dialogue, liberation theologians have gone back to their Jewish roots in the Old Testament. In particular, these theologians utilize the motif of the Exodus to explain God's redemption. Thus Christian writers find themselves using the same vocabulary as their Jewish brethern, and this paves the way for a mutual quest to create a better world.

The Exodus Experience

In presenting their message of hope, liberation theologians repeatedly emphasize the centrality of the deliverance from Egypt. G. Gutierrez writes,

> The Exodus experience is paradigmatic. It remains vital and contemporary due to similar historical experiences which the People of God undergo . . . it structures our faith in the gift of the Father's love. In

Christ and through the Spirit, men are becoming one in the very
heart of history.[2]

Thus these Christian theologians look to the history of the Jewish
people for inspiration in their struggle against exploitation and
oppression in contemporary society, and the biblical story of the
Exodus from Egypt provides a basis for a critique of traditional
Christian thought and modern society.

In Egypt, the ancient Israelites were exploited and oppressed. As
E. Tamez notes, this experience involved a degradation so severe
that it caused the people to turn to God for deliverance.[3] The
Egyptians overwhelmed the Hebrew slaves with work; according to
the book of Exodus, they "made their lives bitter with hard service,
in mortar and brick, and in all kinds of work in the field; in all their
work they made them serve with rigour" (Ex. 1:14). Such affliction
caused the people to cry out to God for liberation; in response God
decreed: "I have seen the affliction of my people who are in Egypt,
and have heard their cry because of their taskmasters; I know their
sufferings, and I have come down to deliver them out of the hand of
the Egyptians" (Ex. 3:7–8).

When the demand for the freedom of the Israelite nation was
made, Pharoah rebuked Moses and Aaron. "Why do you take the
people away from their work?," he asked. "Get to your burdens"
(Ex. 5:4). Pharoah's response to the people's request was to intensify
their suffering: The same day Pharoah commanded the taskmasters
of the people and their foremen: "You shall no longer give the people
straw to make bricks, as heretofore; let them go and gather straw for
themselves. But the number of bricks which they made heretofore
you shall lay upon them, you shall by no means lessen it" (Ex. 5:6–8).
Such affliction, however, was to no avail, and to diffuse the impend-
ing conflict Pharoah granted the Israelites various concessions. The
ancient Israelites refused all these offers. As E. Tamez notes:

> the dialogue breaks off (10.28–29); the confrontation intensifies and
> leads finally to the liberation of the enslaved people. If the Hebrews
> had accepted Pharoah's concessions, the struggle would not have
> become increasingly radical and the Hebrews would not have gained
> their freedom.[4]

A Liberation Theology

In the exposition of the biblical account of the Exodus, liberation
theologians emphasize a theme which has become one of the central

features of liberation theology: God is on the side of the oppressed. "If there is a single passage that encapsulates the liberation themes of the Bible," R.M. Brown writes, "it is the exodus story, describing a God who takes sides, intervening to free the poor and oppressed."[5] The Book of Exodus declares that God hears the groaning of the people and remembers the covenant He has made with them. God takes sides with his people, declaring that they will be liberated from their oppressors: Moses is to lead them out of bondage. From this act of deliverance, Third-World Christians derive a message of hope: If God was on the side of the poor in ancient Israel, surely He still takes sides with the downtrodden. Thus if God has a bias today it is with the poor and oppressed and against the pharoahs of the modern world. Who are these pharoahs? According to R.M. Brown they are

> the tiny minority at home who are in collusion against the great majority; they are the churches and churchpersons who give support to such oligarchies; and they are the rich and powerful from other nations who keep national oligarchies in power, thereby becoming complicit in the ongoing exploitation of the poor.[6]

In the view of liberation theologians God works to liberate those who are oppressed by injustice. And those who seek to be co-workers with God in creating a just society must side with whatever forces are working for the liberation of mankind.

Liberated theologians stress that the Exodus was not simply an event in the history of the Jewish people; instead, it evoked a deep response on the part of future generations. As J.S. Croatto writes: "This word [Exodus] was recharged with fresh meanings by successive hermeneutical re-readings up to the time that it was fixed permanently as expressing a whole world-view in the Exodus account in its present form."[7] The profundity of the Exodus, therefore, consists in its significance for later generations; the past holds a promise for those who understand its relevance. The Exodus is fraught with meaning: For Third-World theologians, it is an account of liberation of oppressed peoples. From this perspective they believe it is possible to understand the plight of those who are presently afflicted—peoples in economic, political, social, or cultural bondage.[8]

In this context, liberation theologians point out Moses' crucial role in the process of liberation. E. Dussel, for example, begins his study of the history and theology of liberation by focusing on Moses' call to lead his people out of captivity. Moses fled to the desert because he had killed an Egyptian. He lived comfortably as a herdsman with his wife, his father-in-law, and his flocks. But one day he heard God speak to him out of a bush. Here God revealed Himself to Moses: Moses heard God's command: "Liberate my people out of Egypt." Established in the totality of fleshly, daily life, Moses responded by becoming the liberator of his people. We, too, are being called continually, Dussel contends, but we do not hear anything. Yet like Moses, we must awaken ourselves to the divine command. As Dussel writes: "God . . . keeps on revealing himself to us as the Other who summons us. He is the first Other. If I do not listen to my fellowmen in bondage, then I am not listening to God either."[9]

Liberation theologians also utilize the Exodus narrative to explain that God guides the destiny of the persecuted. In the flight from Egypt, the Bible stresses that God leads the Israelites: He does not take them out by way of the land of the Philistines—although that is near—"Lest the people repent when they see war and return to Egypt." Instead, "God led the people round by way of the wilderness towards the Red Sea" (Ex. 13:17). When the Egyptian army attempts to capture the Israelites, God intervenes so that they are saved. Once Israel has crossed the Red Sea, God sustains them in their wanderings: He gives them sweet water at Marah; He sends them mana and quail in the desert; He gives them safe passage through the Transjordan; He delivers the Amorite kings into the hands of the Israelites. Not only does God deliver and protect his people, He also leads them to their own land where they are no longer oppressed. Before Moses' death, God proclaims to Joshua: "I myself will be with you" (Deut. 31:32). He will be with Joshua as He was with Moses. The conquest is thus the second stage of God's deliverance.

According to some liberation theologians, a central element of this process of liberation is the use of violence. Paradoxically, love and virtue are interconnected, as J.S. Croatto writes:

> Love can be violent when the loved object cannot be retained or recovered except by force. . . . The history of the Exodus is eminently instructive in this respect. God acts with vigour . . . "I will bring you out from under the burdens of the Egyptians (Exod. 6.6); "I know that the king of Egypt will not let you go unless compelled by a mighty hand (Exod. 3.19).[10]

Here oppression is opposed by a liberating act which is violent— God has acted in this manner because there was no other option. At first, He sent Moses to try to persuade Pharoah to release the

Hebrews, but Pharoah's refusal left God no choice. As the upholder of justice and freedom, He intervened to save his people; violence was inevitably required. As Croatto writes:

> Justice is a radical good that demands of love (paradoxical as it may seem) a violent action. This is a truth so limpid that it shocks us because we have disfigured the image of love. Freedom, for its part, is a gift so intimate and exigent that, when it is obscured or lost, it requires liberation at any price.[11]

As we can see, the Exodus is a pivotal event for liberation theology; it is regarded as the salvation experience par excellence. To the Hebrew mind, salvation involves a historical experience on the political and social plane; God is viewed as saviour because He acts in human history. In the unfolding of the divine plan of deliverance, God reveals Himself through Moses, and, as Croatto notes, "Moses [has] to assume that historical and personal vocation to freedom."[12] So, too, Jesus is viewed by liberation theologians as an emissary of God; he is the typological correlate of Moses. The Exodus experience is, therefore, a central event in the life of the Jewish nation, and it serves as a fundamental model of divine activity in liberation theology. The departure from Egypt, as A. Fierro states;

> is much more than a mere image designed to enrich theological representations; it became the primeval and fundamental happening of the history of divine revelation itself. The Exodus comes to constitute the prototype of divine revelation, the privileged moment in which God once manifested himself and now continues to do the same.[13]

Within this framework, a number of liberation theologians connect the Eucharist with the struggle of the Jewish people for liberation. Like Moses, Jesus found his people oppressed and persecuted and, therefore, took on the task of liberation. He protested against injustice and iniquity; He sought to break down barriers between social classes and between Israel and the gentiles. Carrying out such a ministry, He had to face great hostility, and according to T. Balasuriya, it was then that He established the Eucharist.[14] He realized He would soon leave his followers, and He wanted them to have a symbol of his work. To do this, He used the traditional Jewish Passover meal, giving it new meaning. As Balasuriya states,

> To Jesus' mind the Eucharist was essentially action-oriented. It was a prayer and an offering in the midst of his public life at the height of his involvement in the political and social issues of the time. It signified

his irrevocable contestation of the religious leaders of his people and the narrowness of their message.[15]

Conclusion

Confronting oppression in modern society, liberation theologians rely on this category of Old Testament theology: ancient Egypt is not a civilization past, it lives as a symbol of oppression in the modern world. D. Solle, for example, contends that Christians living in today have become contemporary Egyptians. "We have adjusted ourselves, to the Egyptian lifestyle," she writes. "We have adopted the basic beliefs of the Egyptians."[16] Furthermore, we have tried to Egyptize the whole world: "We see countries that have not yet adjusted to the capitalistic lifestyle and value system as not yet developed."[17] Yet, we in the modern world fail to recognize the fact that we are oppressors. On the contrary, Solle advances, "we have adapted ourselves to it to such an extent that in the very midst of Egypt, under the domination of Pharoah, we feel quite at home."[18] God as emancipator can liberate us from such tyranny and lead us to a vision of a world freed from exploitation. "To remember Jerusalem in the midst of Egypt," Solle writes, "means defining our need for liberation and denouncing the Egypt in which we live."[19] Through the Exodus experience, God has spoken to all men: in making the cause of the oppressed His own, God reveals that He is working toward the creation of a just society. The Exodus is the long march toward the promised land—a world free from misery and alienation.

From this brief survey, it is clear that the experience of the Exodus is typologically significant for liberation theology; it is the paradigm of divine liberation of the oppressed and persecuted. Like Jews, liberation theologians have found renewed strength and hope in the message of the Exodus, and in this way Jews and Christians share a common biblical heritage and vision of the transformation of society. The Exodus event unites them in a common hope and aspiration for the triumph of justice. Remembering the divine deliverance of the ancient Israelites, they can work together for the goal of the emancipation of the enslaved. Ideally, such a shared vision should enable both the Jews and Christians to set aside previous theological barriers to interfaith encounter and concentrate on a shared hope for the creation of a better world. Instead of rejecting Jesus as a blasphemous heretic, Jews can see in Jesus' life a reflection of Moses' liberating mission. In this fashion, the Jesus of the New Testament can be understood as Jesus the Jew, who, carrying on the tradition of Moses and the prophets, struggled to redeem the persecuted. Here, then, in this Christian interpretation of the Exodus is a link which can draw Jews and Christians together in a mutual quest for the elimination of oppression and injustice in the modern world.

NOTES

1. See J. Pawlikowski, *What Are They Saying About Christian-Jewish Relations?* (New York: Paulist, 1980)

2. G. Gutierrez, *A Theology of Liberation* (New York: Orbis, 1981), p. 159.

3. E. Tamez, *Bible of the Oppressed* (New York: Orbis, 1982).

4. Ibid., p. 44.

5. R.M. Brown, *Theology in A New Key* (Philadelphia: Fortress, 1978), p. 88.

6. Ibid., pp. 89–90.

7. J.S. Croatto, *Exodus* (New York: Orbis, 1981), p. 14.

8. Ibid., p. 15

9. E. Dussel, *History and The Theology of Liberation* (New York: Orbis, 1976), p. 7.

10. J.S. Croatto, op. cit., p. 29.

11. Ibid., p. 31.

12. Ibid., p. 28.

13. A. Fierro, *The Militant Gospel* (New York: Orbis 1977), p. 141.

14. T. Balasuriya, *The Eucharist and Human Liberation* (London: Orbis, 1977).

15. Ibid., p. 17.

16. D. Solle, "Thou Shalt Have No Other Jesus Before Me," *The Challenge of Liberation Theology* (New York: Orbis, 1981), p. 5.

17. Ibid.

18. D. Solle, *Choosing Life* (London: SCM, 1981), p. 1.

19. Ibid., p. 4.

12

Markets and Morality: The Catholic Bishops' Pastoral Letter on the Economy

FREDERICK J. MAHER

The Catholic bishops' pastoral letter on the American economy, *Economic Justice for All: Catholic Social Teaching and the U. S. Economy,* and the response to it by the self-appointed Lay Commission on Catholic Social Teaching and the U. S. Economy, will be the focus of this chapter. It will be shown that the Lay Commission proceeds from a model that essentially renders moral judgments irrelevant to the discussion of public policy.

The Bishop's pastoral takes the form of laying out what are described as moral standards derived from traditional Catholic teaching on the economy. These are used as the basis for judging a variety of conditions that currently obtain in the United States and in that country's relations with the rest of the world. Among other things, the bishops mention the importance of "fundamental fairness in all agreements and exchanges between individuals or private social groups."[1] They see a moral obligation for all to be active and productive participants in the life of society. A normative requirement is the establishment of a floor of material well-being on which all can stand. They see the "ultimate injustice" to be when a person or group "is actively treated or passively abandoned as if they [sic] were non-members of the human race."[2] These forms of "marginalization and powerlessness" are seen as socially created and are therefore a "form of social sin." A moral requirement exists to work to establish "minimum levels of participation in the life of the human community."

Probably the most striking of the moral priorities is the "obligation to evaluate social and economic activity from the viewpoint of the poor and the powerless." This "option for the poor" is hardly the primary basis for evaluating policy proposals in the United States or anywhere else. The poor and the powerless are, by definition, not major players in the public policy game. The bishops do soften the radical sound of this by asserting that the "option for the poor is not an adversarial slogan that pits one group or class against another." Instead "the deprivation and powerlessness of the poor wounds the whole community."[3]

In the area of policy specifics, the bishops call for a true full-employment policy. The government should see to it that "everyone who is seeking a job" can find employment. In other words, the current acceptance of unemployment rates in the 6 to 7 percent range as "full employment" should be regarded as "intolerable."[4]

Noting that according to the government's own figures, one in seven Americans is poor, the bishops assert that dealing with poverty is a matter of urgency, and not something to be dealt with after other problems have been addressed. The degree of inequality between the "haves" and "have-nots" is found to be unacceptable.[5]

The bishops endorse full-employment programs and income-support programs for those who will not be helped by job programs. They endorse efforts to end discrimination in jobs on the basis of race or sex. Special attention, they add, should be paid to the education of the children of the poor.[6]

The bishops specifically endorse farming as an occupation and as a way of life. This is also linked to an effective stewardship of natural resources.[7]

The international situation is noted with the grim reminder that 800 million people in the world "live in absolute poverty beneath any rational definition of human decency." This leads to a call for a just international order and a recognition of the link between foreign and domestic policies. Applying the preferential option for the poor in a world with 800 million in absolute poverty is obviously a daunting task. The bishops do not attempt a full-blown analysis of that situation. There are perfunctory remarks about the inability of the United States to save the world by itself, and recognition that Third World countries are not "entirely innocent with respect to their own failures or totally helpless to achieve their own destinies."[8]

The bishops do note that armaments spending diverts resources from human needs to security needs. They note that in 1985 the United States budgeted twenty times as much for defense as for foreign assistance (and most of the latter took the form of military assistance).[9]

The most serious challenge to the bishop's pastoral letter on the economy has been the pamphlet *Toward the Future: Catholic Social Thought and the U. S. Economy—A Lay Letter*. The importance assigned to this by its sponsors, a self-appointed lay commission, can be seen in the fact that the Lay Letter was rushed out as a sort of preemptive public relations strike. It was issued after the first draft of the bishops' letter was released, but before the final draft.[10]

The emphasis in this document is on liberty, competitive markets, and the absence of any governmental intervention in a free economy. Little attention is paid to the fact that free and unbridled competition leads to losers, and that life can be very difficult for them.

The Poverty Issue

Most importantly, the Lay Letter does not come to grips with the "preferential option for the poor" that is central to the bishop's document. Since the economic model that the letter embraces rests on the assumption that the self-regulating economic system will not only clear all markets, but will also clear problems such as substandard wages, unemployment, and assorted forms of economic discrimination, it leads almost inevitably to the idea that economic losers have only themselves to blame.

The bishops, on the other hand, start from the position that there are conditions that exist in society that are not simply the fault of the people who suffer because of them. Despite their emphasis on the importance of liberty, free-market enthusiasts see the self-regulating character of markets as leaving people with the choice of acting rationally (and benefitting), or acting nonrationally (and suffering some deprivation). In such a world, only stupid people lose out, and all who lose are, by definition, stupid. Thus nonrational economic actors suffer from self-inflicted problems.

In terms of the price-auction model, economic actors are basically seen as having a choice between acting rationally under the circumstances that prevail or making nonrational choices which will in the long or short run, impose on them the costs of inefficiency, lower wages, reduced profits, or other negative outcomes. These negative outcomes will serve as an incentive to their victims, causing them to make more rational choices next time or to undo what they have done—if that is still possible. In a perfect world, where there is sufficient knowledge to make rational choices, and where there is sufficient competition to prevent small groups from rigging the market, it might indeed follow that the inexorable market forces would prevent serious economic problems from developing. However, in the real world, it is often the case that prices can be fixed, that there is collusion between putative competitors, and that economic actors, especially the less well placed, suffer from a decided lack of information about available alternatives.

Capital and Labor

The Lay Letter also has some trouble with the relations between labor and capital. It notes that both Abraham Lincoln and John Paul II spoke of "the priority of labor over capital." Since this points toward a path the authors of the Lay Letter do not intend to take, some fancy intellectual footwork is performed. It is granted that "the human person is indeed prior to inanimate capital." Capital, however, "is not only inanimate; knowledge and skills, habits and attitudes are also forms of capital." (Presumably, the authors of the letter would grant that those are also forms of labor, even though their words imply that capital has a monopoly on knowledge and skills.) In a neat twist, the "fact of widespread unemployment" shows that, far from being "prior to capital," labor requires "new investment as its own prior cause." After thus giving the moral priority to capital, it is concluded that "capital and labor are both human."[11]

It would be more accurate to say that capital and labor are both abstractions, and that the laborer is always human, but the capitalist, in the late twentieth century at least, usually is a corporate entity of some sort. The nominal owners of the corporations, the stockholders, are basically gamblers rather than entrepreneurs. The letter has no section on gamblers. It does, however, devote a section to "Entrepreneurs."[12] It is easy to depict the entrepreneur as a moral paragon whose activities produce much socially beneficial fallout. It is more difficult to argue for the redeeming social values of gamblers. Stockholders own pieces of paper. They bought that paper in the hope that it would appreciate in value. Words like "creativity," "energetic," and "hard working" can be applied to entrepreneurs. They are out of place when applied to stockholders.

The laborer cannot be physically separated from the job. Laborers not only hold jobs, but they have families, live in neighborhoods, and establish communities. Capital, on the other hand, knows no community and has no nationality. It can be deployed anywhere in a country or in the world. Capital has mobility. Those corporate executives who make the decisions to move investments across

national boundaries do not need to move from their own neighborhoods and communities. On the other hand, laborers whose jobs
are destroyed by such capital investments are effectively precluded
from moving with their jobs. Indeed, a major motive for much of
the investment that moves across national boundaries is precisely to
terminate the jobs of relatively more highly paid labor. That this is a
rational action for corporate executives to take is not in dispute.
Whether such actions raise moral questions *is,* however.

It is not clear that the authors of the Lay Letter perceive a moral
issue here. Speaking of those who have lost jobs in this manner it is
noted that "business leaders can and should give higher priority to
the long-term security of their associates in the work force." But
there are "costs in doing so." The costs will impair "economic
dynamism [so] prudence is required."[13]

As is customary in exercises of this sort, the Lay Letter places
great stress on principles not in dispute, ignores conditions that are
embarrassing to the argument, assumes that things that ought not
to happen will not happen in fact, and vigorously attacks and
demolishes straw men. Three "principles of political economy" that
have grown out of American habits are invoked. These are (1) the
practice of free association—the liberty to form voluntary associations of various sorts to accomplish various desirable ends; (2) the
habit of cooperation, which smoothes the functioning of all organizations and which makes for a higher level of accomplishment than
would be achieved by coercion; and (3) the principle of self-interest
rightly understood, which, following Tocqueville, emphasizes
those aspects of self-discipline and self-denial in the short run which
are beneficial in the long run.[14]

One would have to look far and wide to find someone who was
seriously critical of these ideas. No one is suggesting that such ideas
and practices be abandoned. However, it does not necessarily follow
from the desirability of these conditions that things always work
this way, or that major difficulties, such as the free-rider problem,
are swept out of the way.

Ethics and Stupidity

For the Lay Letter, the emphasis on individuals is carried through to
the analysis of areas where economic shortcomings may be found.
Shortcomings in the American economic system are described as
the fault of persons not of the system. "A free system can do little

more than offer human beings the liberty to act morally."[15] Good results flow from the free system, but bad results are products of the actions of bad people. Given those premises there is no need for any action except moral exhortation.

In the long run, even moral exhortation is not necessary since "greed is typically its own punishment." Even if some succumb to greed, it should not be thought that greed is central or essential to the profit system. Greed "is a corruption which injures those who give way to it."[16]

To those who say that "markets are cruel and that ethics and religion must be left behind," it is reassuring to know that "over time, however, in this arena as in every other, vice often brings in train its own destruction."[17] It would follow from this that rational participants in such a system, given to thinking about the long run, would choose to act in a moral way since that is the most likely to be advantageous to them.

That unethical or immoral behavior brings its own retribution is a popular idea. A public advocate of this position is John Shad, chairman of the Securities and Exchange Commission from 1981 to 1987. Shad has presented the Harvard business school, his alma mater, with a gift of $30 million for the purpose of establishing a program in ethics in business. At the time of the gift and in a later article, Shad has found it particularly disturbing that "the rash of insider-trading cases on Wall Street" has involved so many "recent graduates of top business and law schools." This leads Shad to the view that these schools have a social obligation to teach the importance of ethics in business. Among the concepts to be taught should be the following:

> executives, bankers, and lawyers who properly serve their customers, clients, employees, and communities do a better job for themselves, their companies, and partners than those who take unfair advantage of these groups . . . the marketplace rewards quality, integrity, and ethical conduct. . . . Integrity and ethical conduct make good business sense [in addition to being their own reward; and finally] ethics pays: It's smart to be ethical.[18]

Shad makes the problem of ethics disappear by reducing unethical behavior to stupidity. More money can be made, and more business success achieved, by acting honestly and ethically than by acting fraudulently or unethically. Anyone who fails to understand, and act upon, this idea is being shortsighted and nonrational. Shad and the Lay Letter are in agreement that if everyone acts rationally the problem of ethics disappears. In the case of the Lay Letter, this leads to the idea that there is no need to have any concerns about the seeking of profit as the fundamental institutionalized motivation in a free-market system since, in the long run, only the ethical will profit.

If it were demonstrably true that departures from moral expectations are self-penalizing, then if we assume rational, free actors desirous of maximizing benefits the system would truly be self-regulating. To believe that to be true of the American, or any other, economic system requires a leap of faith that many are unable to make.

What is overlooked in these optimistic assessments of the consequences of cheating and other ethical lapses, is that the long run can be very long indeed. As Lord Keynes reminded us, in the long run we are all dead. To the extent that actors do not anticipate a long career in particular business activities, the long-run impact of their actions is not likely to be very important to them. A loss of customer confidence is more important to the entrepreneur who hopes to run the same business indefinitely.

Equally important is the extent to which monitoring of activities is possible. Both the Lay Letter and John Shad make much of the importance of reputation. Reputation is more relevant in those activities where monitoring of activity is possible through first-hand observation, gossip, news coverage, or other means by which the word gets around. Where the nature of the situation makes monitoring impossible, or very difficult, the situation is very different.

Many perfectly legitimate business activities are not very visible at all. Not all business activities are conducted in public, as are customer-dependent stores with a fixed physical location. Many services—for example, banking—are customarily surrounded by an aura of confidentiality. Integral to the success of these businesses is that no questions be asked about where the customer's money comes from. Great efficiencies and profits flow from the attitude that money is by its nature anonymous. It can be moved quickly and quietly from one part of the country to another, or from one part of the world to another. This is after all the age of the numbered bank accounts and of money laundering. Even at the government level, where money matters are certainly more carefully scrutinized than in the private sector, improprieties occur regularly. And certainly, a great many private business activities are conducted with virtually no public scrutiny at all, and with reputations unlikely to be affected one way or another by the manner in which these affairs are conducted.

Indeed, there is a division of labor along reputational lines. Relatively visible activities can be conducted by high-profile entrepreneurs conscious of their reputations. Other activities, no less important to social functioning but less respectable, are carried on by entrepreneurs for whom reputation is not as important an asset. Ownership of slum and near-slum properties is an example. This is unlikely to be handled by socially prominent business people who make profits from housing the more prosperous segments of the society.

Individual Exchanges and Collective Goods

We have yet to mention the most serious flaw in the argument that morality is a strategy that advances self-interest. The whole area of analysis of what Mancur Olson has called the *Logic of Collective Action* and the free-rider problem points up the fact that it is often rational for the individual to act in ways that could be called immoral or unethical.[19] The free-rider problem becomes central in connection with collective goods. The Lay Letter confines itself to a discussion of private goods. Market analysis applies to private goods. It falters in the analysis of collective goods.

Markets can be very efficient in allocating resources. There is no longer any very serious argument about that. Even the Soviet Union has a leadership group that is attempting to act on that premise. Market efficiencies, though, are limited to those areas where markets can function—that is, in the satisfaction of the demand for private goods, as opposed to public or collective goods. ("Collective" is clearly the word that makes the most sense, although it has acquired some ideological baggage that sets off Pavlovian responses in many quarters.) Collective goods are those that are indivisible in character. If they are available at all they must, by their nature, be available *to* all. Clean air and national defense are two obvious examples. Individuals cannot decide for themselves how much clean air they wish to have, in the way that they may decide how much ice cream they might like to have. Those who do not want ice cream, need not buy any. Those who prefer beer to ice cream can indulge their preference. However, the people who might prefer that the air be left in a polluted state cannot continue to breath polluted air once it has been cleaned up. Either it is polluted for all, or it is cleaned up for all.

Obviously, with collective goods and the collective action required to achieve them, we are in the realm of politics as well as economics. Collective decisions must be made. We cannot proceed through the simple accumulation of individual preferences that works so well for private goods in the marketplace. Collective decision making involves all the arts of politics, persuasion, log rolling, compromise, and voting. In addition, it involves taxation to pay for the collective goods that are to be acquired. The analysis of collective action supplies what is probably the strongest defense of compulsory (as opposed to voluntary) taxation.

There is obviously coercion in compulsory taxation, but if paying taxes were not a legal requirement it would clearly be rational (which is not to say admirable) to refrain from contributing. The most rational course is to persuade others to pay, while refraining from paying yourself. If everyone else pays, presumably enough money will be collected to finance the undertaking and the collective good will be achieved. Everyone will have the full benefit of it, since its indivisible nature does not permit its benefits to be denied to anyone. Of course, if everyone acted rationally (i.e., did not pay their taxes) in this manner, then the collective good would not be achieved. That is precisely the point of the analysis. In a world of rational actors, compulsion is necessary if collective goods are to be available.

These are the same rational actors, being rational in the same way, that are celebrated in the usual analysis of free markets. This analysis of collective action applies with the most force when the groups involved are large. This is also the situation in which market analysis applies. For free, competitive markets to exist, there must be a sufficient number of buyers and sellers so that collusion to fix prices or limit supplies cannot be carried out, and each individual buyer or seller has only a negligible effect on market conditions. The advantages of markets will be realized under these circumstances. As we move to smaller numbers—and the possibility of collusion for larger market shares—the efficiencies in the allocation of resources diminishes.

Thus the same large number of economic actors that makes competitive markets possible also makes the successful provision of collective goods on a voluntary basis extremely unlikely. With large numbers, the contribution of one individual is so negligible a part of the total needed, that for practical purposes it makes no difference if the contribution is not made. The large size of the group also increases the sense of individual anonymity by reducing the possibilities of mutual monitoring. Therefore, people can decline voluntary participation in large groups secure in the knowledge that little if any social stigma will attach to their nonparticipation, and that the size of the project makes it certain that one person's absence will not have any practical effect on the outcome.

A very obvious example is what has come to be called the "infrastructure" of the modern economy. While infrastructure is not a term with a precise meaning, it is generally used to refer to collective goods, such as road and rail networks, sewer systems, educational systems, communication systems, and so on. (If "collective" did not carry such heavy ideological baggage, it probably would not have been necessary to coin "infra-structure" as an alternative to avoid any left-wing connotations. In that event, "collective goods" could be used and clarity increased.) The existence of these facilities is presumably beneficial, directly or indirectly, to all individuals and enterprises; but such facilities are unlikely to be developed by market forces. Governmental actions are needed to generate an infrastructure that is up to contemporary standards.

Does such governmental action represent a threat to individual freedom? Clearly, there is coercion in taxes, but facilities are provided that would otherwise not come into existence. Once in existence, they enhance the productive opportunities available to all. If decisions to take these actions are made in a democratic fashion, it is not obvious how freedom is restricted. While this point may not seem very significant, the tone of much of the Lay Letter makes it clear that its writers have a major objection to increasing the role of government in social matters. For instance, it is acknowledged in the Lay Letter that poverty is a serious problem, but "poverty is not primarily a problem for the state, it is a *personal* and a *community* problem."[20] In the Lay Letter, the economic system seems to exist apart from the government and to function in spite of government actions. Generating new jobs is described (as all would agree) as "one of the best ways to help the poor." Creating new jobs is a task "proper to the economic system itself." Jobs are created by entrepreneurs with their "enterprising intellects." What is the role for government in this area? It must stop penalizing savings, control inflation, and control its expenditures and deficits.[21] Government can contribute by ceasing to do bad things, which are presumably making matters worse. If government would get out of the way, the economic system would probably straighten things out by itself.

This is obviously a very naive conception of government, and one which ignores the role of government in providing collective goods. While it is not unusual for people on the conservative side of the political spectrum to see no value in governmental provision of collective goods in the economic sphere, these have usually been the most prominent supporters of governmental provision of collective goods in the national security arena. Taxes to support a huge defense establishment are not seen as infringements upon liberty by most conservatives. And it is no secret that the self-appointed Lay Commission is composed of members drawn from this political spectrum.[22]

An emphasis on markets and on the importance of individual freedom from any sort of governmental constraint has a crowd-pleasing ring to it, but it ignores the realities of a society in the modern era. It is in fact advantageous to individuals and to corporations to lie and to cheat. There are entire industries devoted to lobbying and public relations which have a major interest in manipulating and controlling information flow. This is the age of "plausible deniability." The line, for example, between political campaign contributions and bribery has grown increasingly obscure.

There are unquestionably major efficiencies in resource allocation that flow from markets. However, market principles alone will not create collective goods. A legitimate role of government is the development of collective goods. What constitutes a collective good, or a collective bad, is not given. It must be decided upon by whatever the societal decision-making process exists. The importance of certain collective goods seems indisputable—national security is an obvious example. Nevertheless, even in this area, there is vigorous disagreement about achieving the end. Other collective goods are far more controversial. For instance, should a society free of racial segregation be considered a collective good? History has shown that there is no agreement on that question or how such a society could be achieved.

The existence of disagreements about important matters is not surprising, nor is it a cause for alarm. The major function of political institutions is to provide accepted procedures for resolving disagreements. (The existence of political institutions is itself a collective good.) All procedures for resolving disagreements are going to produce situations where some groups and individuals will find that their preferences are not being adopted, and that their taxes are going, in part, to support goals of which they disapprove. Given the existence of disagreements about indivisible objectives, this outcome is unavoidable. To suggest that it represents some form of tyranny or an unacceptable restriction of liberty is really to say that tyranny is an unavoidable condition of modern life.

In a world where no one disagreed about anything, individual liberty could remain unrestrained and society would still function smoothly. That world does not exist. In the real world, political institutions are necessary. Some political institutions may fairly be described as tyrannical, but some are democratic and respect individual rights. Serious discussion of contemporary issues must recognize the role of government in dealing with the problems of collective action. There is little appreciation of the legitimate and necessary function of the state in securing collective goods in the Lay Letter. There is a grudging acceptance of the state's function in the area of welfare, but little else is seen as appropriate.

In a discussion intended "to make our position clear," it is emphasized that the state has a role in the case of the truly needy who "because of age or disability or other necessity cannot be self-reliant." In addition, the Lay Letter recognizes that no economic system can pretend to do everything sufficient for a good society," but the only specific areas of shortcoming mentioned are "helping the young, the elderly, the disabled, those visited by sudden misfortune, and many others permanently or for a time unable to work." Then, by way of summary after discussing nothing but welfare functions, it is asserted that "it is clear from the foregoing that we are not opposed to the state." After cautioning against the possible abuse of state power, the Lay Letter concludes that "particularly in its welfare functions, as a last resort, the state is an indispensable institution of the good society."[23] It is clear that this was intended to dispel the suspicion that its writers feel the state has no legitimate function in the modern economy. What the discussion in fact shows, however, is that they fail to recognize a major limitation of the model emphasizing free choices of voluntary actors, which is clearly the centerpiece of their analysis throughout. The position of the Lay Letter is that any restrictions on individual liberty are intolerable. (It is clear from the context of the whole Lay Letter that those restrictions on liberty that stem from a lack of property are not intolerable. Indeed, it is not even clear that they are considered restrictions at all.)

The Lay Letter fails to take seriously the fact that in the era of the modern nation-state, the economic and the political are inextricably intertwined. It is not simply the case that the state has a role in taking care of the casualties and victims of the free market, as the Lay Letter would have it. The state is an essential player in establishing the conditions that make a market possible, and in achieving the coordination necessary to secure collective goals. It is an inescapable fact that there are questions of collective policy confronting any society. These are inherently political questions. Once answered, they must be implemented by the state.

Not all these questions are narrow economic questions, but some clearly bear mainly on the area of economic activity. If there is a commitment to more or less equal opportunity in the economic arena, does this imply an obligation on the part of state to take actions designed to restore opportunity where it has been greatly restricted? Is it a collective good to prevent the formation of a more or less permanent underclass? Where a few dozen families own practically all of the agricultural land, is it a collective good to redistribute the land in what has come to be known as land reform? There is no strictly economic answer to questions about whether taxes should be more or less progressive, regressive, or flat.

Morality, Markets, and Baby M

A very interesting example of the points just discussed is the famous case of Baby M, currently on appeal in New Jersey. In a well-publicized trial, parental rights were ruled by a judge to be basically a matter of contract law. Marybeth Whitehead had signed a contract agreeing to conceive and bear a child by William Stern, which would be thereafter turned over to Stern and his wife for adoption. That this was recognized by the court as a valid contract was not in dispute. The law of contract envisions a world of entrepreneurs freely entering into agreements to exchange goods and services for mutually acceptable prices. These are private arrangements, and no heavy hand of government is involved. This is the world of which the Lay Letter speaks. This a casual observer might think that the enforcement by the court of the contract between the Sterns and Mrs. Whitehead would appeal greatly to the authors of the Lay Letter.

Not so. Michael Novak, generally acknowledged to be the principal author of the Lay Letter, has taken vigorous issue with the decision that this was just another contract. "Is not such a contract immoral on its face?" he asks. Novak finds it "almost inconceivable that the courts could decide such a case merely on the strength of existing contract law." Why is that?

> Many of us would have thought that it is against American Law to buy or sell human beings. . . . Many of us would have thought that moral relativism would go so far in our society, and that in the end some things would be universally seen to be simply and absolutely wrong.

Novak concedes that despite his enthusiasm for free markets, he does believe in limited markets. "It is simply not the case that everything is permitted or that everything has a price."[24]

To this the obvious question is, Why not? The logic of free markets, where everyone is free to enter into exchanges thought to be advantageous, is toward the commodification of everything. Even if 90 percent have some moral or other reasons for feeling that certain goods or services should not be for sale, the remaining 10 percent will make a market if mutually advantageous deals can be struck. There is nothing in the workings of free markets to prevent this. Markets are inherently amoral. Any moral standards that are brought to bear derive from factors external to the market.

As the furor aroused by the Baby M case made clear, not everyone agrees that contracts such as the one between the Sterns and Mrs. Whitehead are "simply and absolutely wrong." Many people see nothing wrong at all. In a secular society (and probably also in formally religious societies), it is to be expected that there will be disagreement about important matters that cannot be resolved empirically. Presumably, Novak would regard it as an exercise in tyranny for the state to take the position that contracts that treat children as commodities (and women as baby-making machines) are unenforceable. If it did that, the state would be saying that while markets in general are a public good, a market in pregnancies is a public bad. Novak does say that the law ought to "discourage such surrogate parenting, except in certain rare cases." Since the state deals in legalities, not morality, it cannot take such action because surrogate parenting is "immoral," however, but because it makes a political decision to discourage the practice. When the state makes such decisions through law, it is imposing a standard of legality on all. Assuming the political process is an open and democratic one, this is not tyranny, though it does to some degree infringe upon the liberty of those who would prefer to enter into such contracts.

Summary

The bishops propose that public policies and economic outcomes may and should be evaluated in terms of moral standards. The Lay Commission uses the language of morality, but nevertheless argues in effect that moral considerations should have no practical effect on policy judgments or the assessment of economic outcomes, since any effort to reduce freedom of choice among economic actors is unacceptable. The liberty of individuals is the greatest moral good in the view of the Lay Commission. Governmental actions are seen as being detrimental to liberty, no matter how lofty the avowed purposes of the policies.

NOTES

1. United States Catholic Conference, *Economic Justice For All: Catholic Social Teaching and The American Economy.* (Washington, D.C., 1986), Sec. 69.

2. Ibid., sec. 77.

3. Ibid., sec. 88.

4. Ibid., sec. 152.

5. Ibid., sec. 185.

6. Ibid., sec. 204.

7. Ibid., secs. 236–8.

8. Ibid., sec. 254.

9. Ibid., sec. 289.

10. Lay Commission on Catholic Social Teaching and the U. S. Economy, *Toward the Future: Catholic Social Thought and the U. S. Economy—A Lay Letter* (New York: 1984).

11. *Toward the Future*, p. 27.

12. Ibid., p. 28–9.

13. Ibid., p. 69.

14. Ibid., p. 17–24.

15. Ibid., p. 35.

16. Ibid., p. 39.

17. Ibid., p. 44.

18. John Shad.

19. Mancur Olson, *The Logic of Collective Action* (Cambridge, MA.: Harvard University Press, 1965).

20. *Toward the Future,* op. cit., p. 65.

21. Ibid., p. 65–6.

22. The principle author, and vice-chairman of the self-appointed Lay Commission, is Michael Novak, who has become a defender of right-wing positions since the late sixties. The chairman of the Commission is William Simon, who was a cabinet member during the Nixon and Ford administrations. When Alexander Haig, who also served in those administrations, announced his candidacy for the 1988 Republican presidential nomination, he listed William Simon as one of his national advisers. In an almost immediate clarification, Simon announced that he was "backing all the Republican presidential candidates." (*The New York Times,* July 28, 1987, p. A11.) Haig was also a member of the Lay Commission. While the membership list of the Lay Commission includes several Republican stalwarts and conservatives, (not necessarily Republican), there are no known Democrats or liberals.

23. *Toward the Future,* op. cit., p. 32–3.

24. Michael Novak, "Buying and Selling Babies," *The Commonweal,* July 17, 1987, pp. 406–7.

13

Political Talk: Critics of the Bishops' Pastoral Letter on the Economy

FREDERICK J. MAHER

The pastoral letter of the Catholic bishops deals with two areas of acknowledged importance and of great inherent ambiguity. These are the areas of politics and morality. These are areas in which objectivity and truth are often spoken about but never attained in the sense that serious disagreement ceases. As a practical matter efforts in these areas are aimed at achieving agreement rather than discovering truth. Analysis in this chapter will focus on verbal struggles in the realms of public morality and politics.

The language of morality consists of claims that particular actions, or particular outcomes, are good or bad in moral terms. None of these claims are capable of being demonstrated to be true or false empirically. Moral values are not themselves observable.

What is observable is the fact that people talk about morality. People claim to be moral. People claim to hold positions that rest on moral principles. People may accuse political opponents of ignoring the claims of morality.

For purposes of sociological analysis, morality is a tricky area. Since moral values cannot be observed directly, they must be inferred from actions and talk. Indeed, it is not too much to say that moral values exist in so far as people talk about them. If they were not talked about, how would anyone know anything about them?

Not surprisingly, this situation has led to different conceptions of what constitutes moral and immoral behavior. Since morality is not directly observable, arguments about the nature of morality are inevitable. Probably equally inevitable is the development of a variety of self-serving interpretations of the nature of moral demands. There is a tendency for people to adhere to value positions that are self-congratulatory, and moral values are no exception to this.

Political Facts: Objectivity and Ambiguity

It is in order at this point to make note of the inherently political nature of social and economic statistics. It is a rare political issue on which there are not some perfectly "objective" official statistics available which can be used to bolster whatever point is in need of bolstering. Since there is no objective way of determining which comparisons are the most appropriate to make, there is no way to settle anything with statistics unless the parties agree, and if they agreed, there would be no need for all the statistics in the first place.

This situation is responsible for the Catch-22 problem facing the Catholic bishops, and any other group attempting to enunciate a moral position that it intends to apply to contemporary social, economic, or political reality. Basically, the bishops have two choices. The first option is to confine themselves to a narrow discussion of what they take to be the moral principles involved, without making any attempt to specify how these principles apply in the empirical political world. The second option is to claim that particular policies and actions follow from the analysis of moral principles. This would lead to support for particular courses of action, opposition to other courses of action, and the endorsement or denouncing of certain conditions or situations that presently obtain. All this would be done in the name of moral and ethical principles, and it would be presented as some form of moral guidance, indicating the practical meaning of the general moral principles on which the religious leaders rest their claim to leadership roles.

If the bishops select the first option and discuss moral principles without any reference to specific applications, then they will surely be charged with uttering platitudes. There will probably be little public argument about the moral principles themselves, but there will be tacit agreement that those principles are clearly irrelevant to the serious, real-world problems of the day. Thus the first option yields little controversy and virtually no effect.

If they select the second option and spell out what they feel the practical implications of their moral position are, then they will be embroiled in intense controversy. This is not unique to churchmen in politics. One of the characteristics of contemporary media-based politics is that anyone, or any group, that takes any sort of public stand on issues, and bases that stand on principles rather than self-interest, will have his or her motives impugned and judgment challenged. In the case of groups claiming a moral authority for their pronouncements, there is the easy charge that they are over-stepping the bounds of their competence. It is a simple debating trick to grant the proposition that the bishops are indeed experts in their sphere—morality—but are not experts in economics, tax pol-icy, race relations, military policy, arms control, or any of the many areas that have spawned their own experts. The bishops can be credited with good intentions, but everyone knows that good inten-tions are not enough in the complex world in which we live. Con-temporary issues and problems are extremely technical matters that are best left to those who are able to devote full-time to their analysis.

The second option then yields a very high degree of controversy, and it has the further consequence of thoroughly politicizing the position of the bishops and the bishops themselves.

There is no way for the bishops to take moral positions on the issues and problems of the day without first taking some position on what the facts are with regard to those issues. What the facts are is the central issue of contemporary political disputation. Seemingly straight forward empirical questions (e.g., How many homeless people are there?) get bogged down in definitional issues that make it possible for anyone to adopt whatever standards are most conge-nial. Even when the facts are not in dispute, it is still the case that facts must be interpreted. Disputes about the meaning of facts are ultimately not empirically testable.

This is so because there is no clearly right way to define politically important terms. Despite all the trappings of scientific methodol-ogy, there is no clearly objective way to measure social and eco-nomic phenomena when there are, as there almost always are, two or more plausible and defensible ways to measure them. When, as is often the case, comparisons and time series are relevant to the issue at hand, there is no objectively correct way to decide which of several possible comparisons is the most appropriate or in what year a time series should start. Even a statistical neophyte knows that the magnitude of percentage changes depends on the base with which numbers are compared. Even a political neophyte can see that the choice of a base is a political act.

Political Drama: Truth and Credibility

Despite the efforts by participants to make the analysis of social and political issues appear to be a detached seeking after truth, it should be recognized that the enterprise bears more resemblance to an adversary proceeding—a trial—than it does to a laboratory experiment. When the bishops or any other principled group get involved, they will draw fire from any of the adversaries whose cause is not helped by that group's intervention. Since the credibility of participants is a crucial factor in adversary proceedings, opposition to the position of the bishops will almost certainly involve attempts to discredit them. As Birnbaumn has put it, "No argument has been too crude or too vulgar if it were thought likely to denigrate the Bishops and their work."[1]

In adversary proceedings, the purpose is not to arrive at the "truth," but to persuade a relevant audience to come to a conclusion that advances the interest of one of the parties. In a courtroom, the audience is the jury. What anyone else may think is irrelevant; if the jury finds that a party is not guilty, that is all that matters. In the court of public opinion, it is less clear just who constitutes the relevant audience. Some people's opinions make no practical difference one way or the other. The opinions of presidents and of members of the congress are obviously more important. However, in this age of opinion polls, the opinions, or at least the public positions, of elected officials are influenced by their perceptions of the popular mood. What shows up in opinion polls is a complex outcome of the activities of assorted gatekeepers of public opinion: teachers, preachers, editors, TV reporters, friends, and even comics. When Johnny Carson and others start ridiculing a person or idea, the credibility of the person or idea is in jeopardy.

This has various consequences. For one thing, it means that participants have to be more concerned with being persuasive than with being "right." Public relations skills are in demand. The importance of manipulating the impressions they make on others becomes apparent to those in the public eye. When new facts or developments arise, these are not seen as vehicles for the testing of hypotheses in the spirit of truth seeking. Rather they are seen as possible threats to credibility. It becomes necessary to engage in "damage control" or to "put a favorable spin on things" (to use two of the currently fashionable phrases of self-conscious political technicians) in the hopes of preventing support from eroding.

In public debate about policy issues, like the courtroom, the accuracy of facts and the scholarly quality of the arguments are often of less importance than the demeanor and the credibility of the witness. For example, during the Contra hearings, more attention was paid to the demeanor of star witness Oliver North than to his testimony. Ultimately, support for North began to fall off in the opinion polls. Had support remained high, his appearance as a witness would have been a great success and the accuracy of his testimony barely relevant.

The Language of Morality

While there is a great deal of emphasis placed on morality in standard political rhetoric there is no agreement in political circles on what morality means. To some, morality simply refers to the essentially nonrational behavior of members of religious groups. Fasting, wearing yarmulkes, opposing abortion, supporting TV evangelists, are examples of such behavior, which is tolerated as long as it is done privately and does not impinge on the activity of others. Since opposing abortion does most definitely involve attempting to change a situation which involves others, this is often denounced as an attempt to impose one's morality on others. This kind of denunciation rests on the idea that morality should remain a private matter, since it consists of beliefs that are not rationally defensible. They are tolerated in a secular society as long as they remain private.

Morality also has its own cadre of specialized experts who ponder moral questions in the abstract. Unfortunately, these experts address the same problems as do experts in other, more practical realms. Thus moral experts talk most successfully to each other. Morality's connection to the real world is severed and it winds up being irrelevant.

Another position is that morality should govern individual rather than collective behavior. Individuals ought not to lie, cheat, or steal, for instance, but organizations or whole societies cannot be evaluated according to such standards. Corporate spokespersons, executives, or lawyers are seen as living up to role obligations in doing what they can to suppress, deny, or otherwise obfuscate the truth in cases where the interests of their clients or their organizations are served. It certainly is not expected that such people would resign their jobs as a matter of moral principle over expectations that they not be duplicitous.

Political Morality Plays

When moral disasters occur and no one is responsible, morality is not a very meaningful concept. The morality plays and degradation ceremonies of public life have the function of delineating the moral boundaries in a society.

Who can be held morally accountable for collective outcomes that can be construed as moral disasters? The public fixing of blame can delineate the boundaries of the morally acceptable. If no blame is assigned publicly, either because no serious attempt is made to fix blame or because the situation is deemed to be too complex, then the boundaries of the morally acceptable become less clear.

The various senses in which morality is used in public discourse do not supply much support for the idea that morality has a clear meaning or that it is a plausible guide for choosing between alternative policy possibilities. Everyone recognizes that the language of morality and principle is used to justify and defend policy choices that are self-serving. How morality serves to guide political choices in the absence of self-interest is not clear. Given the cynical spirit of the times, there are few, if any, policy choices made by governments or other entities that have not been exposed as being based on ulterior motives, no matter how high sounding the original rationale. The language of morality is deemed to be appropriate on ceremonial occasions, but few believe it is actually a basis for making policy.

Reactions to the Pastoral Letter

The symposium edited by Thomas M. Gannon, "The Catholic Challenge to the American Economy," presents a variety of views about the pastoral letter. Among other things this symposium serves to highlight several questions that are basically unanswerable empirically. One question is whether poverty is best looked at as an absolute or a relative condition? As even casual students of sociology know, there are plausible arguments either way. However, a choice must be made, if statistics are to be developed and policy proposals made. A second question is whether the poor, however defined, will benefit more from programs targeted specifically at them, or whether they will benefit more from general economic expansion. Third, and perhaps most important for present purposes, does it make any sense to speak of economic rights as being on a par with civil rights? We will consider these points separately.

Defining Poverty

As is generally recognized, people who consider themselves liberals favor definitions of poverty in relative terms, and conservatives tend to favor definitions that have a more absolute quality. It is also generally recognized that on matters of economic welfare, liberals and conservatives disagree profoundly over the matter of equality. On economic issues liberals tend to favor positions that will reduce the degree of economic inequality that exists. Conservatives, on the other hand, tend to favor policies that will maintain existing inequalities or widen them. The struggles over defining poverty are continuations of the long-standing, and very fundamental, disagreements about policy that are unlikely to be resolved anytime soon, since these disagreements are not over empirical matters and there is no evidence that can be gathered that bears on the issues.

The bishops clearly focus on a relative definition of poverty, and they regard the degree of inequality between rich and poor as a more important factor than the overall level of income. They speak disapprovingly of the degree of concentration of financial wealth, deplore the fact that "the gap between rich and poor" has grown, and find "unacceptable" the "disparities of income and wealth in the United States."[2] This is certainly a position that can legitimately be assailed in the political arena by those who feel that it overlooks the impact of a rising per capita GNP. People less critical of inequality than the bishops are likely to feel that the pastoral letter overlooks the obvious economic benefit to the poor if the standard of living is rising, even if the poor do not benefit from it. For those who feel that absolute, and not relative, deprivation is the problem, confidence in the bishops as social analysts is not enhanced.

Programs to Alleviate Poverty

A second unanswerable question that has been a staple of political argument for decades is whether the poor are better served by policies aimed at them or at overall economic growth? Implicit in the latter is a kind of benign neglect. It is assumed that overall economic growth will ultimately provide more for the poor than will redistribution. This is basically a "trickle-down" approach. There have been many vigorous critics of trickle-down policies, but the importance of productivity in contemporary societies cannot be ignored. The differences of opinion are almost entirely ideological. The positions seem to be untestable and there is a struggle of competing faiths.

The bishops clearly favor targeting programs toward the poor. They are not opposed to programs aimed at general economic growth, but they obviously feel that such programs alone are not enough to deal with poverty on a national scale. This is a legitimate political position, and it is also a position that may legitimately be criticized. The bishops have been criticized for embracing it.

Is Economic Equality a Basic Right?

Probably the most important question raised in the Gannon symposium is whether it makes sense to speak of economic and social rights as being on the same level as civil and political rights. The bishops clearly assert that there are such rights: "rights to life, food, clothing, shelter, rest, medical care, and basic education. These are indispensable to the protection of human dignity." In addition the bishops endorse a right to "employment" and to "security in the event of sickness, unemployment, or old age." These are "all essential to human dignity and to the integral development of both individuals and society, and are thus moral issues."[3]

In a generally supportive article, William J. Byron emphasizes the centrality of this issue. Arguments that "deny the existence of economic rights will block the letter's implementation."[4]

In keeping with his well-established positions on such matters, Milton Friedman explicitly denies that economic and social rights are of the same character as civil and political rights. Civil rights (freedom of speech, of assembly, of religion) are rights that all can enjoy simultaneously, according to Friedman. One person's exercise of the right to free speech, for example, does not interfere with another's. There is no problem of scarcity, in other words. The situation is different with regard to jobs, clothing, or food. Unless there is some "cornucopia" from which jobs will flow, "everyone cannot simultaneously have the right to adequate" employment. If someone has an economic right to a job, for instance, then someone else has an obligation to provide it. The "relation is one of master and slave, not mutual freedom." In Friedman's view,

> the designation of a "right" to food, housing, adequate nutrition and the like to be on a par with the rights of free speech, religion, and assembly, reflects a collectivist moral vision, a vision that is wholly inconsistent with designating "the dignity of the human person, realized in community with others as the criterion against which all aspects of economic life must be measured."[5]

This is a fundamental disagreement. It raises the direct question of whether moral analysis has any relevance in the economic realm.

For the bishops it is clear that the language of morality includes the language of moral obligations that people have to one another. To Friedman, any talk of obligation that interferes with an individual's freedom to make whatever economic decisions are desirable smacks of the dread "collectivist moral vision."

Peter Steinfels addresses the question that is raised by Friedman and other critics who favor the bishops' goals but attack the way they propose to attain those goals.[6] Steinfels notes that the criticisms of the bishops have largely focused on the policy recommendations that they present. The Bishops are taxed with failing to recognize all the complexities that are inherent in the contemporary economic situation. They are criticized for basically adopting the policy agenda of liberals and Democrats which, in the view of critics, has been discredited by events. They are also accused of being arrogant and being unwilling to dirty themselves in the political arena. The bishops are, in short, assailed from all directions. Their policy proposals are utopian, vague, and at the same time proven unworkable by past experience.

Implicit in almost all this criticism, as Steinfels notes, is the idea that there is general agreement on the broad principles that the bishops advance, and that the argument is about the best way to realize these principles. "But does everyone really agree?" is the pointed question that Steinfels raises. Is it really agreed "that an economy is to be evaluated not simply by the aggregate or average wealth it produces but by the way that wealth is distributed so that none experience exclusion"? This is a major standard advanced by the bishops as a basis for the moral evaluation of the current economy. Is it really agreed that the production of wealth should be so organized that "the everyday activity of all is imbued with meaning"? Is it agreed that institutions should be judged by how they "foster participation and solidarity rather than passivity and isolation"?

To ask such questions is to answer them. As Steinfels concludes, these standards "sharply challenge the deeply rooted assumptions of the present moment." Any suggestion that the "needs" of the less privileged should take precedence over the "rights" of property and of the privileged are not taken very seriously by the established makers of policy and the established analysts of those policies. It is generally taken for granted by serious people that economies should be evaluated by rates of growth, productivity increases, inflation control, and other accepted measures. Efforts to bring changes in these areas should rely on the manipulation of incentives, which will increase the likelihood that people choose to do those things that will enhance system performance. Serious people are rather generally persuaded that government has shown itself to be singularly ill-equipped to deal effectively with the problems of the have-nots. Such persons are best left to the charitable impulses of churches and volunteers. Indeed, it is something of an indication that one *is* a serious person if one holds these views. The bishops have clearly stamped themselves as not serious in the minds of many, and their views are in danger of being regarded as irrelevant to discussions of serious matters.

If the workings of the modern economy are not to be regarded as proper subjects for moral evaluation, then there is obviously no point in the bishops, or anyone else, attempting to advance a moral critique. Certainly, the modern age is not one in which moral judgments are seriously advanced as the basis of public policy. The significant tests in these areas are profit, winning, and efficiency. The argument that a practice should cease because it is wrong, *mala in se,* is not an argument that is likely to get very far against the counterargument that the practice is profitable.

Summary

The language of politics is filled with code words and shibboleths. Code words enable speakers to suggest meanings without actually saying anything. A mastery of this technique is essential for any one interested in political success. Shibboleths enable speakers to convey their solidarity with various political constituencies. An important aspect of coalition building and mobilizing support is communicating the acceptance of group goals.

In American politics manifestations of concern for the poor are taken to be a symptom of liberalism—being soft on welfare, likely to support more government programs. The Democratic party, which once prided itself on its concern for the poor and the outcast, has toned down its stance in the last two decades. The ideological struggle over whether the "war on poverty" was a success or a failure has been won by those who would classify it as a failure. No one on the American political scene is using language that suggests that anything like a war on poverty should be launched again. Democratic politicians who wish to be taken seriously as national figures today emphasize that they are practical, pragmatic, and in

the mainstream, and that they have left behind all pipedreams about
the "Great Society."

At the present moment in the United States, the secular political
Left has virtually collapsed. Language that suggests concern for the
poor and the excluded, and which symbolizes an identification with
their interests, is language that places the speaker on the outer
fringes of the political spectrum. What was the language of the
political mainstream during the brief period following the assassination of John Kennedy is now the language of the outsiders. The
religiously based Left is the only organized force on the Left in
American politics. Old-time Leftists have drifted toward neocon-
servatism, neoliberalism, and neo-Marxism.

The bishops are taking what amounts to an heretical position
with regard to the modern economic system by stating that moral
judgments are relevant to the modern economy and that economic
outcomes can be evaluated in terms of Christianity.

Accordingly, it is not surprising that the bishops' letter is viewed
with deep suspicion in some quarters. Frank Hurley, archbishop of
Anchorage, alluded to this when he noted that

> the preferential option for the poor phrase comes out of Latin Amer-
> ica where there are only two classes, rich and poor. To use it in
> reference to American middle-class people is to risk polarizing them.
> The middle-class is the mainstay of the Catholic Church in this
> country.[7]

Whether the middle class is in fact the mainstay of the church is less
relevant for present purposes than that the middle class is clearly the
decisive battleground in American politics.

The sense of moral superiority felt by the middle class toward the
poor is not something that it is politically prudent to challenge. But
the bishops do challenge this by the clear suggestion that the poor
are not the cause of their own problems, and that those who are not
poor have an obligation to assist those who are. Any political
adviser would suggest that it is much more prudent to tell the
middle-class that they deserve what they have, and that the poor
have an obligation to help themselves by measuring up to middle-
class standards. The most that is owed to the poor, sage political
advisers would suggest, is an opportunity to make the grade. The
best of all middle-class worlds would be one in which opportunity
is provided but relatively few succeed.

NOTES

1. Norman Birnbaum, "The Bishops in the Iron Cage: The Dilemmas of Advanced Industrial Society," *The Catholic Challenge to the American Economy* (New York: MacMillan, 1987) p. 153.

2. United States Catholic Conference, *Economic Justice For All: Catholic Social Teaching and The American Economy* (Washington, D.C.: 1986) sec. 184.

3. Ibid., chap. 3.

4. William J. Byron, S. J. "The Bishops' Letter and Everyday Life," *The Catholic Challenge to the American Economy*, p. 248.

5. Milton Friedman, "Good Ends, Bad Means," *The Catholic Challenge to the American Economy*, p. 99–106.

6. Peter Steinfels, "The Bishops and Their Critics," *Dissent* (Spring 1985) 176–83.

7. Eugene Kennedy, *Re-imagining American Catholicism* (New York: Vintage, 1985) p. 175.

Part IV

ANALYTICAL CONSIDERATIONS: CONCEPTS OF GOD AND SOCIAL THEORY

The final contribution to this volume differs from the others in the sense that it is self-consciously and exclusively analytical-theoretical. The central thesis of the paper contributed by William R. Garrett is that conceptions of God invariably result in differing conceptions of the nature and possibilities of religious life. A tripartite typology is proposed which ranges from scientific reductionism (the most secular), to religious humanism (a civil-religion stance), to theistic transcendentalism (which includes most organized religions today). This typology is not unrelated to the central theme of micro/macro levels of religion, since each of these types is related differently to that problem—in much the same fashion that secularization theory, generally, is related to the division of religious life into its micro and macro dimensions. Indeed, one of the overriding purposes of this essay is to make clear that the rapprochement between social theory and theology has profound ramifications for both macro and micro views of reality and assessments of the consequences of religious belief.

14

Theological Reflection and Social Theory: An Emerging Rapprochement

WILLIAM R. GARRETT

A backward glance at the last several decades of Christian development reveals a rather remarkable innovation in the methodology by which theologians have pursued their cardinal task of giving expression to the fundamental meanings of the faith. This change can be succinctly summarized in the observation that, with accelerating frequency, social scientific theories have been appropriated by theologians as a framework for ordering their discourse. Whereas philosophical schemes provided the main infrastructure for the articulation of theological confessions throughout most of Christendom's initial eighteen centuries of development and expansion, historical rubrics emerged in the nineteenth century to provide an alternative set of categories for organizing theological systems.[1] In this century, theoretical paradigms derived from the social sciences have presented yet a third, and ever-more attractive, option for theologians striving to attain a heightened relevance for Christianity in contemporary social life.

There appears to be no a priori reason why social scientific theories should not serve as a handmaiden to the development of theological reflection in this century, as did philosophy and history in previous eras. Indeed, the creative accomplishments of H. Richard Niebuhr in *The Meaning Of Revelation,* wherein the role theory of George Herbert Mead has supplied the covert analytical structure for his argument; Paul Tillich's pervasive utilization of depth psychology; and the more recent work of Peter Berger, especially his *The Heretical Imperative,* in which the intellectual tools supplied by the sociology of knowledge lay the groundwork for his inductive theological argument, all suggest that significant breakthroughs in theology may well be achieved through this approach.[2] And while Niebuhr, Tillich, and Berger may be among the more proficient in this regard, they are by no means the only scholars engaged in theological construction who have imbibed deeply from the well-

springs of social theory. Harvey Cox, from *The Secular City* to his
most recent, *Religion in the Secular City,* has made consistent use of
the social scientific theories of religion, especially as these pertain to
the macro-social processes of secularization.[3] Others within those
schools of thought known variously in the late 1960s and early 1970s
as secular, radical, and later, revolutionary theology—for example,
Richard Shaull, Paul Van Buren, Thomas J. J. Altizer, William
Hamilton, Gabriel Vahanian, and a host of others—also borrowed
heavily from the available stock of social scientific theories or interpretations as a means for discerning the "world's agenda" and then
fashioning an appropriate response.[4]

Similar patterns are discernible in European theological reflection. Jurgen Moltmann, Johannes Metz, J. M. Lockman, and their
colleagues among the political-radical theologians have made extensive use of the theoretical contributions of the Frankfort or critical
school of social theory, the muted Marxism of Ernst Bloch, as well
as the more standard forms of Marxist and Freudian analysis. Indeed, when the radical theologians experienced a period of dramatic
eclipse after the demise of the counterculture in the United States,
the political-radical tradition continued to prosper—and even dominate—in Europe.

Perhaps the most obvious utilization of social scientific theory as
an infrastructure to theological construction in the contemporary
age, however, is to be found among the liberation theologians in
Latin America. For this coterie of activist thinkers, various forms of
Marxist and neo-Marxist theoretical constructs—including, especially, neocolonial dependency theory—have been widely embraced
as the analytical frameworks for liberationist thought.[5] The Marxist
connection with respect to liberation theology has been downplayed
a great deal by its leading proponents, to be sure, and largely for
reasons of political expediency (to placate both the Roman Catholic
Church and the temperamental governments of Latin America).
Such denials of Marxist theoretical influence are no longer taken
very seriously by either the critics or supporters of this style of
theologizing, however, since it is patently obvious to even the casual
observer that these rubrics of Marxist inspiration serve as the ori-
enting paradigm for the movement.

The foregoing review of the rising influence of social theory in
theology provides the context for two interlocking conclusions: one
substantive, the other of a more critical character. We have already
noted that there is nothing inherent in the character of theology or in

the nature of social theory which renders these two intrinsically antithetical. Depending on their substantive content, however, specific theoretical constructs often possess subtle implications which can ultimately confound theological interpretation. In order to avoid such inimical consequences, theologians need to become intimately familiar with those background assumptions embedded in the theories which they appropriate for their own purposes.

A critical conclusion follows hard on the heels of this substantive observation. Whereas theologians seemed to appreciate the need to master the nuances of those philosophical systems which were employed to give organizational structure to their theological affirmations, a similar sort of critical wariness has not generally attended the integration of social scientific theories into the warp and woof of theological construction. This problem manifests itself in two discrete areas. In the first instance, there has been a generalized tendency by members of the theological community to extend wider approbation to the validity of social scientific concepts than social scientists themselves have typically been willing to concede. Accordingly, a Freudian image of selfhood, or a neocolonial theory of dependency, or, again, one of the many varieties of secularization theory, have frequently been facilely adopted as if these constructs enjoyed an empirical cogency. If they continue to embrace these concepts without scepticism, theologians may well discover that their forays into interdisciplinary construction have the effect of rendering them vulnerable to a whole battery of criticisms devised by scholars in alternative schools of social scientific thought.

In the second instance, there has been a marked tendency among those adventurous theologians who have forged an alliance with social science to treat its concepts as though they possessed a kind of value neutrality and could, therefore, be incorporated into theological discourse with relative impunity. Perhaps this problem is most starkly evidenced with Marxism—although it is also apparent in theology's acceptance of Freudian reductionism and Durkheimian functionalism. The risk here is overlooking the systemic dispositions innately structured into a given body of theory. Consequently, concepts inimical to theistic doctrines of God, for example, frequently crop up in theological accounts where the image of God is clearly depicted in theistic categories, and without any lucid indication of how these otherwise antithetical thought forms are to be reconciled.

Complications occasioned by these problems set the stage for the argument to be developed in this essay. Essentially, the analysis to follow proposes a typological model for delineating the ramifications which devolve from particular frameworks for conceptualizing the nature of religious reality. What this typology makes possible is the correlation of certain styles of social scientific analysis with particular theological positions. The basic stances comprised in this typological model have been derived from Gordon Kaufman's pioneering efforts to delineate the conventional worldviews or interpretive contexts of ordinary people within which "life as a whole is experienced and lived."[6] For our purposes, however, each type has been significantly modified and embellished in order to give fuller definition to the self-contained character of each position. For one of the more crucial consequences arising from this analysis is the suggestion that each orientation possesses a coherence which all but excludes the others. If, indeed, this proves to be the case, then we are afforded a vehicle for discerning the "elective affinity" whereby certain forms of social theory can be effectively linked to corresponding types of theological reflection. By the same token, however, we can also identify those occasions wherein one type of social theory is coupled with an incompatible theological orientation, so that the assumptions underlying the two perspectives work at cross-purposes with one another, and thereby frame an internal contradiction.

Three Worldviews: Scientific Reductionism, Religious Humanism, and Theistic Transcendentalism

The labeling of typological categories is always something of a nominalistic enterprise. Kaufman gave his three worldview categories secular, religious, and theistic frameworks. The alternatives suggested in this essay—scientific reductionism, religious humanism, and theistic transcendentalism—have the singular virtue of being somewhat more precise. Substantively, however, these categories and those employed by Kaufman remain fundamentally the same. Moreover, where Kaufman placed a great deal of stress on the three ordering principles of reason, feeling, and revelation as the distinguishing characteristics for the secular, religious, and theistic worldviews, the differentiating principle employed in this essay turns more directly on the definition of, and attitude toward, ultimate reality found in each orientation. The difference is really more a matter of emphasis, however, than a fundamental disagreement.

Scientific Reductionism

The orientation of scientific reductionism is a direct legacy of the Enlightenment, with its naturalistic, scientific conception of the world and the place of human beings within it. Not only do proponents of this worldview rule out the existence of any other realms of being beyond the immediately present and empirically observable world, but its advocates also regard human beings as the sole architects of their existence. Embedded in this perspective, then, is a starkly—and self-consciously—antitheistic component, along with the erstwhile assumption that culture represents the highest achievement or level of knowledge which humankind is capable of attaining.

For persons so committed, knowledge is derived primarily from the exercise of our cognitive capabilities. The two preeminent forms of reflective activity by which the world is understood and subdued are philosophical reason and scientific calculation. Both comprise a means for coping with those powerful environmental factors which impinge on human existence, so that some measure of control over the blind forces of nature is rendered possible. Philosophical reason eventuates, according to this viewpoint, into systems of meaning and value which allow persons to set purposeful objectives and select among an almost bewildering array of potential courses of action in everyday life. Cultural systems of rules and norms permit selves to rechannel their natural urges arising from physiological needs and drives into socially prescribed patterns of behavior. Similarly, scientific knowledge allows for the development of at least some measure of technological dominion over the physical world. And in both instances, human destiny is determined by the operations of the intellect, since there is no supernatural being or force to which mere finite beings can appeal.

Within this frame of reference, persons are thrust back upon their own resources to devise a system of ethical norms and moral values to order their lives. Some may select strictly aesthetic criteria for determining what is ultimately meritorious in human existence, while others may chose humanistic, hedonistic, or even rationalistic premises upon which to ground their ethical conduct. Whatever the basis, however, this perspective remains fundamentally anthropocentric in its specification of ethical precepts and value commitments. The final court of appeal in all such matters is human wisdom, with all its shortcomings, lacunas, and potential for misjudgment.

The corresponding sociological approach toward religion in this worldview entails a radical demythologizing or debunking stance whereby religious claims are declared untrue from the outset. Symbols which point to supernatural forces or beings are reinterpreted as mystifications designed to mask purely human forces. That is to say, the sociocultural world of human meanings is overlaid with mysteries whose purpose is to obscure the fact that religion is merely a human projection.[7] In Freudism, for example, religion is not dismissed as sheer superstition, but as a defense mechanism which variously shields societal members from the terror of chaos or affords a means of dealing with the neurotic anxieties inherent in the very nature of human experience. Proceeding from somewhat different presuppositions, Durkheim denied the validity of religious truth claims, while, nonetheless, portraying the function of religion as essentially benign—namely, through its ability to forge integrative bonds between societal members and collective social forces. Marx not only declared religious ideas false, but he also excoriated religious movements for their malevolent role in both giving expression to and perpetuating dehumanizing patterns of alienation.

The common theme running through these alternative styles of scientific reductionism is the stalwart conclusion that the divine reality posited by religious ideas simply does not exist. Rather, religion serves to camouflage more basic psychic, societal, or exploitive human forces. The overriding purpose of social scientific analysis, then, is to identify the "real" causes of religion, now that its supernatural origins have been discredited. Where proponents of scientific reductionism part company is over the issue of whether religion ought to be eradicated in order to rid society of its pernicious social consequences, or whether it should be tolerated—in spite of its errors—because its beneficial functions for societal members. Marxist-Leninists have generally opted for the first alternative, while Durkheimian-Freudians have normally favored the latter course of action. It should be underscored, however, that whenever the various theories of this social scientific stance are related to theological ideas, the rapprochement is inevitably a matter of practical expediency, since substantively no one committed to the scientific reductionist position can accord any measure of validity to the substance of theological ideas.

Religious Humanism

The worldview of religious humanism rests securely on a distinctive set of anthropological assumptions wherein religion is identified as a distinct and legitimate domain of human culture. Gone is the sharp rejection of religion on empirical and positivistic grounds so characteristic of scientific reductionism. The perspective of religious humanism fosters at once a more sympathetic response to religious sentiments and a more positive evaluation of the influence of religious organizations. Yet, there is a limit in terms of how far religious humanists are prepared to go with respect to affirming, for example, the orthodox doctrines of the Judeo-Christian tradition, including its classical images for explicating the nature and being of God. Religious humanists are more at home with concepts of religion which treat all theological efforts as evocative symbols whose purpose is to give cultural expression to the ultimate meaning of existence. The accent in this instance falls, then, on conceiving religion primarily as a human enterprise. Both methodologically and noetically, the point of departure for religious reconstruction is the human condition as it is experienced in the everyday world of men and women. Indeed, that metaphysical beings actually exist, a belief implicit in most religions, is less significant than the crystallized meanings embodied in theological constructs through which persons strive to express to themselves the ultimate nature of reality.[8]

The this-worldly character of religious humanism effectively precludes the adoption of certain noetic procedures in favor of knowledge derived through intuitive reason and feeling, with the latter understood more in the sense of Schleiermacher's *Gefuhl*. Whereas scientific reductionism embraces technical reason and positivistic conceptions of reality, religious humanism turns to the inner consciousness of humankind, with all its sentiments of estrangement, ectasy, and the constraints on existence imposed by the human condition. The symbols which arise out of this are, to be sure, extremely varied. Since everything human has potential religious significance, revelatory disclosure may occur as readily in secular poetry or art, in philosophical speculation or political engagement, in family interaction or play, as in scripture or the inner history of a religious tradition. Indeed, any experience which fosters a profound insight into, and a more comprehensive understanding of, the fundamental order of things, which allows for some measure of transcendence over the inherent meaninglessness of human existence stands, perforce, as an expression of religious sentiment and a contribution to the store of religious knowledge. Within the parameters of this point of view, therefore, all religious sentiments are considered to be true in the sense that they represent authentic expressions of the human spirit; but not all are of equal worthiness or efficacy in coping with the perplexities of the human condition.

The ethical postures associated with religious humanism are likewise as varied as the religious expressions surfacing from its worldview. Given its generally liberal orientation, however, most of its ethical systems place a great deal of emphasis on the social dimensions of moral conduct. Such a concern is manifested most notably in the political sphere, where moral values and schemes of societal reformation are joined. Indeed, even where politics does not play a very significant role in ethical calculation, the latent tendency is for moral reasoning to flow logically toward the collective pole of human interaction and away from a strictly individualistic or pietistic ethical stance. Individual responsibility typically gets defined in terms of one's obligations to the common good, and moral virtue consists in that which enhances the well-being of humanity as a whole. Indeed, impiety finds its clearest expression not in declarations of unbelief in a supramundane deity, but in those actions which range from wholesale neglect to outright aggression against one's fellow human beings. And by the same token, benevolent conduct toward others constitutes the highest form of worship, since it is primarily through the fulfillment of moral obligations that one is able to express a sense of love, harmony, and unity with ultimate reality.

The general sociological approach most compatible with this orientation is to be found among the several, closely related varieties of functionalist analysis. The tendency to define religion as that about which one is ultimately concerned—as typified, for example, in Yinger and Bellah's sociology of religion—is altogether consistent with the anthropological emphasis pulsating through religious humanism. Furthermore, the functionalist notion of civil religion as that abstract, politico-cultural framework for expressing the meaning and destiny of a people emerges as a powerful concept for delineating how a religious perspective can be conjoined with a public-spirited social ethic. Civil religion affords the opportunity of taking religion seriously without having to delve into the more troublesome theological issues associated with orthodox affirmations of faith. One can, in other words, be religious without necessarily being sectarian.

Perhaps the most significant ramification deriving from sociological approaches consistent with this religious worldview is that religious symbols are treated as purely human constructions. Transcendent realities are not so much denied—as in scientific reductionism—but treated as if the realm of culture is the highest domain of human experience. Whether one approaches the ultimate in terms of Talcott Parsons's telic dimension of the nonempirical, Robert Bellah's concept of symbolic realism, or Daniel Bell's notion of the sacred, the end result remains very nearly the same: to wit, religious symbols are construed as an effort to find answers which will reconcile human existence with the boundary situations imposed on us by the human condition.[9] Religion is, in short, an inductive and innerworldly enterprise. And as such, it is one of the nobler cultural activities in which we participate, an activity which lifts us above the baser passions and focuses our attention on the higher "goods" that enrich our collective experience. The value of religion inheres, therefore, not so much in its intrinsic nature as in its pay-off in social life. Without religion, human culture would undoubtedly degenerate into a Hobbesian world of a war against all. The real power of religion is that it can induce us to forego our will to power, our hedonistic urges, and our demonic passion for self-destruction by showing us yet a more excellent way to preserve our cultural traditions and transform our destructive vices into redemptive virtues.

Theistic Transcendentalism

Whereas the former type of worldview represents a homocentric approach to religious reality, the third type represents a theocentric alternative. The point of departure in this final perspective is not the world as apprehended through reason or feeling, but the purposive reality of an active being who stands over against the world in a transcendent relationship—namely, God. Accordingly, that ordering principle which bestows meaning and purpose on human existence cannot inhere in humanity itself; it must necessarily lie beyond the world in the transcendent "will of God." The notion of an agent who is capable of volitional activity is altogether crucial here, for God is above all else that being who intentionally created the world and all those who dwell therein, and the being who now stands over against the created world as the potential redeemer of human beings. The condition from which persons are being saved differs markedly in this worldview and the former type, however, for religious humanists seek salvation from the wages of existence, while theists seek deliverance from the wages of sin. In the theist paradigm, therefore, finite creatures are interpreted as dependent agents who encounter the self-disclosures of deity through the historical process and who may, then, elect either to accept or reject the demands flowing from this experience of the Wholly Other. For those who are able to make common cause with the purposes of this transcendent agent, there is afforded the opportunity for participation in the transforming community of the kingdom of God.

The key to understanding the salient orientation of the theistic worldview is volitional activity, both on the divine and human level. For this reason, revelation—understood as a voluntary disclosure of God's fundamental nature and will to the world—constitutes the noetic principle upon which this perspective is predicated. The medium through which revelatory insights proceed may vary quite decisively. A person, a book, an event, or even an experience of sudden illumination, all hold the potential for serving as the parabolic occasion wherein deity manifests its nature and intentions. The unavoidable liability attending this noetic approach, of course, is the troublesome matter of determining whether a believer has genuinely apprehended the will and purpose of the divine revealer or the experience merely represents the wayward yearnings of the human spirit. The normal litmus test by which selves confirm or discredit revelatory occasions is to measure their perceptions against the tradition and witness of other believers in the community of faith. Such a strategy presumes that God's nature and will does not change radically from one revelatory occasion to the next. Hence, social corroboration provides some measure of protection against the possibility that believers are the victims of sheer delusion when they experience revelatory events.

The larger problem encountered in theism generally, however, pertains to the declining credibility which persons nurtured in a secular, scientific ethos are willing to extend to disclosures from a transcendent being. Theism effectively requires the suspension of ordinary epistemological procedures in favor of a way of knowing which presupposes the existence of an agent who stands ontologically over against the world. Theism entails a leap of faith over a broader chasm than exists in the other two worldviews. Some believers have managed to drive a wedge between religious and other forms of knowledge, so that the scandal of belief—while not entirely mitigated—is at least partially muted. Others who resist the bifurcation of reality into two mutually exclusive spheres and who desire to correlate faith affirmations with empirical reality, seem committed to the notion that human experience is one totality and must be confronted as such. Whether such a posture can be sustained in face of modern thought forms and will attract more than a few adherents remains one of the crucial questions of our time.

The ethical stance typical of the theistic worldview resembles that mode of moral conduct long ago described by Weber as characteristic of innerworldly asceticism.[10] That is to say, persons informed by this orientation regard themselves as instruments of the divine will, whose mission is to transform the earthly realm more nearly into the kingdom of God. The divine imperative requires of believers that they adopt a disciplined life style for this purpose. Hence, this ethic is not only activist, but also transformational, in the sense that it takes as its ultimate aim the subjection of the world to the canons of religious virtue and to divine intention. This sort of ethic requires, therefore, close attention to one's individual conduct in interpersonal relations, vocation, and the cultivation of private virtues. Yet it also requires the development of a sense of ethical responsibility, wherein the very structure of the empirical world is subjected to critique and ultimately reformation.

To be sure, in the many varieties of concrete ethical systems originating from theistic presuppositions, the pendulum swings back and forth between the development of individual piety and a radical reconstructionist posture. Both individual and social ethics derive logically from the premises of the theistic worldview. The difference lies largely in how persons are ushered into the kingdom of God. For example individuals may be converted one by one or social institutions may be altered for the better—both bring humankind closer to God's kingdom.

The vision of the world with its transcendent and natural dimensions is not compatible with the paradigmatic assumptions implicit in several varieties of social theorizing. For example, a theistic worldview clashes with the fundamental presuppositions of a reductionist social theory which finds the explanation for religious forces in the empirical, psychosocial processes of human experience. Likewise, a strict functionalist stance which limits religion to the realm of human expressive behavior cannot be accommodated with, at least, the potential existence of nonempirical realities. It should not be assumed from this, however, that the only social theory which is appropriate to the theistic worldview is one which affirms the existence of the supernatural. Social theory is incapable of providing a warrant for or against the existence of a transcendent reality. Accordingly, those theoretical approaches within social science which are amenable to the theistic worldview include perspectives which bracket or assume an agnostic stance on the supernatural. A number of theoretical perspectives meet this criterion, among them several varieties of phenomenological, symbolic interactionist, historical, hermeneutical (or interpretive) sociology, and functionalist analysis. Ironically, just as a theistic worldview is becoming more difficult to sustain in our space-age society, many of the leading social theorists today—and even some within the Marxist camp—are showing themselves to be sympathetically predisposed toward religion. Nevertheless, it is becoming ever more difficult to devise a credible sociological approach to religion which resists the temptation to make human experience the measure of all things. The religion garnering favor among contemporary scholars in the social sciences is, by and large, a religion of culture and tradition, a religion which addresses the emptiness and futility of much human striving and which serves the meritorious function of pulling us out of our self-centeredness and into an altruistic concern for others. Put somewhat differently, then, it is an altogether fair judgment that sociological theorists have of late gravitated toward a stance which is markedly proreligion. But they have managed to do so, for the most part, without relinquishing those antitheistic biases subtly interwoven with the substantive paradigmatic structures through which the nature of social reality has conventionally been interpreted.

The conclusions embodied in the foregoing comments are intended as purely cautionary. There are viable theoretical models within the social sciences that do not require from the outset that one deny the existence of nonempirical forces or treat religion as nothing more than expressive human behavior. Such a declaration must also be followed by an equally important caveat, namely, that the center of gravity insofar as contemporary sociological theorizing is concerned tends more in the direction of religious humanism than the theistic orientation. The result is that paradigms amenable to theistic assumptions remain critically underdeveloped. As a general rule of thumb, however, theorists who employ a substantive—as opposed to a functional—definition of religion can be expected to develop a theory of religious processes more compatible with theistic assumptions than those who elect alternative definitions. The reason for this is, quite simply, that when substantive definitions are employed, the sacred is typically treated as a reality which is not reducible to empirical examination. This does not mean, of course, that social theorists take believers' definitions of the sacred at face value, but theorists who employ substantive categories in demarking the boundaries of the religious are more willing to stipulate that there are limits to the demythologizing process beyond which sociologists cannot properly proceed. And, we might add, this is all that theists should expect of scholars engaged in empirical, scientific analyses of the impact of religion on sociocultural existence.

Conclusion: Theological Reflection and Social Theory

The analysis undertaken in this essay has no hidden agenda. Our intent has not been to disclose the superiority of one of the three types of religious orientation over its alternatives, nor has it been to castigate sociological theorists for their development of a stance which has a greater affinity for one orientation than another. Indeed, the overriding concern of this research has been much more restricted and circumspect. What we have sought to demonstrate is that certain types of religious orientation are compatible with certain types of social scientific theorizing—and incompatible with others. Put in just this fashion, some might question whether we have not demonstrated a point which is patently obvious to anyone who has labored along the boundary line between theology and the social sciences. Perhaps so. But the evidence is certainly less than overwhelming. Not only do we find theologians from the theist orientation, for example, appropriating constructs from scientific reductionism and religious humanism, but we also find social theorists with avowedly theistic commitments attempting to develop theories of religion on strictly anthropological foundations.[11] The consequences in all these instances is less than salutary.

The ultimate justification for the creation of any typological structure, however, must be the heightened analytical clarity and precision which such models are capable of expressing. In the realm of everyday experience, of course, the pure stances for conceiving ultimate reality which we have defined here are only approximated.

The utility of such ideal typical models derives from their ability to identify salient tendencies and central motifs which distinguish one orientation from another. On this basis, it becomes clear that the vocabularies employed by religious persons carry quite different significations according to the frame of reference within which faith is being articulated. When a religious humanist uses the symbol "God," for example, it does not convey the same denotative meaning as when a theist utters the same word. Accordingly, we can apprehend more fully the subtle nuances attending religious speech if we can locate the speaker within the broad types of orientation to the world developed in the main body of this essay.

More particularly, these types also disclose where logical problems and systemic contradictions are likely to arise when certain forms of social theory are integrated with alternative categories of belief structures. This problem is clearly most pronounced for theologians and lay believers who hold theistic assumptions. At the very least, one ought to be suspicious when persons who confess a belief in a supramundane deity seek to articulate their theological affirmations with reference, say, to Marxist, Freudian, or civil religious constructs, since these theoretical concepts derive from orientations inimical to theistic assumptions. This conclusion also cuts in the other direction. If the vast majority of societal members who hold religious beliefs conceive of the God they serve in terms of some theistic image, then this would tend to cast serious doubt on whether civil religion aptly describes a pervasive religious outlook for that population.

These limited conclusions represent only a small portion of those insights which can be teased out of the typological models suggested above. It may well be, of course, that additional types need to be adduced to encompass the full complexity of contemporary religiosity. Attaining closure of a typological construct was not really the purpose behind this research, however. What we hope to have demonstrated is that the appropriation of social scientific concepts by persons engaged in theological reflection not only affords some real opportunities for creative advances, but it also entails some substantive risks. Both theologians and social theorists need to focus more attention on the latent implications arising from these frameworks for their critical reflection. A failure to take these matters seriously can only result in a trivialized theology and an ever-more superficial scientific study of religion.

NOTES

1. See Van A. Harvey, *The Historian And The Believer* (New York: Macmillan, 1966).

2. H. Richard Niebuhr, *The Meaning Of Revelation* (New York: Macmillan, 1941). See also, William R. Garrett, The Sociological Theology of H. Richard Niebuhr. Pp. 41–55 in William H. Swatos, Jr., ed., *Religious Sociology: Interfaces and Boundaries.* Westport, CT: Greenwood Press, 1987; and Peter L. Berger, *The Heretical Imperative* (Garden City, NY: Doubleday, 1979).

3. Harvey Cox, *The Secular City,* rev. ed. (New York: Macmillan, 1967); and Harvey Cox, *Religion in the Secular City* (New York: Simon & Schuster, 1984).

4. For a concise summary of these schools of theological persuasion, see Sydney E. Ahlstrom, "The Radical Turn in Theology and Ethics: Why It Occurred in the 1960s," Pp. 19–39 in *New Theology,* vol. 8, ed. Martin E. Marty and Dean G. Peerman (New York: Macmillan, 1971), pp. 19–39, as well as the other volumes in this series; and William R. Garrett, "Politicized Clergy: A Sociological Interpretation of the 'New Breed,' " *Journal for the Scientific Study Of Religion,* vol. 12, no. 4 (December 1973): 383–399.

5. The literature of liberation theology is much too extensive to cite here, but two central contributions merit mentioning. These are: Gustavo Gutierrez, *A Theology of Liberation* (Maryknoll, NY: Orbis Books, 1973); and Juin Luis Segundo, S.J., *The Liberation of Theology* (Maryknoll, NY: Orbis Books, 1976). For further references and a critique of the Marxist role in framing liberation theology, see William R. Garrett, "Religion and the Legitimation of Violence," in *Prophetic Religion and Politics,* ed. Jeffrey K. Hadden and Anson Shupe (New York: Paragon House Publishers, 1986).

6. Gordon D. Kaufman, *God the Problem* (Cambridge, MA: Harvard University Press, 1972), pp. 203–25.

7. See Peter L. Berger, *The Sacred Canopy* (Garden City, NY: Doubleday, 1967), p 90

8. See Robert N. Bellah, *Beyond Belief* (New York: Harper and Row, 1970), pp. 216–29; 237–59.

9. See Talcott Parsons, *Action Theory and the Human Condition.* (New York: Free Press, 1978), pp. 352–433. See also Robert N. Bellah, *Beyond Belief,* op. cit., pp. 237–259; and Daniel Bell, *The Winding Passage* (New York: Basic Books, 1980), pp. 324–54.

10. See Max Weber, *The Sociology of Religion* (Boston: Beacon Press, 1963), pp. 166–83.

11. Two significant cases in point are: Peter Berger, *A Rumor of Angels* (Garden City, NY: Doubleday, 1970); and Andrew M. Greeley, *Religion: a Secular Theory* (New York: Free Press, 1982).

CONTRIBUTORS

DANIEL COHN-SHERBOK, Director, Centre for the Study of Religion and Society, University of Kent, Canterbury, United Kingdom

FRANZ G. FEIGE, Executive Director, New Ecumenical Research Association, New York, New York

WILLIAM R. GARRETT, Professor of Sociology, St. Michael's College, Winooski, Vermont

IRENE KHIN KHIN JENSEN, Professor of History, Augsburg College, Minneapolis, Minnesota

FREDERICK J. MAHER, Professor of Sociology, St. Michael's College, Winooski, Vermont

ARMAND L. MAUSS, Professor of Sociology, Washington State University, Pullman, Washington

WILLEM NICOL, Minister of Religion, Universiteitsoord (Dutch Reformed Church), Pretoria, South Africa

RITA MATARAGNON PULLIUM, Adjunct Assistant Professor of Psychology, Rensselaer Polytechnic Institute, Troy, New York

RICHARD A. QUEBEDEAUX, Author, Senior Consultant, New Ecumenical Research Association, Berkeley, California

JOHN K. ROTH, Pitzer Professor of Philosophy, Claremont McKenna College, Claremont, California

RICHARD L. RUBENSTEIN, Robert O. Lawton Distinguished Professor of Religion, Florida State University, Tallahassee, Florida

JAMES R. WOOD, Professor of Sociology, Indiana University, Bloomington, Indiana

Index

Humanitarianism, 30; anti-
humanitarianism, 39–40,
42; belief in God as basis of
leverage of religious
leaders, 36–38; church
participation and, 33–34;
devotionalism and, 32–33,
39; impact of church on
society, 34–36
Humphrey, Hubert, 36
Hunter, James Davison, 140
Hurley, Frank, 204

Ideology, 159; of white South
Africans, 161–63
"Imperial Rescript: The Great
Principles of Education,
1879," 116, 117
India, 111; Christian Medical
College Hospital in Vellore,
92–93, 95, 98; education for
women in, 97–98
Individual, relationship of the,
and society, 10–11, 12–13
Individualism: American,
69–71, 72; self-interest
and, 70
Internal locus of control, 87–88
Intolerance, religiousness and,
80–89; authoritarian per-
sonality and, 85–86;
extrinsic versus intrinsic
religious orientation, 81–
83, 88; just-world belief,
83–84; locus-of-control
concept, 86–88; overlook-
ing of situational
attributions, 84–85
Intrinsic religious orientation
and prejudice, 81–83, 88
Iran, 41, 42

Islam, 41
*Is the Homosexual My Neigh-
bor?* (Scanzoni and Mol-
lenkott), 136
Ito, Prince, 114

Jacksonian America, 48
Jacob, Walter, 171
Japan: Christian missionaries
in, 119–20; emperor in,
111–23 *passim;* emphasis on
collective interests, 110;
father-son conflict in biblical religion, 107–11; filial
piety in, 111, 115–16; lim-
itations of, 123–24; Meiji
restoration in, 112, 113–14,
116; modernization of, and
preservation of traditions,
111–24; Protestant ethic
and rise of capitalism, 106–
108; religious significance
of economic challenge of,
105–24; *senjoku jidai* period
in, 113; Tokugawa period
in, 113
Jefferson, Thomas, 8
Jensen, Irene K. K., 27–28,
91–99
Jensen, Marius B., 112
Jesus Christ, 110, 176–77; in
Mormonism, 46, 48
Jesus freaks, 17
Jesus People movement, 135–
36
Jews: Mormons and, 55–56,
58, 59; mortal missions of,
55–56; Nazi Germany and,
146, 147, 150, 154; *see also*
Judaism
Joshua, 174

Workshops, church, 94, 96
*Worldly Spirituality: The Call
to Take Care of the Earth, A*
(Granberg-Michaelson),
95
World War I, 144

Yinger, 218
Young Reformation move-
ment (Yungreformatorische
Bewegung), 151

Zionism, 56